THE BILLBOARD GUIDE TO
CONTEMPORARY
CHRISTIAN MUSIC

BARRY ALFONSO

BILLBOARD BOOKS
An imprint of Watson-Guptill Publications/New York

First published in 2002 by Billboard Books,
an imprint of Watson-Guptill Publications
a division of VNU Business Media, Inc.,
770 Broadway, New York, N.Y. 10003
www.watsonguptill.com

Library of Congress Cataloging-in-Publication Data
Alfonso, Barry.
        The Billboard guide to contemporary Christian music / Barry Alfonso.--
1 ed.
                    p. cm.
Includes index.
"Chronology of contemporary Christian music"--P.
        ISBN 0-8230-7718-7
1. Contemporary Christian music--United States--History and criticism. 2. Contemporary Christian musicians--United States--Interviews. I. Title.
        ML3187.5 .A44 2002
        782.25--dc21   20022010375

Senior Acquisitions Editor: Bob Nirkind
Senior Editor: Julie Mazur
Designer: Cheryl Viker
Production Manager: Hector Campbell
The principal typeface used in the composition of this book was 10-pt Adobe Giovanni.

Manufactured in the United States of America

First printing, 2002

1 2 3 4 5 6 7 8 / 09 08 07 06 05 04 03 02

TABLE OF CONTENTS

ACKNOWLEDGMENTS

Researching and writing this book turned into a far more involved project than I'd originally anticipated. The idea took shape through conversations with such old Nashville friends as Gerd Muller (my long-time song publisher), who has worked with some of the best talent in the Christian music industry. Craig Bickhardt (my songwriting partner since the mid-1980s as well as composer of the wonderful Christmas musical *Precious Child*) shared his knowledge and insights as well. Artist/producer Dave Perkins was extremely helpful in sharpening my perceptions about Christian music at the start, and served as a sounding board as the book was being written. Singer/songwriter/producer Johnny J. Blair of Williamsport, Pennsylvania, also gave me early guidance and important contact information. Jay Swartzendruber (former publicist for Squint Entertainment, now with Gotee Records) went out of his way to set up interviews and put me in touch with the right people. Chris Estey (of Tooth & Nail Records) and Jason Dodd (of *HM* magazine) steered me toward some of the more interesting outer frontiers of Christian music.

Special thanks go to those who agreed to be interviewed for this book, including Nick Barre, Margaret Becker, Pastor Bob Beeman, Brent Bourgeois, Steve Camp, Steven Curtis Chapman, Bruce Cockburn, Brandon Ebel, Peter Furler, Norman Greenbaum, Phil Keaggy, Sarah Masen, Toby McKeehan, Larry Norman, Matt Odmark, Charlie Peacock, Michael Roe, Rebecca St. James, Randy Stonehill, Michael Tait, Steve Taylor, Terry Taylor, Doug Van Pelt, Jaci Velasquez, and Matthew Ward.

Listing everyone in the Christian media who lent assistance over the last two years isn't easy, but some of these helpful folks include Rick Hoganson (publicist for Jars of Clay and Jaci Velasquez); Stacie Vining, Jennifer McVey, Tim Frank, and Brian Dishon (Sparrow Records); Rich Guider and Lee Ann Mangen (Word Records); Jen Bockman, Lainie Miller, and Suzanna Parish (ForeFront Records); Jacquelyn Marushka (Provident Music); Jennifer Hanson (Essential Records); Laurie Anderson (Third Coast Management); Michelle Murphy and Brenda Biseau (True North Records); Jonathan Cargill (Secretly Canadian Records); Tom Gulotta (Stunt Records); Tricia Whitehead (Spinhouse Public Relations); and Jennifer Alexander (Gospel Music Association).

I'm grateful to the photographers who allowed usage of their images in this book, including Kristin Barlowe, Matthew

Barnes, Allen Clark, Scott Greenwalt, Sandra Johnson, Chris Knight, and Michael Wilson.

Rolling Stone press editor Holly George-Warren gave me early encouragement to pursue this project. Vance Wilson and the staff at the Belmont University library in Nashville always came through for me as a ready source of research materials.

At Billboard Books, senior acquisitions editor Bob Nirkind displayed the biblical virtues of patience, wisdom, and mercy in standing by me through this two-year project. He believed in the book from the beginning and has been unstinting in his support. Senior editor Julie Mazur provided discerning and judicious guidance during the book's final stages. She was always there for me in grappling with editorial decisions great and small (including the almost metaphysical dilemma of whether "Sandi *Patti*" or "Sandi *Patty*" is correct).

Finally, my wife, Janet Ingram, provided invaluable help as editor/researcher from start to finish. I would have fallen into a slough of despondency long ago if it hadn't been for her sense of humor, sound artistic judgment, and ready blue pencil. (It was red, actually.) Her abiding love and faith made this book possible.

Introduction

Americans are a religious people. Despite enormous changes in family patterns and cultural life, the United States leads the Western world in percentage of active believers. According to a December 2001 survey by the Graduate Center of the City University of New York, 81 percent of Americans claim a religious identity. Part of the story has been the rise of fundamentalist and evangelical Christianity from the 1970s onward. Popular culture has reflected this trend in recent years—from *Touched by an Angel* and the CBS-TV *Jesus* miniseries to films like *The Apostle* and *Moses: Prince of Egypt,* there's been renewed interest in Christian-based themes.

Music has been no exception. Once derided as a fringe genre, Contemporary Christian music has emerged as a commercial force to be reckoned with. Building upon the early 1990s breakthroughs of Amy Grant and Michael W. Smith, a wave of fresh Christian artists has increasingly gained exposure. Such acts as Sixpence None the Richer, Jars of Clay, and P.O.D. have achieved impressive success at attracting non-Christian fans. Other artists—including Steven Curtis Chapman, Carman, dc Talk, the Newsboys, and Rebecca St. James—have achieved comparable success without reaching a large mainstream audience. By the end of the 1990s, Christian music sales exceeded those for classical, jazz, and New Age music combined. And the market keeps growing. According to figures announced by the Gospel Music Association (GMA), nearly 50 million units were sold in 2001, an increase of 13.5 percent over the previous year.

For all this acceptance, Contemporary Christian music continues to be stigmatized, ridiculed, and dismissed by many mainstream listeners. It rivals gangsta rap in the levels of hostility and misunderstanding it arouses. Those who dislike it consider it illegitimate as art and/or a cheapened form of evangelism. TV's *Seinfeld* touched upon this stereotype some years back. In one episode, Elaine Benes is horrified when she discovers that her boyfriend listens to Christian pop music radio stations. When told about this, her pal George Costanza comments, "I like Christian rock.... It's very positive. It's not like those real musicians who think they're so cool and hip."

Is Contemporary Christian music something less than "real"? Is it a tool for ministry rather than creative expression? Or is it the equivalent of decaffeinated coffee, lacking the kick of unfiltered secular pop/rock? Can it ever hope to be more than a safe alternative to the genuine article?

This book is an attempt to answer such questions. It also seeks to place this music into the larger context of the cultural divide in America between conservative fundamentalist Christians and liberal secularists. In recent decades, it's seemed as if these two camps have had little to say to one another beyond exchanging slogans. Could the fitful efforts of Christian artists to cross over into the secular mainstream be an attempt at a more meaningful dialogue?

The question of whether Christian artists should try to appeal to secular record-buyers is a contentious one. The urge to remain separate is strong. More than one observer of the Christian music industry has called it a "parallel universe" to the mainstream entertainment business. Business and religion—definitely an unstable mix—come into play here in sometimes conflicting ways. An extensive network of record labels, radio stations, and industry publications combine the sacred and commercial to varying degrees. The fans themselves range from socially conservative Middle Americans to tattooed Gothic rockers who have embraced the Christian faith. The connection between artist and audience is a close one, often involving a sense of pastor-like responsibility. When these artists prove fallible, the repercussions are different than in the secular music realm.

Beyond all this is the nature of the music itself. How creative and interesting is it as artistic expression? How many artists record definably Christian music that has anything to say to someone outside the faith? Can Contemporary Christian music be held to the same critical standards that are applied to secular pop/rock?

The more I examined these issues, the more complex they seemed. I discovered that many of the artists themselves had a hard time defining what Christian music was or should be—some felt it shouldn't even exist as a separate category. One theme kept reoccurring in the interviews I did for this book: Christian musicians felt that the secular media rarely got their stories right. They considered themselves victims of bias. Some of them also acknowledged that Christians themselves helped to encourage this prejudice by withdrawing into a subcultural ghetto. For whatever reason, they felt it was hard to get a fair hearing.

By and large, pop music critics have ignored Contemporary Christian artists. Very few music encyclopedias include entries for Christian musicians—if they do, they lump the rock bands in with the old-fashioned gospel groups. Lyrically, this might make some sense, but musically it makes none at all. There is no good reason why artists like Jennifer Knapp or Third Day (to pick just two recent examples) shouldn't be considered alongside the likes of Fiona Apple or Son

Volt. The more Christian music I heard, the more I felt that its exclusion from critical scrutiny was arbitrary and based on prejudice.

The Billboard Guide to Contemporary Christian Music is an attempt to take an evenhanded look at what's good, bad, bland, and outstanding in Contemporary Christian music. It also explores the development of the industry and some of the larger social and cultural issues involved. The history of American fundamentalist and evangelical Christianity is covered to some extent, though this is not a book about religion per se. Neither is this a scandal-sniffing expose or an "inspirational" book designed to lead anyone to a particular faith. What's intended is to examine this multifaceted and paradoxical genre of music with as few preconceptions as possible.

The boundaries for inclusion in this book are broadly drawn. Some have argued that Contemporary Christian music is primarily a marketing term—strictly speaking, it only includes artists who record for identifiably Christian record companies. This seems unnecessarily narrow. For the sake of diversity—and because it's just more interesting—I've included musicians like Bruce Cockburn and T-Bone Burnett, who have never released albums on Christian labels. On the other hand, traditional gospel isn't within the scope of this study—the issues and aesthetics involved are different. White southern gospel quartets and African-American church musicians are rooted in different traditions and stand distinct from contemporary sounds. For the purposes of this guide, Contemporary Christian music is a blending (sometimes a blurring) of a faith-based message and secular pop music styles.

More than anything, it's the amazing diversity of the performers within the Christian music world that made me undertake this project. They run the gamut from the blistering extreme metal of Mortification to the contemplative orchestral folk of John Michael Talbot, from the giddy ska of Five Iron Frenzy to the mature gospel/pop of Dallas Holm. Shared beliefs aside, many of these artists are light years away from each other musically—it's hard to conceive of a Carman fan being able to listen to a Danielson Famile album, for instance. It seems as if the differences between Christian art-rockers and pop hit-makers and grindcore post-punks are as pronounced as those between Southern Baptists and Seventh-Day Adventists.

What's striking is how much worthwhile music has gone unheard by mainstream audiences—and, in some cases, by most Christian listeners as well. There's a subgenre within Contemporary Christian music of gifted writer/artists who are too left-of-center for Christian radio and too faith-oriented for secular record companies. These include Daniel Amos, the 77s, Michael Knott, and the late Mark Heard—important maverick talents who deserve far more exposure. Some of the most powerful music in the genre was recorded by the first wave of Christian artists. Today, pioneers like Larry Norman are only sporadically heard on Christian airwaves. In the A–Z Encyclopedia portion of this book (pages 107–266), I've included representative artists from all segments of Christian music, from current stars to neglected innovators and interesting fringe characters. Hopefully, the full range of expression within the genre is shown, even if some artists aren't covered.

I'd like to imagine Elaine and George discovering this book and reconsidering some of their opinions. Maybe they'd even get up the nerve to pick up a few CDs by Phil Keaggy or MxPx or Out of Eden. They might find that Christian pop music can be very real after all. It's not going to happen for Elaine and George, I know. But any open-minded musical agnostics out there reading these words ought to give it a try.

CONTEMPORARY CHRISTIAN MUSIC:

A HISTORY

"Why should the devil have all the good music?" It was a simple enough question when asked by singer/songwriter Larry Norman back in 1969. At the time, rock-'n'roll was being denounced by conservative preachers as a satanic tool used to corrupt the young. In a time of revolutionary musical change, perhaps the ultimate rebellious act was to tap the energy of rock in the service of a Christian message. The combination of rock and religion didn't seem like a marriage made in heaven to everyone—but slowly, over the following decade, a distinct new genre took shape that came to be known as Contemporary Christian music. It continues to grow, and it continues to be controversial.

For all its acceptance, pop music with a Christian underpinning still seems like a strange animal to many. After all, hasn't most of the popular music of the last 60-odd years been based around throwing off inhibitions, getting crazy, shocking your elders? The answer is yes—and it is this radical spirit that connects it with American religious tradition.

There's a clear link between Contemporary Christian music and the great American religious movements of the past 200 years. The key is the concept of "revival": a dramatic, convulsive event that is both a break with

tradition and a return to a long-lost past. From the country's earliest days, Americans have hungered for intense personal revelation to transport them out of the mundane present and connect them with something greater than themselves. The most uniquely American strains of Protestant Christianity have embraced this form of worship as a way of getting closer to God. The only thing in this country's history to approach this kind of experience has been rock'n'roll.

REVIVALS: ROCKING THE NINETEENTH CENTURY

The first of the great American revivals is said to have been held in the early nineteenth century in Logan County, Kentucky (not far, interestingly enough, from Nashville, Tennessee, the center of today's Christian music industry). The fervor of repentance and surrender that erupted here and in later meetings was extreme, almost as wild as the sinful behavior that the sinners were renouncing. Those attending these revivals expected to feel the presence of God, to be "slain in the spirit" and touched by the Lord instantly. Members of more established denominations back East were scandalized by such carryings-on: This was religion as raw and passionate as frontier life itself.

The most famous of these revivals was held at Cane Ridge, near Lexington, Kentucky, on August 6, 1801. Some 20,000 people attended this sprawling outdoor marathon of preaching and testifying. Descriptions of the event invite comparisons with legendary rock concerts like Woodstock, except that Cane Ridge was wilder, more life-changing. Thousands of laughing, crying, convulsive men and women dedicated themselves to Jesus as the rain poured down and the ground turned to mud. Hecklers vied with preachers in a bedlam of shouts and prayers; those overcome with the spirit spoke in tongues, barked like dogs, lost the power of speech, or fell unconscious.

Extraordinary events like Cane Ridge had a significance beyond theology. They were enthusiastic outpourings of desire that weren't afraid to break normal bounds of propriety. Attendees tapped into both a private connection with a higher power and the collective energy of those on a similar quest. For all its attempts to transcend the flesh and its temptations, the revival experience was highly sensual—an experience that gripped the body as well as the spirit.

The revivalists were seekers and, in their own way, rebels against the prevailing culture. Early nineteenth-century preachers like Charles Grandison Finney became celebrities comparable with today's pop idols. In an era when many Americans were forbidden from dancing or attending the theater, Finney and his colleagues provided a much-needed emotional release for thousands. Finney was denounced by more conventional clergymen for unduly stirring up passions and breaking down barriers between the sexes—charges that would be lodged against rock'n'rollers from Bill Haley onward.

Revivals continued to stir the spiritual fervor of American Protestants for the rest of the nineteenth century. This was particularly true in the South, which would later become the breeding ground for rock-'n'roll. The passion of the Christian faith in the southern states was embraced and transformed by African-Americans, and the black spiritual would become the basis of much American pop music of the twentieth century. American Christianity believed in reaching out to the unsaved, and some believers found creative ways to do this early on. Setting new, biblically inspired lyrics to popular tunes—an early form of Contemporary Christian music—began as far back as the 1850s, when Horace Waters turned several Stephen Foster melodies into Sunday school hymns. Echoing the reaction to Jesus Music 120 years later, hymn composer Thomas Hastings condemned the use of "merry dances, street ballads, bacchanalian songs, and negro melodies" for their power to "bring wicked and irreverent thoughts to mind," even in the service of a godly message. But the blending of religious teachings and catchy tunes didn't end there, of course.

In the 1870s, the Fisk Jubilee Singers began to perform before white audiences around the world, marking the beginning of black gospel music as a transracial phenomenon. Their music was both uplifting and entertaining, combining the earthy and the exalted in a uniquely American way. White and black gospel music would develop along parallel lines into the twentieth century, intersecting at times but retaining distinctive identities. They would begin to draw closer after World War II, when racial barriers began to fall across America. Helping them to blend was a new kind of music that was considered anything but sacred: rock'n'roll.

OF BILLY AND ELVIS

It seems that just about every American musical innovation has come from the wrong side of the tracks. Ragtime, jazz, and the blues were nurtured by African-Americans in red light districts and tar-paper shacks; the tunes of Tin Pan Alley were hammered out by poor Eastern European immigrants; country music was created by hillbillies, Okies, and other marginalized southern whites. It's also true that much of the dynamic force in American religion has come from humble sources, such as poor black and rural white churches and touring low-budget preachers. Whatever one thinks of its theology, the

Protestant movement that came to be known as fundamentalism brought a renewed moral force and personal spiritual commitment to believers around the world.

Resisting the prevailing liberal trend in mainline Protestant churches, evangelical Christians sought to return to biblical basics during the first two decades of the twentieth century. The term "fundamentalist" came about in 1920, following the publication of a series of books called *The Fundamentals*. Adherents put their faith in a literal reading of Scripture and decried evolution and other trends in science and society, which they saw as undermining their faith. The most famous fundamentalist preacher of the early twentieth century was Billy Sunday, a ferociously intense revivalist who barnstormed America, lambasting sinners and calling stray lambs home to Christ. (He also used music in his services, adding an entertaining touch that would be built upon by his successors.)

After a decline of several decades, Fundamentalism gained new converts during the late 1940s, in part by decrying the erosion of American morals. Interestingly, its rise coincided with changes in popular culture, including the emergence of rock'n'roll as a mass phenomenon in the early 1950s. As much as the two trends seemed in opposition, there was common ground between them. Both had deep roots in southern culture and drew upon the emotional passion identified with the region. Both were signs of a break from the bland consumerist conformity of the post-World War II years. Americans, particularly the young, were hungry for something authentic and inspiring. True, rock music was linked with teenage rebellion and sexual promiscuity while fundamentalism advocated conservative morality and patriotism. But both were looking for something more than conformity and materialism, and both placed the heart above mere logic and rationalism.

It's also interesting to compare the rise of the Reverend Billy Graham with that of Elvis Presley. In the late 1940s, Graham was a key field representative for Youth for Christ, a fundamentalist organization. The group's rallies featured entertainment and musical performances; in *Billy Graham: Revivalist in a Secular Age* (Ronald Press, 1960), Graham is quoted describing one event as offering "smooth melodies from a consecrated saxophone." According to Graham, the rallies "used every modern means to catch the attention of the unconverted—and then we punched them right between the eyes with the gospel." When Graham launched his own "crusades" a few years later, he continued to find ways to reach out to restless, spiritually searching youth. Graham exuded tremendous charisma and became a worldwide celebrity who influenced politics and culture on a scale never before seen by the American clergy.

Graham's advent as a national icon roughly coincided with the emergence of Presley. For all of the controversy Presley stirred with the lascivious elements in his act, it's worth noting that he began releasing sacred songs barely a year after his first hit, "Heartbreak Hotel," topped the charts in 1956. *Peace in the Valley*, an EP of religious material, appeared in 1957; four years later Elvis released an entire gospel album, *His Hand in Mine*. Some might have been shocked that this hip-wiggling, lip-curling teen idol would turn around and sing the Lord's praises so early in his career. But at his best, Elvis transmitted passion, whether in the carnal or spiritual realm. His music struck more straightlaced music fans as impolite at first, just as many respectable churchgoers thought fundamentalist worship was crass and excessive.

Presley found a way to reconcile rock-'n'roll with his religious roots; some of his peers found the task more difficult. Jerry Lee Lewis was both a wilder rocker and a more tormented Christian than Elvis appeared to be. Raised in an Assembly of God family, he briefly attended Southwest Bible College in Waxahachie, Texas, prior to his breakthrough as a performer. Lewis didn't dispute that rock'n'roll was the spawn of Satan. During one early recording session (captured on tape and later released on the bootleg album *Good Rockin' Tonight*), he argued about sin and salvation with producer Sam Phillips. Lewis refused to consider Phillips's position that a rock-'n'roller could be a force for Christ—after affirming that the Bible was God's word, Lewis blurted out, "I have the devil in me!"

Little Richard's oscillation between the bandstand and the pulpit was more public. Famous for such outrageous scream-fests as "Tutti Frutti" and "Long Tall Sally," he underwent a spiritual crisis during a 1957 tour of Australia and renounced his rock-'n'roll career. Richard went on to become a Seventh-Day Adventist minister and recorded such scripturally based material as "He Got What He Wanted (But He Lost What He Had)." Frustrated by a lack of success as a gospel artist, he returned to rock in the mid-1960s. By the end of the 1970s, he had renounced secular music once again, telling fans at church revivals that "God wants you to give up rock'n'roll."

It was not only the raucous, rebellious sounds of rock and other pop music forms that made Christian musicians and fans alike uneasy. From the mid-1950s onward, secular entertainment in general was taking on a disturbing cast for believers. The emerging rock culture seemed to embrace just about every sinful thing imaginable: sexual freedom, drugs, political subversion, blasphemy. When John Lennon declared that the Beatles were more popular than Jesus, the line was clearly drawn. If hell had a soundtrack, it was psychedelic-era rock.

Still, some ministers perceived that pop music could be the means to bring a gospel message to the young. Among them was Billy Ray Hearn, a minister at the First Baptist Church in Thomasville, Georgia, who created the musical show *Good News* in 1967. Modeled after the relentlessly cheerful touring musical show *Up with People*, this folk-slanted review overcame initial doubts by more conservative Baptist leaders and went on to sell thousands of copies in print and disc forms. After initial resistance, the Baptist establishment accepted the show; one production brought together 1,300 singers for a performance at the Southern Baptist Convention as a warm-up for Billy Graham. *Good News* was tame by the standards of Christian music today, but it nevertheless opened the door for greater creative risk-taking in the future.

Word, Inc. became interested in Hearn's project. Founded in 1950 by Jarrell McCracken, Word had been an important force in Christian music from its inception. The record company shared Hearn's desire to reach the younger generation and signed him up as its director of music promotion, with a mandate to create more projects like *Good News*.

Hearn enlisted the help of Ralph Carmichael, another key figure in the rise of Contemporary Christian music. An experienced composer and arranger, Carmichael had been trying to update church music as far back as the late 1940s. He had found the restrictions grating; in those days, just about every instrument except for piano and organ was considered unfit for sacred songs. Things loosened up, though, and

Carmichael was able to use bass and drums on the soundtrack to Billy Graham's 1965 youth-slanted film *The Restless Ones.*

At Hearn's urging, Carmichael and fellow composer Kurt Kaiser created *Tell It Like It Is,* a musical utilizing a choir and electric instrumentation that was released in LP and music folio form in 1970. As with *Good News,* the musical approach was different enough to raise protests from some in the Baptist community. But a line had already been crossed, and further musicals of this type followed.

By any estimation, these works were a far cry from acid rock. But at that time *anything* that smacked of late 1960s secular pop music raised the hackles of fundamentalist Christians. The sex, drugs, and radicalism that rock music embodied gave preachers plenty to crusade against. Among the most active of them was Reverend Bob Larson, a former rock musician/songwriter who attacked the music he'd played in his younger days in *The Day the Music Died* (Creation House, 1972) and other books. Larson condemned rock on many fronts, from the false idolatry of pop-star worship to the sinful content of its lyrics. He laid particular emphasis on the music's rhythms, charging that they derived from the demon-invoking beat of African religious ceremonies. "It is obvious to any qualified, objective observer that teenagers dancing to rock enter hypnotic trances," he wrote in *The Day the Music Died.* "When

control of the mind is weakened or lost, evil influences can often take possession. Loss of self-control is dangerous and sinful."

Larson saw little value in trying to convey God's message through such satanic entertainment: "For a song and dance, today's liberal church leaders seem to be ready to deliver the soul of America to the devil on a gold record. Unfortunately, many of their evangelical counterparts aid and abet the cause by suggesting that rock can be used to communicate the fundamentals of the gospel." (In recent years, Larson has softened his stance and offered guarded praise for Christian rock artists. In his book *Your Kids and Rock* (Tyndale House Publishers, 1988), he noted that "much Christian music today is both musically sophisticated and well-grounded theologically," but warned that "the music is still the same—it's got that THUMP-THUMP beat.")

SAVED FREAKS AND SANCTIFIED HIPPIES

That beat—so identified with youthful rebellion—would lie at the heart of what came to be known as "Jesus Music" at the start of the 1970s. Unlike *Good News* and the other stage productions previously mentioned, this music was not created by those in the church for a targeted audience. Jesus Music was a true grassroots phenomenon launched by an assortment of musicians and counterculture types operating outside of the bounds of accepted church policy. In appearance, many of them resembled the psychedelic rockers of San Francisco and Los Angeles—and in their fervor and excess, they resembled even more the evangelists of the nineteenth century era of great revivals, spurring on their audiences to ecstatic devotion.

Many of these musicians and their fans fit the "hippie" stereotype: long-haired, living in urban youth ghettos or rural communes, at odds with the older generation, seeking something to believe in. They were drawn to (and in some cases founded) independent evangelical ministries. Those who accepted Christ brought an outsider's attitude to their beliefs and were often attracted to extreme teachings. For many, millennial prophecies of Jesus' imminent Second Coming seemed to match the events of the times. What came to be called Jesus Music had an end-of-the-world cast to it that made it sound both jubilant and (to some observers) a little scary.

There's some dispute as to who the first Jesus Music artist was. Certainly, a number of Christian pop musicians began appearing in scattered spots around the United States by the late 1960s, working independently of one another. One of the first—and among the strangest—examples was the All Saved Freak Band, a group which grew out of the ministry of street evangelist Larry Hill. Preaching an apocalyptic brand of Christianity, Hill organized his own

Church of the Risen Christ (CRC) in the Cleveland, Ohio, area in the mid-'60s. He began broadcasting his *Time for the Risen Christ* radio program to spread end-time prophecies, which included a war with Communist China on American soil. By 1968, some of his followers had formed a rock group as a way of attracting young followers to the church.

The band gained a stellar member when guitarist Glenn Schwartz joined the group a year later. A former member of the James Gang and of Pacific Gas & Electric, he had announced his acceptance of Christ as his savior on stage at a 1969 rock festival. This was a bizarre thing for a rock guitar hero to do at the time—so much so that Schwartz's wife and parents had him committed to a mental institution after he began spending time with Larry Hill. Once released, he joined the Church of the Risen Christ and became a member of the All Saved Freak Band. In 1970, sisters Pam and Kim Massmann were added on cello and violin, lending a classical touch to the band's blues/rock base. The group released several albums on small labels and toured extensively in the Midwest and Canada.

Though the band was reaching a widening audience, the CRC was drawing inward, with Hill showing the classic signs of cult leadership. His visions grew more apocalyptic, including the Catholic Church as well as the Soviet Union and China as enemies of America and Christianity.

Church members moved to their own communal farm in rural Ohio and began stockpiling firearms for the expected "last battle." Hill became increasingly dictatorial and abused his followers physically and mentally. The All Saved Freak Band began to splinter by the late 1970s; a final LP appeared in 1981. Hill and the Massmann sisters remained together, and were reportedly still living on their farm in the 1990s.

Several other groups active in the late 1960s are still remembered today. Agape was an early Christian hard rock group based in Southern California, releasing a pair of albums in the early 1970s before disbanding in 1974. Another group, the Exkursions, played jazz/rock and appeared at Billy Graham Crusade–sponsored events and on college campuses.

These bands were far cries from the clean-cut, church-sponsored productions that Hearn and Carmichael had created. What the likes of the All Saved Freak Band lacked in polish, they made up for in sheer intensity and weirdness— qualities that many of the best secular bands of the late 1960s displayed. It would take artists with more finesse and professionalism to bring Jesus Music to a mass audience, however.

Foremost among these artists would be Larry Norman, whose 1969 Capitol album *Upon This Rock* is considered pivotal in the development of Contemporary Christian music. Both a maverick and outsider from the start of his career, Norman is not shy in asserting his place in Christian pop music history. His role in helping to define what Christian music could be, as well as his own considerable strengths as a songwriter and performer, are undeniable.

Norman recognized the direct connection between gospel music and rock'n'roll as far back as 1956: "I was just a kid when Elvis Presley came along. The music he was singing was hailed as something new. But I had grown up in a black neighborhood and knew that this style of music was from the black church. The kids at school seemed impressed with Elvis. None of them accepted my invitations to go to church. So one day I brought church to them. I started singing during lunchtime, walking around from bench to bench singing. I was nine and in the fourth grade."

Based in San Jose, Norman first gained notice as a member of People, a theater-rock combo that shared stages with the Grateful Dead and Janis Joplin, among others. The band scored a number 14 hit with "I Love You" in 1968, but Norman's desire to record explicitly Christian songs led to his embarking on a solo career. He soon became the most visible exponent of what was labeled "Jesus Music," and won respect for the quality of his songs and the energy of his performances.

"I Wish We'd All Been Ready" (on his LP *Upon This Rock*) remains Norman's most enduring song, a stirring depiction of the "rapture" (the fundamentalist belief that the Lord's faithful will be carried bodily to heaven, leaving unbelievers to suffer seven years of tribulation on Earth). He was able to address sex, drugs, and rock'n'roll in songs like "Why Don't You Look into Jesus" with an ear for street language. Stepping outside of the boundaries of traditional gospel music, he advocated helping the poor and criticized materialism as well as preaching the need for salvation.

Norman blazed the trail that many other Christian rockers would follow in the early 1970s. He is even credited with inventing the "one way" gesture (the index finger pointing straight up) that became a trademark of believers around the world. Looking back, he maintains that he didn't particularly identify with the youth-oriented "Jesus movement" of the time: "I was not one of the kids who had recently become a Christian. I did not have any scintillating 'testimony' of getting high on Jesus and then giving up drugs, girls, and the pursuit of material possessions. In fact, I felt that I was neither a part of the 'establishment' or part of the alternative lifestyle enclave which felt itself so superior to their parents and our civic leaders....

"I felt more comfortable at secular concerts and rallies than I did when invited to appear at Christian events.... I tried to suppress my laughter when one of the 'leaders' of the Jesus movement decided to open up a concert for me with a 'Jesus cheer.' He

yelled out, 'Give me a "g"!' The crowd did not respond. It was a few seconds before he realized that 'Jesus' starts with a 'j.'"

Unlike Norman, many early exponents of Jesus Music were newly minted Christians who set their 'scintillating testimony' to music. Randy Stonehill was among the best of this bunch. An active San Jose musician since his teens, his early work combined folksy melodies with a boyishly awkward sincerity. "Norman's Kitchen," a 1970 composition, captured his conversion experience in (literally) Larry Norman's kitchen with vulnerability and humor. His first album, *Born Twice*, appeared in 1972. Stonehill compensated for an occasional oversweetness with an appealingly innocent song delivery—he sounded like the quintessential Jesus freak, the kid high on God. Rather than sounding like a preacher, he came across as an ordinary believer trying to make sense of his life.

Stonehill's story was duplicated by many of the first wave of Jesus Music artists—raised in an agnostic household, he embraced fundamentalist Christianity with a fervor that propelled him out into the world as a singing advocate for Jesus. He saw the same spirit spurring others onward: "I got the hint that God was raising up musicians and creating something for everyone. Rock'n'roll was our vernacular, and we were going to share Jesus with these songs." The rebellious energy of rock seemed a natural vehicle for his message:

"I figured, if anyone had a license to rebel against a world gone mad, it's Christians. This is the source of real life, not just a distraction of the culture."

This was still a controversial idea in many fundamentalist circles in the early 1970s. "I found that I was running into some pretty intense opposition," Stonehill recalls. "I would be really wounded by those people who would call me a tool of Satan. I'd go back to my hotel room after a concert feeling like I'd been mugged.... I got so frustrated, I said to myself, 'I'm done—who needs this aggravation from these loveless, judgmental people? Who needs the grief?' But I couldn't just walk away from sharing the hope of the gospel with my audience. I turned back around to God and said, 'You're right, I'll try to speak the truth of love to my critics.'"

Christian rock musicians had uneasy relations with the secular music industry in those days. As an artist signed to Capitol and, later, to MGM, Norman attempted to share his faith with record executives: "The challenge I often was aware of was, how do I bring these people closer to the cross without offending them and getting thrown off the label? Years later, when I read a book on the industry titled *Hit Men*, I discovered that 'allegedly' many of these men had ties with the Mafia. In hindsight, perhaps their Catholic upbringing created a special warm spot in their hearts for my attempts to save them."

GOD GOES TOP 40

Christian references in songs—if not the Christian faith itself—became somewhat trendy in mainstream pop music circa 1969 to 1972. Suddenly, God's name began turning up on Top 40 radio. From the Beatles' "Let It Be" to James Taylor's "Fire and Rain" and Jackson Browne's "Rock Me on the Water," it became hip to add a spiritual tinge to a pop/rock lyric. A few hits of the day—among them "Put Your Hand in the Hand" by Ocean (number 2, 1971) and "Jesus Is Just Alright" by the Doobie Brothers (number 35, 1973)—were unmistakable declarations of faith set to bouncy pop tunes. Traditional gospel, as evidenced by Judy Collins's version of "Amazing Grace" and the Edwin Hawkins Singers' uplifting "Oh Happy Day," made it onto the airwaves as well. There was also the phenomenal success of the stage musicals *Godspell* and *Jesus Christ Superstar*, productions that tapped into biblical themes in unorthodox ways.

And then there's the strange case of "Spirit in the Sky," a number 3 hit single for Norman Greenbaum in 1970. For more than three decades, this enduringly popular tune has been taken by some listeners to be a sincere celebration of Christ, by others as a sarcastic parody. Something about "Spirit in the Sky" left room for interpretation in either direction. Maybe it was the recording's nasty, distorted guitar or boogie-rock groove that made some question the piety of the lyric, or the slightly odd choice of words (e.g., Jesus "is gonna *set me up* with the spirit in the sky"). Was this meant to be reverent, or mocking? According to one rumor in the evangelical community, Greenbaum was a part of a demonic cult when he wrote this song. There was also talk that he was a Jew for Jesus.

"I didn't write it with tongue in cheek," Greenbaum insists today. The inspiration came from watching country singer Porter Wagoner perform a Christian song on his syndicated television show: "I'd never written a religious song, so on impulse I wrote the words in about five minutes. Why did I choose Jesus? I thought it would be easier for people to relate to. It wasn't cold, but it was calculating." It took Greenbaum months to come up with the right music for the song. Released by Warner Brothers Records as a single, "Spirit in the Sky" almost died on the charts until one key Los Angeles station agreed to keep playing it at the behest of a record distributor. It went on to become one of the biggest hits of 1970. Since then, it's been a staple on oldies radio, has appeared on numerous film soundtracks, and has turned up in commercials for everyone from Toyota to Enron.

Over the years, the curious have tracked Greenbaum down and asked him about his beliefs: "I get letters from heavy-duty Christians who really lambaste me. They're thinking that I was sarcastic, but I wasn't....

The Scriptures say, 'We're all sinners.' Well, in the song I said, 'I've never been a sinner,' and that pisses people off. It wasn't a personal statement at all—it just sounded like it belonged there."

In fact, "Spirit in the Sky" has more explicit religious content than do many recent Christian radio hits. Its odd journey through American pop culture took another turn when dc Talk recorded it for the soundtrack to the *Jesus* miniseries, broadcast on CBS-TV in 2000. Through it all, Greenbaum has stood a little in awe of his own creation: "Was I a channel for the song? Could be. I mean, where did it come from? I wasn't a Christian.... I was a songwriter and I hit on something. There is something about this song that's extraordinary. It's almost eerie. It did have a rebirth and it's not finished yet. There's always *Spirit in the Sky: The Movie*. It'll just happen."

THE SLOW TRAIN ARRIVES

Notwithstanding the wave of Christian-slanted hits in the early 1970s, there was little indication that fundamentalist believers were being welcomed by the mainstream music industry. Few outspokenly Christian artists were signed to secular record deals; in Larry Norman's case, he left MGM to found his own Christian label, Solid Rock.

Working outside of the secular music industry appeared to be the best approach. All across America, it seemed, Christian rock musicians were beginning to emerge, independent of one another but united in purpose. Some had experience as recording and touring artists; among the best of these was Phil Keaggy, an Ohio-born guitarist whose fluent style had won the praise of no less than Jimi Hendrix. Keaggy had become a Christian just as his band, Glass Harp, began to record for Decca in 1970. The group became a fairly successful act, but was a less than ideal forum for Keaggy to express his faith. Leaving the group, he joined a small Christian community called the Love Inn in upstate New York, founded by disc jockey Scott Ross. Ross, a pioneer Christian radio personality, released Keaggy's first solo album, *What a Day,* on his New Song label in 1973.

Meanwhile, in Southern California, Chuck Girard and his bandmates in Love Song were tapping the surf music sounds popularized by the Beach Boys to advance the Christian message. Girard had gained some notoriety in the early 1960s as a singer with the Hondells ("Little Honda") and the Castells ("So This Is Love"). After he embraced Christianity and began attending Calvary Chapel in Costa Mesa, California, he formed a harmony-centered folk/rock quartet with Tom Coomes, Jay Truax, and Fred Field. Tunefully mellow, Love Song proved an influential band in Christian music circles of the '70s. (The Calvary Chapel became a center for early Christian rock and went on to launch its own record label, Maranatha! Music.)

Music and ministry were inseparable for most of these artists; their role as entertainers was definitely secondary. In a few cases, evangelism was linked to social activism. This was true of Resurrection Band, connected since its inception with Jesus People USA, a communal ministry organization on Chicago's south side that offers food and shelter to the needy. Rez Band (as it came to be known) was assembled by singer/guitarist Glenn Kaiser, whose bluesy playing style had more grit and muscle than that of most of his Christian rock peers. Kaiser and his group were not afraid to rock hard, and they performed at the Cook County Jail, among other venues. A bit too loud and heavy for some ears, the band wasn't signed to a label until 1978, when Star Song released *Awaiting Your Reply.*

The sonic parameters of Larry Norman, Love Song, and Resurrection Band—to cite only three examples—show the diversity of Christian rock from its inception. All of these artists reached devoted but limited audiences during the first half of the 1970s. For all their talent and fervor, their efforts were hampered by limited resources and opportunities for airplay. This began to change when Christian bookstores started featuring albums by these artists. The rise of Christian summer music festivals also raised their visibility. Among the first of these was Explo '72, held June 17 to 22, 1972, in Dallas, Texas, and sponsored by

Campus Crusade for Christ. Billed as a "World Student Congress on Evangelism," this event featured performances by Jesus Music artists Larry Norman, Randy Matthews, and Barry McGuire, as well as Johnny Cash, Kris Kristofferson, and Rita Coolidge.

Still, by the standards of the secular music industry, Jesus Music—or, as it came to be known, Contemporary Christian music—remained a fairly small and isolated genre, ignored by most American audiences. What gained more notice were the famous pop music personalities who embraced Christianity by the end of the 1970s. This wasn't completely new—there was Pat Boone, of course, and British rocker Cliff Richard, who had first proclaimed his belief in Jesus on stage in 1966. In 1971, the news that Fleetwood Mac guitarist Peter Green had quit his band to join the Children of God (held by many to be a Christian cult) caused some ripples of comment. But when the likes of Richie Furay (a founding member of the Buffalo Springfield and Poco) and Dan Peek (from the group America) began writing and recording outspokenly Christian songs, a younger generation of rock fans began to pay attention. When hit-making disco diva Donna Summer followed suit, there was even more comment.

It was the public announcement in 1979 of Bob Dylan's conversion to the faith that had the greatest impact. It was genuinely newsworthy that this Jewish-born icon of 1960s rebellion had accepted Christ as his personal savior. The first album to follow his born-again experience, *Slow Train Coming,* confirmed the importance of his spiritual shift. The LP contained "Gotta Serve Somebody," which reached number 3 as a single and earned Dylan his first Grammy Award (for best rock vocal performance, male). Some rock critics gasped at the album's uncompromising Bible-based lyrics, but others noted that Dylan's music seemed rejuvenated by his faith. Overnight, the man who'd written such protest anthems as "Blowin' in the Wind" and "The Times They Are a-Changin'" had been transformed into rock's most famous advocate of fundamentalist Christianity.

All of this took place in the context of a larger cultural change. Evangelical Christianity had become increasingly visible, even mainstream. Jimmy Carter's campaign for the presidency in 1976 was something of a watershed event in this regard. For the first time in recent memory, a candidate for the White House discussed his spiritual life in intimate terms; among other things, Carter helped to introduce the phrase "born again" into American secular vernacular. An active layman in the Baptist Church, he later fell out of favor with politically conservative Christian leaders like the Reverend Jerry Falwell during his presidential years. Beyond politics, though, Carter's role in helping to make evangelical Christianity a greater force in society at large was undeniable.

Newsweek dubbed 1976 "the year of the evangelical." That same year, former Nixon administration official Chuck Colson published his best-selling book *Born Again* and Billy Ray Hearn left Word, Inc. to launch Sparrow Records. All of these developments marked a greater engagement in the realities of American society, both politically and culturally. Only a few years earlier, Hal Lindsey's book *The Late Great Planet Earth* had reached a vast readership with its predictions of humanity's destruction and Christ's impending return. Now the emphasis in the fundamentalist and evangelical communities was on making a difference in a sinful world. Like their brethren in politics, Christians in music wrestled with the question of how far to reach out to secular America without compromising their beliefs.

SUCCESS AND SOUL-SEARCHING

Christian pop music began to change noticeably by the late 1970s. The rawness and radicalism of the Jesus Music period gave way to artistic sophistication and a less apocalyptic stance; the days of the All Saved Freak Band and Larry Norman's early work seemed far behind. Some of the now-familiar subgenres of Contemporary Christian music began to emerge—such mainstays as hard-rocking combo Petra and country-turned-New Wave band Daniel Amos were already well established by the dawn of the 1980s. Recording budgets started to rise and production quality improved as well. Mainstream labels began to make forays into the Christian market, drawing criticism from purists that has continued to the present day. Word Records was acquired by ABC in 1974; Sparrow signed a distribution deal with MCA in 1981; Light Records agreed to be distributed to the secular market by Elektra/Asylum in 1982. Several major labels picked up newly launched Christian labels as well, including Exit Records (distributed by Island) and What? Records (a joint project handled by A&M and Word). In 1981, CBS Records launched its own short-lived Christian label, Priority.

Most of these ventures proved disappointing. Elektra/Asylum's deal with Light (which included albums by Resurrection Band, among others) fizzled out after only a year, for example. Mutual misunderstanding of the aims and methods by both parties were often to blame. But more than anything, the Christian artists marketed by the major secular companies simply lacked the star potential to reach a mass audience.

The first to break through this barrier was Amy Grant. It's hard to overemphasize the impact this Georgia-born singer/songwriter has had on the course of Contemporary Christian music. Her rise to stardom became a model for every young

Christian: Discovered while working at a Nashville recording studio erasing tapes, she was signed to Word at age 15 and scored her first Christian radio hit in 1978. Her 1982 album *Age to Age* became the first by a solo gospel artist to reach the gold sales mark (sales of 500,000 units). It was 1985's *Unguarded*, though, that would push Grant into the mainstream. The album conveyed its spiritual themes with enough tasteful restraint to appeal to a broad listenership, and even earned Grant a Top 40 hit with "Find a Way," making her the first Contemporary Christian act to score a pop crossover hit.

Grant's appeal was not hard to understand. She was worldly enough in her approach to music and fashion (favoring faux leopard-skin coats and other hip apparel) to make her attractive to secular audiences, yet deeply rooted enough in her faith to retain the loyalty of her Christian fan base. And, not incidentally, she was also an above-average songwriter and an expressive, distinctively individual singer. For all of these reasons, Amy Grant quickly became a highly effective spokesperson for the evangelical Christian community as well as a hugely popular entertainer.

Unfortunately, there were few Christian artists who were able to duplicate Grant's success in the secular world during the 1980s. The colorfully clad heavy metal band Stryper—known for tossing Bibles out to their audiences—won a good deal of secular press. Many others, including such talented artists as Charlie Peacock, Margaret Becker, the 77s, Mark Heard, and Daniel Amos, had potential; some tried and fell short, others disdained the attempt altogether.

The prospect of secular success led to much soul-searching among the Christian music community during this time. This confusion and ambivalence over how to proceed was mirrored among evangelical leaders. The face that Christianity presented to the world was not a happy one during the 1980s. In 1987, Jim and Tammy Faye Bakker were brought down in a huge scandal involving financial and sexual improprieties; the fallout from the collapse of the Bakkers's PTL Ministries injured the credibility of prominent Christians in the mainstream media. The Bakker debacle was followed by Jimmy Swaggert's highly publicized downfall after an encounter with a prostitute near New Orleans. Swaggert— a cousin of the similarly conflicted Jerry Lee Lewis—had been a critic of rock'n'roll for years, including the Christian variety. No matter—the Bakker and Swaggert scandals were black marks on the reputations of evangelicals across the board, musicians included.

The larger theme in all of this was the role Christians chose to play in the world at large. Was interaction with secular America, in all its pleasure-seeking consumerism and obsessions with fad and fashion, a healthy thing? Was the gaudy spectacle of Jim Bakker's Heritage U.S.A. theme park so different from the increasingly slick and glitzy Contemporary Christian music emerging in the mid-'80s? Was this music effective preaching, mere entertainment, or, worse, a diversion from truly spiritual forms of art and worship?

The difference between the militant millennialism of a Larry Norman and the far less confrontational stance of an Amy Grant was striking. The apocalyptic urgency of the Jesus Music period had been largely supplanted by a more moderate, worldly subculture that attempted to work within pop music conventions in the service of Christian faith. How well they had succeeded by the 1980s was debatable. The same may be said for those purporting to represent evangelical Christians in the political arena. It was a long journey indeed from Jimmy Carter's 1976 campaign to the presidential bid of televangelist Pat Robertson in 1988. At one time, the idea of a television preacher running for the White House would have seemed unacceptable; by the mid-'80s, it was within the realm of political possibility. Still, Robertson faded after early success in the Republican caucuses, just as Christian rock fell short of the predictions of its mainstream potential. And once again, the question was raised as to whether evangelicals should retreat from the larger political and social culture—or try all the harder to engage it.

SUBVERSIVE SATIRE AND FAST-FOOD CHRISTIANITY

A few Christian artists attempted to offer critiques of these shortcomings and contradictions. Perhaps the best among them was Steve Taylor, a gangling preacher's son who served up biting satirical New Wave–style rock with a jittery Elvis Costello–like edge. He first gained notice in 1983 with "I Want to Be a Clone," a punk-slanted tune that attacked church conformity. Later that year, he stirred up trouble with "We Don't Need No Color Code," a not-too-subtle attack on Bob Jones University's segregated dating policies. He kindled further controversy four years later with "I Blew Up the Clinic Real Good," an ironic sketch of an antiabortion extremist that was mistaken by some as a defense of clinic bombings. A former youth pastor, Taylor's commitment to his faith was as clear-cut as his outrage at the hypocrisies he saw among his fellow believers. In a way, his presence on the Contemporary Christian music scene testified to its diversity and willingness to allow dissent.

Still, Taylor's role as "evangelical rock's court jester" (as *Newsweek* once dubbed him) wasn't always a comfortable one. His debut EP sold 150,000 copies (good numbers for a Christian rock act in those days), mostly through word of mouth. Unlike many Christian artists, Taylor performed at secular venues rather than touring on the church circuit. His songs eventually began to gain airplay in the mid-1980s, though the degree of exposure he received through Christian media channels was rarely equal to the influence he had among his musical peers.

Even today, Taylor feels that "a lot of Christians have problems with satire. I would go back to Scripture and say, 'When Jesus said, "take a log out of your eye," what is that?' But they had a problem with that, and in general with this notion of subversive communication, of not saying what you really mean bluntly." Like most good satirists, there was serious intent behind Taylor's sharp tongue: "Christians have notoriously been good at finding the fault of things outside the church, but not particularly good at looking at the church as an institution and pointing out the problems. But I thought it would be a good thing to be willing to say, 'We've got our dirty laundry, but that's not what it's all about.'"

A critique of the flaws in the American evangelical subculture was not everyone's idea of what Contemporary Christian music should be. Taylor was seen as something of a loose cannon; suspicions were aroused by the cover artwork of his 1987 album *I Predict*, which some felt resembled a tarot card. Seeking a wider audience, he formed the band Chagall Guevara and signed with secular label MCA. Chagall Guevara (which included such Christian music veterans as guitarist Dave Perkins)

was an eclectic modern rock unit, aggressive in sound and darkly comic lyrically. Unfortunately, the group failed to reach a wide audience, though its 1991 album received favorable reviews in *Rolling Stone* and elsewhere. Frustrated, the band folded and Taylor returned to the Christian music world.

The failure of bands like Chagall Guevara to make the leap into the secular market didn't mean that Christians were completely unrepresented. Canadian folk singer/songwriter Bruce Cockburn was a prime example. Since the mid-1970s, Cockburn had recorded albums filled with highly literate and strikingly personal testimonies to his Christian faith. His 1981 album *Dancing in the Dragon's Jaws*, for example, was successful both as an expression of spiritual belief and a collection of inspired song-poetry. Ireland's U2 also made no secret of its belief in the redemptive power of Christ; such early hits as "Sunday Bloody Sunday" (1983) referenced God explicitly. Cockburn and U2 worked with a freedom that artists on Christian labels often lacked; they sang of their faith but didn't proselytize and didn't need to cultivate squeaky-clean images. Lesser-known examples of Christians working in the secular mainstream included T-Bone Burnett, Sam Phillips (formerly Christian recording artist Leslie Phillips, and no relation to Elvis's first producer), and the Mercy Seat (a gospel/punk hybrid which included Gordon Gano of the Violent Femmes).

"The history of Christian music has probably been the conflict between 'ministry' and entertainment," Steve Taylor notes. "In my career, you can see skid marks from trying to ride down that very slippery road." In his case, a conscious decision was made to create entertainment rooted in Christian values. Others saw this as a watering-down of a Christian musician's mission and went in the opposite direction. "Praise and worship" music, emphasizing songs extolling the Lord and based explicitly on Scripture, became an increasingly important subcategory of Christian music toward the end of the 1980s.

The split between art and message was not always complete, although the lines became increasingly evident. For some, the problem was not a lack of artistic freedom, but a weakening commitment to spreading the gospel in a plain and direct form. Singer/songwriter Steve Camp was among those artists who grew into a minister's role after a long and successful career as a Contemporary Christian recording artist. Along the way, he came to feel that too many of his peers were falling away from their mission and cheapening their message with inappropriate music.

Camp himself wasn't afraid to tap into modern rock and R&B sounds during the 1980s and early '90s. At times his sound recalled the pop/rock of bands like Loverboy or REO Speedwagon, at other times the sleek R&B of Whitney Houston. But unlike those of artists like Taylor, Camp's recordings left the impression that the music was always there to serve the evangelical message. What Camp had to say was primarily addressed to the believing Christian; his anthems of faith and condemnations of secular society had little chance of reaching an unsaved audience. "I don't wanna be friends with the world," he sang on his 1984 Myrrh album *It's a Dying World.* Such sentiments harked back to the uncompromising stance of Larry Norman's early work; there was no bid for crossover listeners here. If Taylor was a Christian satirist, Steve Camp was a no-nonsense preacher with little time for jokes.

In the late 1990s, Camp gave up a full-time recording career and went on to serve as a pastor at Grace Community Church in Sun Valley, California, a move spurred in part by the purchase of his longtime label Sparrow by corporate giant EMI in 1992. Camp felt that partnering with a secular music company was spiritually wrong, no matter how much business sense it made. "People can try to justify it in a cold and calculated way, but biblically it doesn't wash," he insists. "Nowhere in Scripture are the apostles commanded to join hands with Nero in the work of the gospel.... Having alliances with unsaved people where you've surrendered your spiritual autonomy in a relationship that exists only for money is spiritual adultery. Even people who don't know the Lord know that's wrong."

Contemporary Christian music came to reflect this unholy alliance, Camp says: "There's been a watering-down of the gospel message. We are flooded today with what I refer to as 'God-is-my-girlfriend' songs.... You have songs now that sound like romanticism between a man and a woman, and they try to take a sort of 'I want to fall in love with Jesus' attitude." Such songs, he feels, fail to provide real spiritual nourishment. "If you eat at McDonald's every day, we call it junk food," he says. "Spiritually, if you give people a fast-food Christianity, they end up with a faith that lacks biblical moorings. It's the quintessential adaptation of post modernism in music: a lack of absolutes, no standards, no rules to live by....

"There's a loss of the transcendent in the [Christian music] industry today, a loss of reverence. You see music that is not producing a high view of God. It's mostly man-centered: 'my needs, my wounds, my pain.' So what we have brought into the industry is that God exists for my needs, not for His glory. The question is, what does it mean to bring God glory, and to honor Him with music that is claiming to represent His name? That has to be the foundational issue in what we are doing in Christian music."

Looking back to the early 1990s, it would seem that Steve Taylor and Steve Camp were in polar opposite camps in a great debate over creative freedom versus biblical literalism. Yet both were reacting to tremendous changes in a rapidly expanding industry that appeared to marginalize them. The temptation to tap into the secular market had the potential to undermine the entire premise of Contemporary Christian music. You could say—at the risk of using a pagan metaphor—that Amy Grant's popularity opened a Pandora's box of troublesome issues that the Christian music industry has wrestled with to the present day.

CONTEMPORARY CHRISTIAN MUSIC TODAY:
CHALLENGES AND CONTROVERSIES

Pop music has always been liberal in its definitions. Rock music's boundaries have been flexible enough to include everything from Bread to Limp Bizkit. Country music has moved far from its earthy roots, and jazz's permutations now stretch from the avant-garde to easy listening. Overly precise labels tend to be shunned by both those who create the music and those who wish to market it to the widest possible audience.

Contemporary Christian music is another matter. From its beginnings, it was defined by the content of its lyrics; without an identifiable Christian element present, it ceases to have a reason to exist as a category. The whole idea of the genre was to provide an alternative to "the world." That was a concept on which everyone could agree.

It's not that simple. Thirty-plus years after the Jesus Music uprising began, there are fewer and fewer points of agreement on what makes a pop song Christian. This may be an indicator of success—the genre's diversity represents both artistic vitality and a broadened listenership. But does it also indicate a falling away from the music's fundamental mission?

The Gospel Music Association (GMA) brought this issue to a head in January 1999, when it announced new lyrical criteria for its Dove Award nominations. On first examination, the standards seem plain: "Gospel music is music in any style whose lyric is substantially based upon historically orthodox Christian truth contained in or derived from the Holy Bible; and/or an expression of worship of God or praise for His works; and/or testimony of relationship with God through Christ; and/or obviously prompted and informed by a Christian worldview."

It just so happened that one of the songs up for Dove eligibility that year was Sixpence None the Richer's "Kiss Me," not only a hit on Contemporary Christian radio but the biggest pop single in the secular market during 1998 as well. The band had won praise both for its wistfully tuneful folk/rock sound and its ability to hold its own as an unashamed Christian act in the secular media empire. None of this seemed to matter to the GMA; it passed over "Kiss Me" for a song of the year nomination, not a popular move in many Christian music circles. (To complicate matters further, the song's nomination for best video was announced, then retracted the following day.)

GMA president Frank Breeden later told *The Wall Street Journal* that Sixpence None the Richer "are great Christian guys and a girl, but they've made a great mainstream song." He added that the tightened lyric rule for Dove nominations was an "eligibility criterion for an awards show, not an end-all statement about Christian music." This clarification didn't soothe everyone's feelings, however. For many, the GMA's lyric standards were indicative of a host of misdeeds by the Christian music establishment: an insensitivity toward artists, a narrowness of vision of what Christian music could and should be, a misguided belief that "Christian music" should be an easily labeled, standardized product.

The subtext of this debate was the issue of who had the *authority* to determine whether or not a song was sufficiently Christian, a very old point of contention. For well over a millennium, religious bodies have attempted to regulate the content of Christian expression. This has been especially true in the visual arts. In 1563, for example, the Council of Trent cracked down on possible heresies by forbidding "the placing in a church of any image which calls to mind an erroneous dogma which might mislead the simpleminded.... In order to insure respect for its decisions, the Holy Council forbids any-

one to place or to have placed anywhere, and even in churches which are not open to the public, any unusual image unless the bishop has approved it."

Note the concern that a Christian work of art be misinterpreted by a less-than-sophisticated public—these same fears about "unusual images" crop up in today's arguments over Christian pop lyrics. The question of who should set the parameters of creative expression has grown steadily murkier in modern times. This is especially the case in the United States, where Christian denominations have fractured and subdivided for centuries. Being able to interpret God's laws according to personal conviction is at the core of American society. Jesus Music grew out of splinter sects and street ministries, where oversight by established churches often didn't exist.

The GMA, then, could not exclude Christian songs from its canon of acceptable gospel music without challenge. But even those who found fault with how the Dove nominations were conducted felt that Christian music had become increasingly vague and slack in its standards. Singer/songwriter/producer Charlie Peacock was among those who criticized the GMA for its restrictive criteria and even suggested ending the Dove Awards entirely. But he has also criticized Christian artists and those in the industry as a whole as deficient in their knowledge of the Bible and misguided by unsound theology. In his provocative book *At the Crossroads* (Broadman & Holman, 1999), Peacock called for a "kingdom perspective"—meaning a broader and more comprehensive view—about the role of music in Christian life. He stressed the right of a Christian artist to deal with a wide range of topics about the human condition; at the same time, he called for better grounding in what the Word actually says.

So, if not the GMA, then who should pass judgment on what is or isn't Christian music? Peacock and others have suggested that the "gatekeepers" should include Christian radio stations and bookstores. To a large degree, these two entities already define what is acceptable Christian music—they are the primary way the music is exposed to much of its audience. Taking a still larger role in guiding artists on a correct spiritual path might seem appropriate. Then again, it's not to be assumed that a program director or retail store owner has a better grasp on theology than a rock band does.

There is always the implication in the Christian music industry that being a professional is not enough, that there's a ministerial role to be filled as well. That's not to say that a concert promoter is considered a clergyman. But business decisions have moral implications that are simply not issues in the secular entertainment world. It's not just a question of literally spreading the gospel. Among the faithful,

stewardship—the responsibility that Christians have to take care of resources and perform their duties well—is a concern amidst the day-to-day job of selling records.

THE JPM FACTOR

Word Records A&R chief Brent Bourgeois has seen the music business from both its secular and Christian sides. Prior to taking a staff position with Word, he recorded for the secular Island and Charisma labels and released a Christian album on Reunion. You might say he's a "worldly" musician in the most favorable sense of the term. From his perspective, Christian music has been changing for the better: "Before about 1993, if you happened upon a Christian music station, you wouldn't have to know by the lyrics—you'd know by the music. It was thinner, just five years behind the pop curve, [with] drum machines that might've sounded good in 1984 and over-singing and clumsy lyrics. All of that added up to a sound that wasn't very flattering."

Today, the gap in sonic quality between Christian and secular music is far less noticeable than even a decade ago. Bourgeois attributes this in part to the growing sophistication of the listenership:

I think the media is so much more pervasive now that you can't miss it. I don't think you can keep your kids out of it if you wanted to, like you could maybe 15 years ago. Now Christian kids demand that their music has to be as good as the stuff they're hearing out there [in the secular market]. So the quality has risen because it's had to if this industry was going to survive. It had to quit trying to fool people into thinking, "Here's our faux rock band, here's our faux alternative band, here's our faux R&B stuff...."

There were people like me who came along and said, "That doesn't sound very good." The way I discussed it was, God's music ought to be the best. It shouldn't be five years behind the pop culture. It should be the best music, period.... I think it's kind of ridiculous to have a whole industry dedicated to Jesus Christ and the gospel and all that and the music be something you really didn't want to listen to.

Bourgeois is among those who are dubious about Christian radio's ability to help sell records: "We put more into it than it delivers, I think. Because everybody loves to pat everybody on the back and go, 'We had a number one song.' It's something you can hang your hat on; it's good for morale. But it's all in all a very small pond.... The radio, with the exception of a few markets like Dallas and Houston and a few other places, is insignificant to the general selling." Bourgeois has found that, for many mid-level artists, performing at church-supported events is the main way to stimulate record sales.

Many programmers feel that their listeners want to only hear tunes that glorify God in unambiguous terms. There's talk among Christian artists that songs have to meet a "Jesus per minute" (or JPM) requirement on some Christian stations. Newer artists are expected to state their belief in Christ more clearly than are established ones. As Bourgeois explains, "A Michael W. Smith or a Steven Curtis Chapman or an Amy Grant, they don't have to say it at all, because people know. But a new artist sort of has to establish their credentials." A related phenomenon is what's called "Jesus-is-my-boyfriend" songs—pop love ballads written by or for younger female artists and addressed to the Lord with all the naïve sweetness that the term implies.

THE CHRISTIAN MUSIC MEDIA KINGDOM

The checks and balances within Christian entertainment are complex, with economic, spiritual, and artistic concerns intertwined in sometimes curious ways. It's a good point in this narrative to examine the current size and scope of the industry and the market it serves.

Thirty-five years after the birth of the Jesus Music phenomenon, Contemporary Christian music has become an enduring segment of the American entertainment industry. It exists both as a branch of the secular music industry and as an alternative version of it. More than anything, it is defined by its core audience, which expects the artists within the genre to uphold certain spiritual values, both on- and off-stage. As this audience has changed, so has the Christian music industry changed with it.

To be in this world but not of it—that's the goal many Christians strive to attain. Living within the all-pervasive pop culture empire is a tricky proposition for many evangelicals. Increasingly, mass entertainment *is* the world, and rejecting it entirely is not an option. The apocalyptic pronouncements of the Jesus Music movement seem remote to many. Today, an elaborate Christian entertainment industry mirrors trends in the secular media while modifying or deleting their most offensive aspects. The form and texture of pop culture is there, but the content is infused with spiritual ingredients. The whole process might be compared to a vegetarian restaurant that tries to maintain a conventional menu, slipping in tofu and tempeh in place of meat with as much skill as possible.

From the early Jesus Music days onward, the premise of most Christian artists has been that the medium is not necessarily the message, that the hardest rock could carry the Word safely. Naysayers like Bob Larson have largely fallen by the wayside or changed their opinions; today, the idea that Christians can imitate secular pop music in order to spread their message is largely accepted.

This really isn't so surprising. Evangelicals eat the same fast food and drive the same fast cars as their fellow Americans. Very few have equated adherence to fundamentalist Bible teachers with a complete rejection of modern consumerism. Still, even the most visionary among those in the evangelical community couldn't have predicted the scope and extent of Christian media at the dawn of the twenty-first century. A visit to one of the larger Christian book store chains—LifeWay or Family, for instance—shows how nearly every pop culture niche is filled by its Christ-centered equivalent. Slogans and images of pop culture are transformed into Christian paraphernalia (called "Jesus junk" by some critics). T-shirts ask "Got Jesus?"; decals depict Calvin (late of the comic strip *Calvin and Hobbes*) with hands folded in prayer. Market values are smoothly blended with spiritual tenets at these shops, which offer everything from books of Bible-based dating tips to products like Testamints, rolls of little candies with bits of Scripture included.

Bookstores are the most familiar gatekeepers for Christian products, providing a place where believers can feel safe about what they buy. The days of stocking only old-fashioned gospel records are gone, but some retailers still get nervous about carrying some of the Christian rock CDs. One store reportedly refused to carry Jars of Clay's *Much Afraid* because its cover showed a young boy wearing only swimming trunks. In a letter published in the April 2000 issue of *CCM* magazine (more on this publication a little later), an assistant store manager from Arkansas complained about the cover of a recent issue that featured the Newsboys wearing dark eye makeup: "The makeup made them look very secular, and if I didn't know better... very demonic. We have a very delicate clientele. A lot of our customers are against contemporary music in the first place." A little eyeliner goes a long way in the world of Christian marketing—what might seem trivial to an outsider is viewed as a sign that an artist may be too worldly, too loose in upholding his or her faith.

Offending Christian bookstore owners is something the labels want to avoid. But there's more to Christian merchandising than these traditional retailers. Sparrow Records A&R man Nick Barre notes that his label's number one retail outlet is Wal-Mart.

The state of Christian music can also be gauged by its radio outlets. In a 2000 survey by the National Association of Religious Broadcasters, 202 stations in the United States described their formats as "Adult Contemporary" Christian, while 120 classified themselves as "Contemporary Christian," and 69 fell into the "Christian Hit Radio" category. These numbers are somewhat misleading, as many of the stations listed reach a small listenership or devote only a portion of their airtime to Contemporary Christian music formats.

In reality, there are approximately 65 Contemporary Christian stations that reach significant listenerships in major U.S. markets. About 50 of these are Adult Contemporary stations, a format that includes all but the most rock-oriented Christian artists. Most of the remaining stations favor the Contemporary Hit Radio format and tend to be a bit edgier and hipper in sound. With a few exceptions, the highest-rated stations are found in the South, the West, and parts of the Midwest; among the most influential are KLTY (Dallas), KSBJ (Houston), WPOZ (Orlando), KXOJ (Tulsa), WBGB (Jacksonville, Florida) and WAY (Nashville).

As in secular radio, networks and syndicators dominate much of the Christian radio industry. The largest overall network is California-based Salem Communications, which owns nearly 80 radio stations and syndicates music, news, and talk programming to some 1,600 stations. Recently, the company found success with "The Fish," a format that falls between Adult Contemporary and Christian Hit Radio in terms of play list and targeted audience. As of summer 2001, Salem was operating stations with Fish formats in Los Angeles, Dallas, Atlanta, Chicago, Cleveland, and Sacramento.

Salem Communications also owns CCM Communications, publisher of six consumer and trade publications with a combined readership of more than 300,000.

The most important among these is *CCM* magazine, the virtual Bible (so to speak) of the Contemporary Christian genre. *CCM* and sister publication *CCM Update* (aimed at music and radio professionals) combine the functions of *Spin* and *Billboard* in the secular realm—coverage in their pages is essential for all but the most underground Christian act. The look and layout of *CCM* is clean and sleek, a fitting counterpart to much of the music it covers. The magazine is the undisputed leader in its field. In fact, the term "CCM"—the popular acronym for Contemporary Christian music, used for more than 25 years—is actually a registered trademark of CCM Communications.

While *CCM* serves as an arbiter of the genre's artistic and theological standards overall, there are a number of other publications that speak for smaller segments. Among the best known is *HM*, published out of Austin, Texas, and aimed at a youthful, heavy metal/hardcore punk readership. Billing itself as "your hard music authority," *HM* has lively, street-oriented writings, devoting lots of space to little-known but worthy bands as well as Christian underground stars like P.O.D. and Five Iron Frenzy. Also appealing to a younger crowd is *7ball*, which covers everything from neo-grunge rockers to folksy singer/ songwriters. In addition to the print media, Christian music fandom is well represented on the Web on an ever-changing number of sites.

Annual music festivals are another key part of the Christian music infrastructure. Most of these combine preaching and teaching with entertainment—Woodstock meets Billy Graham revival, as it were. Cornerstone, held in rural Illinois every summer since 1984, is probably the most established of these events; it drew 25,000 attendees in 2000. Other festivals of importance include Georgia's Atlanta Fest, Ohio's Alive Fest, Pennsylvania's Creation East, and Washington state's Creation West. These and other festivals provide a performing circuit for artists and are especially important in exposing new acts. Sharing the stage with the musicians are celebrity preachers like Eastman Curtis and James Robison (the latter a familiar name from the Moral Majority political wars of the 1980s).

HEAVY METAL MINISTRY

Not everything within the Contemporary Christian music world is aimed at a mass market. There are also subgenres and underground movements that have existed for years. Among the most significant is what used to be termed Christian heavy metal, which today has diversified to include such splinter categories as Christian Death Metal and Christian Goth, among many others.

First exposure to these artists can be jarring. The CD cover art of long-established groups, such as Mortification and Tourniquet, is as lurid as that of secular counterparts, filled with skulls, knives, serpents, and similarly threatening imagery. The sounds inside are equally uncompromising, built around ferocious guitar riffs and maniacally shrieking vocals. If the music seems derived from the likes of Metallica and Slayer, the lyrics are fervently biblical—even more so than those by softer Christian artists. A dose of these bands challenges the notions of what Christian music can be and should be, even for most believers. Welding the power of heavy/speed/ thrash metal to the Word is not as bizarre an idea as it might seem—the confrontational, in-your-face quality of the music makes it a powerful (if sometimes crude) evangelical tool. The stories of the Old and New Testament are perfect raw material for the melodramatics of heavy metal.

Christian metal and its offshoots remain a minority taste; for many, the satanic connotations of the music's sound and imagery are too much to overcome. No matter—the subgenre remains alive and seething, with its own record labels, festivals, publications, and fan Web sites. Misunderstanding from secular "metalheads" and more conservative Christian musicians has only served to forge tighter bonds between the bands and their fans.

Pastor Bob Beeman has ministered to the spiritual needs of this community for some two decades. A Montana native, he made the transition from keyboardist (working with Larry Norman, among others) to youth minister in the mid-1970s. Ordained as an evangelist in 1980 (by no less than Chan Romero, composer of such hits as "Hippy Hippy Shake" prior to becoming a clergyman), Beeman began pastoring heavy metal musicians five years later in Whittier, California. Among the bands participating were Stryper, Barren Cross, Deliverance, and Guardian—all groups that would become mainstays of the Christian metal scene during the 1980s. A self-described old hippie, Beeman adopted a bit of the heavy metal look himself, sporting "poofy" blue-streaked hair for a time.

What came out of Beeman's Bible classes was a phalanx of spiritually armed hands ready to combine fervent evangelism with head-banging hard rock. Since then, Christian metal has waxed and waned in popularity, just like its secular equivalent. Some bands, like Stryper, enjoyed considerable success but then splintered. Others, like Disciple, have soldiered on, carrying the faith to Christian and secular fans alike.

Pastor Beeman's heavy metal ministry continued to grow, and by the late 1980s took on the name Sanctuary. Currently based out of the Nashville, Tennessee, suburb of Mt. Juliet, Pastor Bob (as he prefers to be known) is at the hub of an extensive musical/theological network active across the United States and Europe. Rather than operate out of a church building, Sanctuary reaches its flock through home study courses, an elaborate Web site, and telephone counseling. It is also heavily involved in recording, distributing, and promoting Christian heavy metal bands, making its exact function hard to classify.

Sanctuary has been viewed with suspicion by outsiders—Jimmy Swaggert once called Beeman "the heavy metal minister from hell." "The whole Christian community looks at us and assumes we're a cult," Beeman responds, "though maybe not so much now as in the beginning. Any kind of fringe movement is suspect. We have a 40-page doctrinal statement so that people know exactly where we stand, that we're legitimate. There are always those people who say we are in sin because our people have long hair or listen to music with a beat that's satanic in origin."

Heavy metal may raise a hellacious din, but it claims a role in extolling heaven. "The Bible speaks of both celebration and of worship," says Beeman. "As I read it, celebration is loud clanging cymbals, lots of instruments, lot of noise.… One of the criticisms has been that the music we have is not worshipful and that you can't praise the Lord with it. That's true, but that's not what it's created for. Celebration is singing about the Lord; worship is singing to the Lord. And we do that differently."

Channeling the testosterone-fueled aggression of heavy metal into Christian service has been a controversial idea ever since the genre's 1980s heyday. Leather,

studs, and shaggy hair are still red flags for many evangelicals. Sanctuary has provided a "ministry on the edge" for those who identify with rock's hard fringe. Still, Beeman worries about the spiritual isolation of his followers: "You can't mentor [without] the older men teaching the younger men. People who are a little older in the faith are not real excited about that [heavy metal] style of music and that style of dress. And so they're not going to come and coexist with a group like that. These people who are marginalized somehow need to be integrated into where the mature Christians are at…so we've forced them to be involved in other groups. We're not an end-all ministry—our goal is to take people who have somehow been affected by music on the edge and help them to get grounded in the Word."

Beeman's work has taken him far beyond traditional pastoring, however. He's promoted bands, organized music festivals, even put groups together from scratch. Intense Records, a Christian heavy metal label active in the '80s and early '90s, was his brainchild. Pastor Bob's seal of approval was highly valued by bands and music retailers alike. "My staff and I made the choice to put my picture along with a little endorsement in a lot of the early albums," he says. "We did that for a couple of reasons—one, so that people would realize this was a valuable ministry, and second, to give stores a sense of validity.

We'd get a lot of letters from the stores saying, 'We don't understand this music very much, but if it has your picture on it, we want to have it, because we know you're established and all that.'"

All of the above blurs the lines between ministry and the music business in provocative ways. If Pastor Bob is less than a cult leader, some critics might accuse him of ego-tripping at the expense of young and spiritually impressionable musicians, though in face-to-face conversation he doesn't come across this way. Hefty in build and quiet in demeanor, Beeman seems an intelligent, reasonable spokesman for his cause. And he doesn't mind admitting his mistakes and limitations.

One of Beeman's most celebrated—and ill-fated—projects was the creation of the 1980s thrash-metal band Vengeance (later renamed Vengeance Rising). Beeman handpicked a lineup of expert players with jazz, blues, and mainstream rock backgrounds for the group, with charismatic singer Roger Martinez selected as front man. "We put Vengeance together for one purpose, and that was to reach the edge at the same time the world did," Beeman says with a distinct tone of pride. "Christian music has traditionally been a few years behind the music on the edge in secular society. When we released the first Vengeance album in the late 1980s, I believe it was the first time in several centuries that we were absolutely current with what was going on in the world's

music. (The cover of the first Vengeance album, *Human Sacrifice*, featured a closeup of Beeman's hand, oozing blood from a spike driven into his palm.)

Vengeance was a bold stab artistically, a full-throttle, thrash-metal exercise with a clear-cut Christian message. The band endured several reorganizations during the early 1990s and continued to release albums despite lineup changes. Beyond his role as lead vocalist and lyricist, Martinez also served as a pastor at Sanctuary fellowship meetings. Gradually, though, he began to drift away from his religious convictions until, in 1995, he renounced them entirely. Today Martinez continues to lead a revamped version of the group while militantly crusading against Christianity via seminars and a Web site. Like an Old Testament rebel angel, he attacks his former faith without mercy, condemning Christians for intolerance and persecution of nonbelievers through the ages.

Beeman is moderate in his response to this apostasy: "I listen to Roger's rants, and a lot of his criticism of the church is valid. You don't have to go far to see the abuses; you just have to turn on the television. But his throwing the baby out with the bathwater is not the answer.... I'm not excited about where he's at, and I think he's a dangerous person at this point."

Currently, Beeman serves on the board of directors (as well as pastor) of Diamante

Servant Distribution, which handles the releases of more than 60 independent record companies. Much of the product could be described as heavy metal or hard-core punk, though a few more sedate artists like Steve Camp and Crystal Lewis are represented as well. "My involvement in Diamante is in a lot of ways to help turn the [Christian music] industry around," he says. "We are the only Christian distribution company that's owned by Christians. We're putting in place more of a Christ-centered relationship, and demanding the same thing from those labels and all the artists."

Some of the most sonically aggressive bands in Christian music are distributed by Diamante. But for all the latitude it gives its artists musically, the company is also the most particular when it comes to lyric messages. Pastor Bob oversees the content of the songs, and certain standards must be met: "I think freedom of speech and creativity are important, and I would never squelch that. But false doctrine and an unresolved message are two things that concern me. By 'unresolved message' I mean that there are some albums that come out that are angry with the church, with society, whatever. And there's no answer there. I think that's irresponsible.... I don't mean that someone has to adhere to my personal doctrinal stance. But a person needs to understand how to be saved, and if there's a blurring of that, then I have a problem with that. The content has got to be clear."

How far can a devotee of extreme music go and still be a good Christian? After two decades as a heavy metal minister, Pastor Bob still isn't sure: "Sanctuary does a couple of music festivals in Sweden. I was at one of them, and I had some people come in from London who call themselves Christian vampires. That's a stretch for me. They have surgically implanted fangs, white contact lenses, and blood-red hair. Their experience with the Lord seems to be genuine. Their focus is on blood, but so is a lot of the Bible. That's uncomfortable to me, but it doesn't seem to be to them.... I've gone through a lot of cultural changes over the years, and every time I draw a line somewhere, it seems like God draws it somewhere else."

BRUTAL BLESSINGS

Ghouls for Jesus? As bizarre as this might seem to the uninitiated, there's an extensive underground fandom for dark-tinged Christian rock. "Brutal music" is a term used by some devotees to describe this subgenre—whether the music is slow and grinding or shrill and assaulting, the effect is intentionally harsh. Unlike this music's secular counterpart, though, the goal is to extract something positive from all this gloom and doom. There's an aesthetic of torment that occurs again and again in the lyrics and graphics of these bands and their followers. Bands like Tortured Conscience, Sordid Death, Crimson Thorn, Grim, and Lament appear to be the modern equivalents of medieval self-flagellation cults, scourging themselves as they await the end of the world. All of this is intended to celebrate Scripture and honor the Lord. As the motto of the Whipping Post, a fan Web site, puts it: "Brutal whipping for our sin…brutal music for our savior."

Diamante distributes a number of these groups. Among the most intriguing is Rackets and Drapes, a pale-faced, leather-clad threesome that has been described as the Christian equivalent to Marilyn Manson. On *Trick or Treat*, the band's third CD (released in 2000), singer/bassist Kandy Kane croaks and shrieks his way through a brace of ominous tunes with insinuating swagger. Trying to find an upbeat "God-is-love" message amidst the campy Halloween posturing that color this album takes more than a little effort. But beneath the self-consciously ugly imagery is a disdain for the material world that *is* decidedly Christian. "The bitter taste of rotten fruit is vomit in the mouth…the taste is sour and is spit upon the ground," Kane slowly intones in "Rotten Apples," giving a Gothic slant to Adam and Eve's temptation in Paradise. Spitting out the vileness of a Satan-dominated planet is the main theme of *Trick or Treat*; the album's rampant disgust for mankind's sins wouldn't be out of place in a fundamentalist sermon.

Rackets and Drapes may or may not be the cutting edge of brutal music, but it does embody some of the paradoxes in today's Christian rock. *Trick or Treat*'s songs castigate materialism, sexual excess, enslavement to pleasure—an almost ascetic stance. Yet the band's look and sound are definitely hip and worldly, steeped in the sort of necrophiliac Goth self-indulgence that would seem the antithesis of a Christ-centered lifestyle. On one hand, Rackets and Drapes is completely defensible as a creative group of musicians trying to prod the consciences of young believers with an unusual treatment of Bible-inspired themes. On the other, the notion that *any* kind of entertainment can present a Christian message effectively is severely tested here—only a few can accept the Word from a messenger in androgynous death-rocker garb.

Another Diamante-distributed act worth mentioning is Saviour Machine. Pastor Bob Beeman has endorsed the band's music, a grandiose brand of Goth metal thoroughly steeped in biblical language and imagery. Since the late 1990s, Saviour Machine has been releasing CDs in its ongoing *Legend* series, heralded as "the unofficial soundtrack to the end of the world." There's some truth to this claim. These albums explore the fine points of the Book of Revelation, painting the ultimate clash of Christ and Antichrist in bold and bloody colors. *Legend Part II*, for instance, surrounds the listener in a soundscape of massed choirs, clanging guitars, and thudding rhythm tracks, with orchestral touches adding some classical grandeur. Lead singer Eric Clayton wails his lyrics with great solemnity, a latter-day prophet of doom. There is hope for the faithful offered in the message, but the pervading mood is one of fear and trembling.

Intentionally extreme, Saviour Machine is significant beyond the relatively small niche market it reaches. Clayton and his bandmates create some of the most unabashedly biblical rock music ever recorded. As blunt lyrically as it is sonically bombastic, it makes no concessions to unbelievers. The group transforms heavy metal's overblown fantasy motifs into a lyric saga that fans can immerse themselves in completely. Artistically as well as theologically, it makes perfect sense. Why dream about some ill-defined "Stairway to Heaven" when Saviour Machine lays out literal paths to salvation or damnation?

A FAR CRY FROM "KISS ME"?

Saviour Machine is far from alone in its obsession with Revelation, of course. Endtime prophecies are central to the world view of many evangelicals. The theory of dispensationism—that Christ's return will be preceded by the rapture of his faithful and a period of tribulation suffered by nonbelievers—is alive and well, and has inspired quite a few Christian pop culture

works of recent years. This deep concern with the end of the world and the battle between ultimate good and evil is definitely a dividing line between Christian and secular entertainment. Some of Contemporary Christian music's best-known artists have supported the advancement of this stillcontroversial interpretation of Scripture.

Of course, this is nothing new—remember that Larry Norman's "I Wish We'd All Been Ready," one of the key songs of the Jesus Music heyday, was a graphic description of the fate of the unsaved. This same concept is at the heart of one of the most phenomenal publishing successes in recent history: the *Left Behind* series, an ongoing multivolume evangelical thriller that has sold upwards of 30 million copies in hardcover and paperback.

Coauthors Tim LaHaye and Jerry Jenkins present the events of Revelation in contemporary terms: A brave-hearted reporter seeks to expose the Antichrist (in the guise of a United Nations diplomat) as millions face salvation or destruction. There are plagues, storms, sinners punished, and wavering believers called back to faith. These world-shaking events made it to the screen when Cloud Ten Pictures, a Canadian company, turned *Left Behind* into a $17 million film starring Kirk Cameron and Chelsea Noble (both veterans of TV's *Growing Pains*).

The *Left Behind* soundtrack album was released by Reunion Records in 2000 in advance of the film. Such established talents as Michael W. Smith, Third Day, Avalon, Rebecca St. James, Bob Carlisle, and Kathy Troccoli contributed tracks to the disc, with several of the tunes used as theme songs for the characters. Reunion senior vice president and general manager George King was quoted on the ChristianityToday.com Web site as calling the album a "once in a lifetime recording [that] has generated a great deal of momentum within the industry and among Christian music artists."

Left Behind initially sold more than three million copies as a video; it received mixed reviews after its secular theatrical release. But whatever its aesthetic merits, the film was highly significant to both Christian and secular culture. Like the novels that inspired it, *Left Behind* blurred the lines between political opinion, biblical interpretation, and adventure/fantasy entertainment.

Relatively few in the secular world are familiar with Tim LaHaye's writings, though he's been a leading force in the evangelical community for a quarter century. A co-founder of the Moral Majority, he has crusaded for a host of fundamentalist and politically conservative causes under various organizational banners. His 1980 best-seller *The Battle for the Mind* (cowritten with wife Beverly, herself a conservative Christian activist) condemned secular humanism as the leading corrosive force in American life.

As he sees it, the anti-God philosophy of the secular humanist establishment is indistinguishable from the satanic forces that will struggle for control of the earth at the time of the Second Coming. Besides the 40-plus novels and nonfiction books he has written, LaHaye has advanced his views through his Family Life Seminars for Christian Couples, the anti-evolution Institute for Creation Science, and, most recently, the Pre Trib Research Center, devoted to the study of end-time prophesies.

According to LaHaye's biblical interpretations, the final confrontation between Christ and Antichrist is being played out on Earth at this very moment. His condemnations of the enemy are blunt and uncompromising. "All thinking people in America realize an anti-Christian, anti-moral, and anti-American philosophy permeates this country and the world," he wrote in an essay featured in the September 1999 edition of his *Pre-Trib Perspectives* newsletter. "It dominates the public school system from kindergarten through graduate school.... It dominates the entertainment industry, and it elects a predominance of liberals to both parties in our national government." LaHaye went on to single out the United Nations, the ACLU, Planned Parenthood, and various other agents of "atheistic socialism" as forerunners of the Antichrist's rule of Earth. (Essentially, this essay reads like *Left Behind*, with a somewhat larger cast of villains.)

Is LaHaye's cause too far outside the American mainstream for the likes of Michael W. Smith or Avalon to lend it their support? Putting pop music in the service of a political agenda is nothing new—there were the antinuclear benefit concerts by rock celebrities in the 1970s, and, during the 2000 presidential election, Melissa Etheridge campaigned for Al Gore and Rage Against the Machine supported Ralph Nader. But linking those who disagree with you to the Beast of Revelations is a bit different from campaigning for votes, as is associating an artist's musical ministry with such assertions.

This volatile mixture of entertainment, religion, and extremist politics might not sit well with secular audiences—assuming they're ever exposed to *Left Behind*. The film's confrontational tone was a far cry from the indirect Christianity of "Kiss Me" or Amy Grant's secular hits, much more extreme than that which the Dove Awards strives to present to secular TV audiences. This suggests that Contemporary Christian music sometimes offers a different message to its core audience than to the world at large. And keep in mind that, according to LaHaye's way of thinking, Reunion Records is in league with the "forces of darkness"—specifically Zomba Music Group, Reunion's secular parent label. There are more than a few paradoxes in all this.

The doomsday visions of *Left Behind* are not the only ones being advanced through Contemporary Christian music. In June 2000, Squint Entertainment released a compilation of songs inspired by the influential book *Roaring Lambs* (Zondervan, 1993), written by the late Bob Briner. A veteran sports publicist and Emmy-winning television executive, Briner became a leading advocate of Christian involvement in the secular world. He particularly focused upon the need for Christian artists to advance their ideas effectively among nonbelievers in the entertainment field.

According to Briner's strategy, "roaring lambs" are Christians who infiltrate the camp of the nonbelievers and help spread the gospel through the quality of their work and the integrity of their conduct. Squint's *Roaring Lambs* CD featured tracks by such Christian luminaries as Sixpence None the Richer, Michael W. Smith, Charlie Peacock, Jars of Clay, and Steven Curtis Chapman, addressing the theme of being a "roaring lamb" from different perspectives. (Note: As a company, Squint Entertainment embodied the Briner philosophy of engagement exceptionally well. Unfortunately, its success with Sixpence None the Richer was not enough to keep the label afloat. Squint chief Steve Taylor's relationship with partner Gaylord Entertainment grew strained and, after a failed attempt to go independent, the label's staff was let go in mid-2001. It currently exists in name only as an imprint of Word Entertainment, which is in turn now a part of Time-Warner AOL.)

BACK TO CANE RIDGE

In the midst of this battle for the soul of American culture, there's been a counter-trend within Christian music that avoids doctrinal fine points in favor of pure celebration of the Lord. This genre has been referred to as "praise and worship music," often known simply as "worship" music. Rather than dealing with human struggles, its songs are modern-day hymns that pay homage to God in direct, fervent terms. Worship music is meant to be participatory and de-emphasizes the role of performing artists. The most talked-about worship events have been those sponsored by the Passion Conference, associated with Atlanta-based Choice Ministries. While praise and worship has been a part of the Christian music scene since the early 1970s, the Passion events are noteworthy for their ability to attract teens and college students with a minimum of show business trappings. They are advertised as "solemn assemblies," not as entertainment.

"Passion is a movement without a face," says Sparrow A&R staffer Nick Barre. "They have these huge events where tens of thousands of people gather, and you don't know who's going to be there—it's like an anti-festival. It's a complete rejection of all the Christian celebrities and rock stars that my generation has helped to promote.... I don't think these kids care about Christian music. These are not performances. In fact, if there's a hint of a performance, that makes

it uncool. It's a real call to holiness—one of the most inspirational things I've seen in a long time."

Sparrow has marketed a series of *Passion* CDs to strong response. Their focus is on the overall message of the music rather than on contributing artists. The featured vocalists are referred to as "worship leaders" or "artist/worshippers"—a clear distinction being made between them and Christian pop singers. Worship leaders like Charlie Hall, Chris Tomlin, and David Crowder— all featured on the *Passion* albums—resemble early Jesus Music artists like Randy Stonehill and Love Song in their musical sweetness and melodic simplicity (though Hall, for one, couches his lyrical prayers in U2-like rock anthems). They blur the lines between pastor and performer almost completely.

The Passion events are aimed at Christians ages 18 to 25 and promote a generational bonding in the name of the Lord. The biggest event so far has been OneDay, held outside Memphis, Tennessee, on May 20, 2000, and attended by an estimated 40,000 people. "It wasn't meant to be a public event," says Barre. "You had no idea who was on the bill, so there was zero celebrity factor. Kids drove in from Alaska, a kid came from Singapore who found out about it on the Internet. There was a kid in Paris who couldn't attend, so they got a church and a real audio card and played what was happening through their speakers. It was like this huge party or rave, where you get a live broadcast of a DJ and have your own dance."

There are definite similarities between gatherings like Passion and the phenomenon of raves, in which young people communally dance themselves into altered states under the guidance of revered DJs. With both, there's a sense of harnessing and manipulating pop culture icons in the service of a counterculture underground. The use of 1960s and '70s icons and slogans (Flower Power imagery, smiley faces) by rave organizers is mirrored in the slick techno-derived imagery found on Passion's CD packaging and Web site. There are even subtle references to the inner liberation of group prayer as being the ultimate high, far beyond Ecstasy (double meaning intentional).

It's fair to say that Passion and similar worship events take cues from pop culture celebrations, while raves have a spiritual element akin to religious surrender. What's common to both is an intense hunger for transcendence, of breaking through the normal and the rational. It seems appropriate that one of the key bands in modern worship music is named Delirious— a phrase that would apply to many an all-night raver as well.

By the end of 2001, worship music had become decidedly trendy. Reacting against their own star appeal, Christian artists tried to tone down their star power

when stepping into a worship leader role. According to a Reunion Records press release, Michael W. Smith and an all-star choir (including Amy Grant and Out of Eden) "dropped all their agendas" and "came clothed in humility" when performing at a worship event in Lakeland, Florida. De-celebrifying one's self is no easy matter—what's important to note here is the recognition that Contemporary Christian music needs to shed some of its glitz and glamour in order to return to its original purpose.

Beyond any pop fad overtones, this latest wave of worship events is a return to something as old as American evangelical Christianity itself. The need to be broken in the spirit publicly, to cry out for God's love among fellow believers, runs back through the Jesus movement to the frontier camp meetings of 200 years ago. Joyous abandonment en masse didn't start with raves.

Imagine this scene: A young man and woman arrive separately at a wild celebration, full of shouting and dancing and singing. Stripping off extra clothing, the man plunges into the crowd, hugging and kissing male and female alike; the woman lets her hair down and starts to gyrate furiously. Finally, the two find each other in the throng and, still caught up in the fervor, embrace. The man begins to loudly sing: "I have my Jesus in my arms, sweet as honey, strong as bacon ham...." This may sound like a crazed techno dancefest, but it's actually taken from an account of Abraham Lincoln's father and mother at a Kentucky revival in 1806.

Contemporary Christian music enters the twenty-first century divided between pop-rock aesthetes and heavy metal Bible-thumpers, tempted by worldly success and chafing at restrictions set by questionable authority. But looming above all this confusion is the long shadow of a deeply rooted American faith tradition. The connection is there—as the old hymn puts it, "the circle is unbroken." A sinner begging for salvation at Cane Ridge two centuries ago would be delighted to see young people surrendering to Christ at a Passion event—even if he or she didn't relate to the electric guitars.

TESTIMONIES: INTERVIEWS WITH CHRISTIAN ARTISTS

MARGARET BECKER

Since her 1987 recording debut, Margaret Becker has released a series of albums that veer from rock to R&B to Third World–influenced pop. Growing up on Long Island, New York, she wrote songs and dreamed of a career as a cabaret singer. Unlike some of her peers, she didn't deliberately set out to be a Contemporary Christian artist—the spiritual tinge of her songwriting naturally led her in that direction. She quickly found herself in demand as a backup vocalist as well as a writer once she arrived in Nashville in 1985. From her first hit, "Never for Nothing," onward, Becker established herself as a distinctive singer with an individual point of view. A series of Charlie Peacock–produced albums in the late 1980s and early '90s saw her developing more artistic subtlety. She also began to explore her Catholic roots, a move that caused some concern among her fundamentalist Christian fans. For the most part, though, radio programmers and her fan base remained loyal during her time of religious exploration. Her most recent album, What Kind of Love, *released by Sparrow Records in 1999, was an elegant, understated song collection. Thus far, Becker has received three GMA Dove Awards and has authored several books aimed at the Christian market.*

Part of your role is to be confessional in your work. Do you see it that way?

MB: I don't see it as part of my job, but it excites me about art in general. The thing that always excites me, whether it's a painting or a movie, or music, is the ability for people to present their experience with their own personal template, and yet allow you to insert yourself to the part where you are moved or changed— art that lifts you out of yourself and gives you a different point of view, and then drops you back a little bit changed. That's the type of art that I try to create.

Margaret Becker
Photo by Matthew Barnes

It does seem, though, that a Christian artist's work needs to be true—you're not just being entertaining. Does that put you on the spot at times?

MB: Oh, absolutely. It's not a comfortable position, and that's probably the beauty and the incredible challenge of it. For the most part, you can't do something that is false or has the least bit of fluff to it and still continue to have the right to make commentary. In fact, that's one of the criteria in defining our music, and I think that's one of the things that has changed as of late—that requirement has not become as stringent. The business itself has fractured, and I think it's a good fracture, because it's allowed people to make what I would call passing commentary that feels good and has great entertainment value but at the core also holds certain values.

Doesn't that kind of music risk getting caught in the middle between the secular and the Christian markets?

MB: Absolutely, but unfortunately that is part of the sacrifice you make when you get into Christian music. There are very few Christian musicians who make a very good living at what they do. You can count them on maybe two hands. I know the secular audience is quite fickle, but the Christian audience is worse, because there are all sorts of factions within an overall faith group. So if you're speaking about something really poignant that happened

to you, you run the risk of offending a good 40 to 50 percent of the people, because you used the wrong terminology.

Have things like that happened to you?

MB: Oh, everything. Every time I would put out an album, we would have to go over the lyrics, which would irk me. Every single lyric is combed over by several different people from several different standpoints for little things that might make people crazy, but even though I've been conscientious to the point where I've regretted it in certain instances, I have still offended people just by who I am. Sometimes I walk out on stage and I offend people. So there's really not a lot I can do, and I realize that now. But as a younger artist I was more willing and eager to think there was a formula, when people can just be critical, period.

You've changed artistically since your first album. Did you change as a person or just in your response to the audience?

MB: I've matured as a person, and the commentary I was making at 26 years old, God forbid it would be the same that I'd be saying at 36 or 38. I don't want to remain stagnant, and that's been part of the challenge, not only as a person, but artistically. So what I did is make commentary relevant to where I was at. For the first album I was in a very evangelical state and I was going to do all that I could to make as many people hear about what I believed was the center of life. As I went on as an individual, I saw how the subtlety of evangelism is really a wonderful tool as well. So I looked for different ways to paint the same picture of the cross without using two pieces of black that look exactly like it.

Do you feel that you still evangelize through your music?

MB: I think it's the participant's choice. But I've been quite humbled in this way. I no longer see it [faith] as something I can bring about. At this point in my life, I think God will have His way, regardless of what I do. And I think the best thing I can do is just be honest. If people are evangelized by that honest commentary, so be it. If they're not, it's not my responsibility.

Is it okay if someone listens to your latest album and doesn't come away with a clear sense that you're a Christian?

MB: I don't see it as a failure. Especially with the last two records I've done, I've tried to write more from a commonality of the human need, and then to pepper that commentary with what I perceive to be the answer that has applied to my life. To some Christians, that sends them running to the hills. They don't want that. They want it really heavy-handed, make no mistake about it. But with the last two records, you're going to know that I'm

speaking about Christ, but you're still going to feel that this maybe isn't the Jesus that our culture has seen in the media, which I think is probably one of the worst faces of Christ since the Crusades.

Where does that place you in Christian music?

MB: I feel that I'm very left of center. I think my audience is very left of center, but I think they're mature people and they've gone along in this life quite like myself, feeling like "Yes, I have a sense of peace and a center here, but by no means is every question answered." Those people are very few and far between, and most of those people don't listen to Christian music. People who are listening to me are listening to Sarah McLachlan or Kate Bush. They include me because they like what I'm saying, but I don't think that for the most part they're Christian music listeners.

Is it difficult to hang on to this audience?

MB: I think a lot of these people at one point did listen [to Christian music]— that's another trend in Christian music right now. The Christian music audience used to be just completely loyal to Christian music, but now the Baby Boomers and the very upper tip of the GenXers have become very diverse. I've made the cut with some of these people. As they've moved on, they've taken me along with them.

Have you encountered any sort of bias as a Christian in the secular music world?

MB: I haven't. I've met people all along the way who I never thought would know me, in record companies that I've never even dealt with. It always astounds me. I've never gotten resistance; in fact, the wheels have been greased on my behalf many times.

Is Sparrow able to get your music outside the Christian market?

MB: We've yet to see that, frankly. I think at one point, when they were first purchased by EMI, there was an impetus to do that, but I think there was a backlash in the industry as a whole and they pulled back.

A backlash from the Christian music community?

MB: Yes. People who cross over are demons—essentially, that was the underlying tone. So they [Sparrow] didn't want to jeopardize their standing. They've always been known as a "ministry label," so they pulled back.

What's been the impact of your return to Catholicism?

MB: It's something that I don't focus on. The truth is, if people were to grade me on my Catholicism, I'd fail miserably. I don't adhere to most of the tenets. I was born and raised Catholic but I was in the evangelical church for years. And it became

oppressive in a sense for me—I was stilted, I wasn't learning anything, and I just felt lifeless. One Sunday, I went down to my local Catholic church out of desperation and I said, "I'm going to sit here and be anonymous and see what I used to feel as a kid." And it was as if the message came full circle for me. When I began to say that to people, all they heard was "Catholic."

There is a huge backlash against Catholics in the evangelical community because they're perceived to be idolatrous and all these other things. It was shocking to me. It became such an issue—you would've thought I'd had nine affairs and six babies out of wedlock and killed somebody. So after that, when people would ask me, I'd say, "I attend a Catholic church, but I'm not a good Catholic—I attend a Catholic church because the one in my neighborhood is very Christ-centered, but they're also very world-view." I'm a very world-view person and I appreciate the history of the established ecumenical churches—Episcopalian, Catholic—because they've already gone through their adolescence, so to speak. They've had all these huge leaders who've done well but have also failed the people in certain instances, so their history allows them now a maturity, whereas I think the American evangelical church is going through a certain gawky adolescence now, and it's bothersome to me at times.

Is it awkward for your records to be sold at Protestant bookstores and for you to play at Protestant music festivals?

MB: No, not at all, because when I look at the true form of Christianity, there are no lines. And I think we'll be amazed at how much bigger He'll be than all of our issues once we encounter Him face to face, and that includes music. I don't want to put on the shackles of other people's expectations—I've carried that to some degree my entire career. It's not because I'm rebellious. I feel like I have a limited time and the older I get, the more I realize I will answer for my compliance. And I have so many silly things to answer for, I don't want to add that to the list.

I have been fortunate at Sparrow. There have been certain personalities there who have been with me from the beginning, and they've been very lenient with me. I think we're all growing and maturing.

Is the Christian music industry becoming more conscious of the bottom line?

MB: Yes. It's emphasized a lot more. I think the mergers have fed into a trend and what you have now are several companies that are not necessarily based on Christian music. These are now music companies driving this industry and they have certain perceptions and they're applying their profit margins to a business that frankly had its own complete legal contractual system before. Signing a pub-

lishing deal with a Christian company used to be a lot different than signing with Sony, but now lower expectations have been sucked up to a [secular] industry standard. What has also happened is that the trends out in the secular marketplace have infiltrated more quickly into Christian music.

Are there still strong boundaries between Christian and mainstream music audiences?

MB: Inherently, when you are writing a body of work based on the Gospel, you're going to be offensive. There's no way that's going to "pop" and people are going to jump on board and not find Christ offensive if that's not what they embrace. So in terms of Christian music becoming the next big thing, I think that's sort of a pipe dream.

Are things improving on that score?

MB: The mainstream has come around to being a lot more tolerant of spiritual themes. I think in the mid-1980s they were pretty intolerant, but in the early '90s, when all these artists were going through interesting discovery periods— from Sting to Peter Gabriel—the tolerance for it was more generous. I think they're very open to spiritual commentary as long as it's not overbearing.

For more on Margaret Becker, see also page 118

STEVEN CURTIS CHAPMAN

In many ways, singer/songwriter Steven Curtis Chapman is the archetypal Contemporary Christian artist. Boyish in appearance, he comes across as both morally correct and fun loving, personally conservative yet reasonably hip. The Christian music world has embraced Chapman from the 1987 release of his debut album, First Hand, through his 2001 CD Declaration.

A Paducah, Kentucky, native, Chapman has been a constant presence on Christian radio, racking up nearly 40 chart-topping singles and selling more than six million albums. Four Grammy Awards and 44 GMA Dove Awards have only confirmed his stature. Through all this success, Chapman has taken his leadership role seriously, retooling his country/pop sound every few years—most recently with modern rock and hip-hop—to keep his Bible-rooted message fresh and relevant. The best of his songs— "Heaven in the Real World," "Lord of the Dance," and "Speechless," to name only a few—convey a sense of spiritual awe amidst ordinary human life. Chapman has never really crossed over into the mainstream, though his contribution to the 1998 film The Apostle earned him some attention. Keeping his core audience happy while making forays into the moral minefields of secular entertainment, he's a role model for younger Christian artists to emulate.

Steven Curtis Chapman with his wife, Mary Beth.
Photo by Thunder Image Group

How has Contemporary Christian music changed since you became involved in it?

SCC: It seems to me that Christian music has artistically grown by leaps and bounds over the last 15 years, the time that I've been a part of it. I think in the beginning it was a lot of folks who were very sincere and had a real desire to communicate their faith, but they were as new and as young in their faith as they may have been as musicians. So, it [the music] was very sincere and very passionate, but still in its infancy. As more and more kids inspired by Christian music grew up, they were able to take that inspiration along with a deeper artistic calling and not have their music all sound similar. When dc Talk first came out, people were going, "You can't rap and be a Christian and say Christian things." But they did. And they did it well, and they did it in ways that had never been done before.… I think, too, Christian music has matured and moved away from this need to say, "We have it all figured out and we have all the answers and let us tell you what's wrong with everything and everybody." Not that Christian music ever really did that, but I think that there's a perception that that's what it was about. It's matured into saying, "Let me express my own struggles and what I have come to learn." But it's still anchored to the hope of the gospel.

As a songwriter, do you think your way of approaching faith-based subject matter has changed over the years?

SCC: I don't think so. I think the way I have approached it has stayed the same. I think my depth of understanding of faith and all of that has changed and certainly grown. And even now I'm in another process of what almost feels like decon-structing much of the faith that I grew up with and really asking tough questions. Life has a way of doing that, and circumstances cause you to reevaluate and say, "Okay, God, how much of this is really true faith and how much of this is the version that I was surrounded by as a kid growing up, and what of it needs to get changed and rearranged and shaken?" My parents' divorce several years ago was a big thing that did that, and it kind of brought on an album, *More to This Life*. I understand grace to be so much more than I maybe understood it to be five years ago. So the songs are going to hopefully represent that. That's certainly my prayer.

You were talking about how Christian music is perceived by people who are not very familiar with it. Are there misconceptions that you'd like to clear up?

SCC: Well, there are still plenty of people who, when they hear the words "Christian music," think that it's the hymns they grew up hearing in church. The fact is, there is such diversity.… There's [also] the concept that these are people who are Bible-thumpers, who want to tell me what's wrong with me. It's the whole "us versus them" kind of thing. And I can't honestly say that's a complete myth; some of that we have brought on ourselves, and it's unfortunate and it's wrong.

Jesus himself said [that] there's part of this gospel that's foolishness to many and it won't make sense, and if we try to make it palatable to everyone we won't really be communicating the gospel. But within that, we see that Christ was the one who spoke in a language that people were drawn to and that people could understand. And He was incredibly poetic and creative in the way He communicated the truth of the kingdom of God.

You've had a little more opportunity than many Christian artists to reach a secular audience through *The Apostle* and some of your other soundtrack work. Still, do you feel like you've had a real opportunity to reach beyond the Christian market?

SCC: You know, I'd be less than honest if I said there wasn't a little bit of a yearning that I feel to have that opportunity to really be heard as a creative artist who writes songs from his heart and his experience and is judged at that level. And yet, I always follow that up with wanting to say [that] I'm not whining and I'm certainly not complaining. Because I've already had opportunities way beyond what I ever dreamed of, with movie soundtracks and having my songs played on the radio and television and those kinds of things. But there is still that part of me that sometimes thinks, "Maybe this record, maybe this time, we'll get that shot at people in the mainstream." For example, we have yet to get on the ever-elusive Jay Leno show My record company and management

have tried to get that when I've had an album out or we've been out [in Los Angeles] for the Grammys. We've gotten real close a few times, but…the question always comes back to, "Well, what's he got on pop radio?" or that…it's not something their audience at large would appreciate. You can't help but think that if we could get that one thing to pop, it would open up a few other opportunities.

Are there signs that you're connecting with that larger audience?

SCC: Yes and no. I feel like my music certainly has had the opportunity to reach an audience beyond the Christian music audience. I just finished a run here where I did several state fairs and county fairs, that kind of thing. The audience was primarily fans of my music, but there are always those who come up and say, "Man, I've never heard of you before—this is really great. I'm hooked. I'm going to go buy your records." But by and large, the audience that I have listens to Christian music, because they connect with the themes of faith.

We within the Christian music community wrestle a whole lot with the old question, "Are you just singing to the choir?" And there's even been at times a sense of "Well, yeah, I'm not one of the real pioneers, I'm just one who kind of does a grade B or grade C career/ministry thing." And I think I've come to realize that all I can do is really be faithful with the gifts that God's given me and, in the sense of the old saying, dance with the one that brought me. All I can do is write out of my own experience and be as honest and non-preachy as I can. That's always the goal: [to] write in such a way that if Joe off the street heard this song, he wouldn't immediately go, "What in the heck is the language he's speaking?" There would be enough that would connect about real life and relationships that we all share in common.

Is there a danger that the entertainment elements in what you do will weaken or blur your message?

SCC: I think they're absolutely dangerous. I think there are dangers any time something has impact. And I'm not one who has navigated these waters with a completely pure heart.... I think I came into this world ready to jump up on the table in the delivery room and put on a show. I've even realized since that I was brought into this world by my parents to help salvage a struggling marriage. So, even from the very beginning, I was kind of here to perform and to fix some things....

Proverbs says a man is tested by the praise he receives. Certainly when you enter that realm of being an entertainer, a performer, there is praise that comes with that. And that's a test. I have been tempted many times to throw the baby out with the bathwater and say I can't do this because

there are too many dangers.... There's a word we throw around a lot in Christian circles and that's "accountability," which basically means that you're not a lone ranger out there thinking you've got it all figured out. I've had to keep myself surrounded by pastors, friends, people who aren't impressed with who I am as an entertainer or performer or any of those things, but really care about me as a friend whom they want to see stay faithful to the things that they know are important.

You mentioned accountability. How does that work in your life? Do you consult with a pastor about specific things that come up as an artist?

SCC: It's kind of changed faces over the course of my career. I've had a pastoral advisory board. It's probably been in place for the last 10 or 12 years. It's been there through some of the real important changing seasons of my ministry, going from churches to theaters to concert halls and wrestling with questions about working with secular mainstream promoters. Do things like that continue to line up with what I'm supposed to be about?

How do you handle these situations, when the involvements might raise some questions?

SCC: More often than not, I tend to follow the motto, "Better safe than sorry." I tend to err more to the side of safety.

Any specific instances?

SCC: Well, there was a time not so long ago when the Baptist Church was boycotting Disney. And several other church organizations of that kind were supportive of that boycott. I had contracted to perform at *Night of Joy*, which is a Christian music festival that's been going on at Disney World for many years, and I began to hear some questions being raised: "Well, are you going to go do this? How are you going to be able to go do this and support your Christian brothers and sisters who are boycotting this?" So that was one of those [situations] where I had to immediately make those calls to different people that I have in my realm of accountability. And it was interesting because I actually got a couple of different opinions. I had some who were saying I absolutely should support the boycott. And then there were several others who said, "Well, let's consider together why you would do that and what do you believe God would have you do, aside from what people are going to say." So, it was one where I really had to take all that information and finally just me and the Lord had to figure it out together. And I went out with a greater sense of calling than I had ever done at a concert before, thinking I really knew why I was there and that this wasn't just a contract that I was fulfilling. I was there for a real purpose.

So there's an accountability that's ongoing?

SCC: The accountability that has probably been most important is in my marriage and private life, apart from the stage. The real danger of being an entertainer and having a platform is that it's a license to isolate yourself. And when you isolate yourself, you can get real stupid in all of those other areas. That's where the accountability has been most important. My wife and I have been in counseling together off and on for the 16 years we've been married. She has the phone numbers of big, strong, good friends of mine who can come and kick my butt if I need it and say, "Hey, you're being an idiot here. You're singing these songs about how much you love your wife and family and yet her opinion is that you're spending an awful lot of time investing yourself in myths and she's kind of getting the leftovers." That's probably the area where it's been most important to have accountability in place.

Were there people who questioned your involvement in secular projects like *The Apostle* soundtrack?

SCC: Yeah, there were. There were some letters from concerned, very well-meaning people who just said, "How could you be associated with this and these kinds of things that don't represent Christianity in the way that it should be represented?" And the reality in all of that is, sure, if I was scripting those things, I probably would've scripted some things differently. Each time the opportunity comes, it's something I have to wrestle with and decide if this is really something that God has presented for me to be a part of. Would it honor Him? Would it dishonor Him? And in those situations I've been able to arrive at a place where I could say that my involvement was something I think God is putting His hand of blessing on.

Do you follow secular music or television? Do you feel comfortable with it and do you deliberately take it and add it to what you're doing to make yourself as contemporary as you can?

SCC: What I really teach my kids is what I teach my own heart: You are what you eat. I tell them there's a lot of junk food and I'm probably as big of a junk-food junkie as anybody. But you know, I can't live on a diet of that. I've tried at times and my album covers will reveal those seasons when I was living more on Snickers bars than salads. The "heavy years," I like to call them. But it is a process of me guarding what I eat in that sense.… I listen to a lot of different stuff. I'm listening right now to everything from [Samuel] Barber's "Adagio for Strings" to Stevie Ray Vaughn to current pop records that have just come off the press. But I'm careful to make the diet

primarily music that nourishes my soul and my faith.

I don't watch television much at all. I watch when I'm running. A lot of times I'll watch VH-1 and get caught up on videos and find out what's going on in the world of pop music. But…there are only so many half-dressed ladies that I can look at in a video before I say, "You know, it's time for me to turn the channel, 'cause I ain't just studying the artwork here." I've got to be guarded and careful about that. And not because I'm some great spiritual giant—actually it's the opposite, because I know how quickly I can be knocked off course. And that's kind of what I talk with my kids about, too. If these are the things that are important to me, to honor God with my mind and with my eyes and with my thoughts, then there are going to be lines that I have to draw.… There's only been one time that I know of when I bought a CD and thought, there's too much going on here and I need to get rid of it. Even though it [the CD] was great musically, I knew it would be an excuse to say that I was just trying to be culturally relevant.

What was the record, if I may ask?

SCC: It was a Paula Cole CD, actually. I thought, "There are just some things here that I think I need to not have going into my brain." Probably because I did like the music so much.

You're talking about the lyrics?

SCC: Oh yeah, exactly. Because again, musically it was a great [CD]. There was one song in particular that had a pretty sexual invitation throughout the song. I just thought, "Man, that's not where I need to be hanging out." So, it's just a process for me of trying to be on guard and yet be aware of what's going on. Music is a very mysterious, powerful gift that God created and I think it's even supernatural in the ways that it can access parts of our hearts that the spoken word could never get to. I know I've experienced that myself. And with that power great good can be accomplished, but that power also can be damaging.

For more on Steven Curtis Chapman, see page 138.

BRUCE COCKBURN

Canadian singer/songwriter Bruce Cockburn has been releasing albums since 1970. Hailing from Ontario, he spent time in Europe and studied music in the United States before launching his recording career. His first half-dozen albums were mostly acoustic folk in sound, highlighting his painterly lyric touch and fluent guitar playing. His music took on more of a rock cast in the 1970s, with jazz shadings and synthesizer touches.

Cockburn's Christian outlook became more evident over time. By 1979's Dancing in the Dragon's Jaws, his work conveyed a powerful sense of reverence and spiritual awe. He continued to record for secular labels, however, avoiding association with the Christian music industry and criticizing Jerry Falwell and other American evangelical leaders. During the 1980s, Cockburn's songs became explicitly political, attacking U.S. policies in Central America and Western oppression of the world's poorer nations. In the 1990s, such releases as Nothing but a Burning Light found him dealing with Christian themes once again. His most recent album, Breakfast in New Orleans, Dinner in Timbuktu, appeared on Rykodisc in 1999.

Do you feel it's important for your audience to know you're a Christian?

Bruce Cockburn
Photo by Kevin Kelly

RC: Not necessarily, no. If anybody asks, they'll hear it. And I think most of my audience does know. At one time I did consider it more important than I do now. But I feel like having made the statement, it's out there on the Internet for everybody to pore over if they wish to. It's not necessary to keep on making it and if somebody comes into it new and doesn't know that about me I figure they'll sort of find out soon enough in their own way.

If it's somebody who's coming from another faith, they may find that something in the songs will touch them, and I'd kind of rather have it touch them unprejudiced first. Then they can decide if they still like it if they find out it's coming from a Christian perspective.

Do you feel comfortable having the term "Christian artist" or "Christian musician" applied to you?

BC: Depends on whom I'm talking to or who's using the term. For myself, yes, I feel comfortable with that. I'm suspicious of hyphenated things, [like] "Christian-artist." I'm an artist and I happen to be a Christian, those two things go together, but so does everything else. I'm a Christian who uses the bathroom, who makes phone calls, and people don't [think] it's necessary to hyphenate those things. So why hyphenate "artist"?

One of the reasons I'm suspicious of that is, when you call someone a Christian artist there tends to be an identification of that person with the commercial Christian music scene, if you're talking about a songwriter. And to me that's a scene that has no particular value at all. There are artists in it who may disagree with me, but it's just another way to sell records and I'm not sympathetic to it. So I don't want to be identified with it, particularly.

I also find that it has a built-in limitation, because if somebody says to me, "Oh,

I've got this CD you should hear; it's a Christian artist," I immediately get suspicious. I don't think I'm going to like it….

There have been a lot of people who are competent but are not that interesting to me because their music lacks a sense of exploration…. There's a lot of music that doesn't have any sense of exploration in it in the world, but to me it's doubly disappointing when it comes from the Christian scene or anybody with a faith-based message. This is a huge adventure that people have embarked on, this adventure of faith, and it should have all the exploration that you can imagine in it— but instead it has none. There's too much reliance on what has been done before and that makes it uninteresting to me.

Did you ever seek to be a part of the early wave of Christian artists in the 1970s?

BC: I tried for a few years to be in some way part of that scene, [though] not commercially. I had my record deal—I didn't need to go to a Christian company to get a record deal, [and] I didn't feel obliged to sever ties with my Jewish-owned record company because I was suddenly a Christian (which I guess some people do feel). Some people feel they need to retreat from the world and surround themselves more with people of like belief, and I never quite had that feeling. So, depending on your point of view, that was either a lucky break for me or a ticket to hell, I suppose. In any case, after a few years of trying to align myself with this tendency I found myself unable to. When my marriage broke up in 1980 after 10 years, it called into question all of the assumptions I'd made about stuff, including the promise I made before God that we were going to be together until we died. And God himself seemed to be not only permitting this parting of ways, but encouraging it, or at least smiling on it.

This was around the time that your *Humans* album came out (1980)?

BC: Yes, it was, actually. The *Humans* album had a lot in it about that, about the divorce and whatnot. But in the end it seemed that at the very least God permitted this. And since he saw fit to permit the breaking of a word given before Him, then I had to question what that meant. And in questioning what that meant, of course I had to question everything else, too. I found at the same time, just because of where my life went at that point, that it was time for me to understand what it meant to love my neighbor, to translate these sorts of interior speculations and growth that had been going on through the 1970s into something more outwardly directed. I figured you can't love people if you don't know who they are, so it was time to become a little more gregarious. I'd always been very much a loner and my wife and I were kind of a package,

traveling around with minimal contact. It was time to get more social, and I did. That characterized pretty much what happened in the early 1980s and in a way has been going on ever since. That's reflected in the songs as well—at that point, some of the conservative Christian folks started thinking maybe I wasn't a Christian after all, because I wasn't talking about Jesus overtly and I was saying things in songs that they couldn't relate to.

Did your old audience have a problem with your political direction, and did your new audience have a problem with your Christian identification?

BC: Well, there was a very interesting kind of flow around all of that…. The audience kept expanding and expanding in the direction of questioning Christians particularly. [These were] people like me, who didn't fit comfortably into a niche with their faith. When I started talking about more political stuff, when the songs started to reflect Third World travel and what I was seeing there, some of the Christian folks got anxious about that and let me know. Other people got attracted to the music who…didn't really care if I was a Christian or not. And it's gone on that way, back and forth, ever since. It's been a very interesting process to watch.

Which songs do you think reflect your faith most clearly?

BC: I like to think they all do in one way or another. Some of them might be a bigger reach for people to figure that out.... I think for instance of *The Charity of Night*. There's a lot about God on that album. It doesn't say "Jesus" because it didn't seem necessary. But "Strange Waters" for instance, that's taking the Twenty-third Psalm and putting in my experience. I haven't gotten to walk by those still waters yet. My faith has led me into turbulent situations and that's what I'm talking about. So, that for me is a song that reflects my faith. The songs that I write that celebrate life do that.

"Great Big Love" (on *Nothing But a Burning Light*) struck me that way.

BC: "Great Big Love," yeah. There's a transcendent thing in there, or at least that's hopefully in there. There are some things about it that are pretty mundane, of course...but the love that's sweeping across the sky is God's love.

Other songs are more direct?

BC: "Lord of the Starfields," that's a bit more blatant, I guess. It was an attempt to write a psalm. The songs that are sort of dealing with the questions that we ask ourselves are the songs where the faith shows up most clearly.

Have the changes in your work over time reflected changes in your spiritual life?

BC: There was a change from sort of interior speculation and exploration into more externally directed things...at the beginning of the 1980s. With the last couple of albums, it's kind of gone back inside again in a way, but informed by what I've experienced in the world. Issues like land mines, some hideous affront to human dignity like that, or the environmental destruction that we see going on around us—to me, these are questions of faith, too.

I've grudgingly come to feel over the last few years that there actually may be such a thing as a spiritual evolution taking place among human beings. If that's the case, now's the time to really push hard on that, and at the moment at least, it doesn't matter to me whether it's pursued in the Christian context or not. The important thing is to realize that we need to be looking for that polarity, that sort of spiritual maypole to dance around, if we're going to survive as a species. I can't predict in advance where my songwriting is going to go, but it wouldn't surprise me if it happened to go in the direction of talking more about spiritual things, because I think that's the key to turning the course of things around on a planetary scale.

Do you feel a greater social responsibility because of your faith?

BC: I think so, yeah, because I've chosen to accept the notion that I'm supposed to love my neighbor, and accept it consciously. I can't love my neighbor and be party to that neighbor being ripped off and starved. "Everybody's my neighbor"—Jesus says that, right? You've been talking about the guy who lives next door behind the picket fence. But it also happens that some of my neighbors are doing really awful things. I've got to wrestle with that, too.

Does that ever come in conflict with your creative instincts?

BC: Not so much for me, but for people who want things out of me it's a source of tension. I'll get complaints—why don't you write about this or that or why don't you put your music at the service of this cause or that cause? I can only do what I can do. The basis of the writing is experience and the muse, whatever that is, so I don't have that much conscious influence over what direction things go.

These are not sermons, in other words?

BC: No they're not intended to be that at all. I'm from a non-Christian background, from an agnostic background, and I was never impressed by the Ernest Ainsleys [an American evangelist] of the world. That way of approaching the sharing of the faith didn't say anything to me. And I felt that there must be a lot of other people like me out there, people who were turned off by jingoistic kind of language, whether it was about politics or about spirituality. So, it was my thought that I could offer [another] option [for] embracing the Christian faith. Because people like me had previously not perceived that as an option. I didn't for the longest time. To me, being a Christian seemed like an idiotic thing to be—why would I want to be that? And so I thought I could probably do people a favor just by pointing out that hey, look, this isn't what you thought it was.

Any other thoughts about being a good artist, Christian or otherwise?

BC: If an artist comes and says, "I'm a Marxist and I have this to say," it's going to turn off a lot of people. I think people are reluctant to be propagandized to. And that's where a lot of it [Contemporary Christian music] is, though I'm not sure all of it. I think to some degree that people who are like me already know we don't need to be spoken to. It's like, we're already the converted. So we don't really need to hear that over and over again.... If your experience is Christian and you're feeling the need to write songs that address spiritual issues, then write good ones. Go deep, go as deep as you can and really get on the edge. Write what you see. Don't write what you think you're supposed to write.

For more on Bruce Cockburn, see page 144.

For more on Bruce Cockburn, see page 144.

MICHAEL TAIT
AND TOBY McKEEHAN

(vocalists, dc Talk)

The trio dc Talk came together at Virginia's Liberty University in the late 1980s. At first, members Michael Tait, Toby McKeehan, and Kevin "Max" Smith gained notice as one of Christian music's few rap groups. Gradually, they diversified their sound, interweaving modern pop and hip-hop styles and emphasizing singing over rapping. Their breakthrough came in 1992 with Free at Last, an album that eventually sold two million copies and won a Grammy. Increasingly, dc Talk's lyrics dealt with how Christians interacted with an often-disapproving secular world. To date, the group's most famous statement on this topic has been 1995's "Jesus Freak," a full-throttle declaration of faith that's become a Christian music standard. While the band scored an isolated pop hit with "Just Between You and Me," the mainstream market has not yet truly embraced it. In 2001, all three members released solo projects, putting the band's future somewhat in doubt.

Did you expect "Jesus Freak" to be the anthem that it was?

Tait: The day we finished "Jesus Freak" —it was the spring of 1995—I said, "Guys, either this record is going to be huge or it's going to bomb." Because it was so

Toby McKeehan
Photo by Christian Lantry

Michael Tait
Photo by Kristin Barlowe

drastically different, it was such a departure from *Free at Last*. We were used to being sporadic and schizophrenic stylistically, but this was like a massive job. So we had no clue. But I did have a feeling that we were on the threshold of something great. Didn't know what. Didn't know it was going to do 2.5 million. It was quite amazing, actually.

Did anything in particular prompt that song?

McKeehan: It came from being ostracized. As dc Talk progressed and the mainstream became aware of us, I think we felt a lot of prejudice because we were a Christian band. We just played off of that and put the magnifying glass on it more directly and said, "Yeah, we're Jesus freaks. We are different, we have a different mentality." We are strangers in this land, but that doesn't take away from the fact that we can make art that can affect our culture and can move people.

It really struck a chord with your audience....

Tait: It just makes a statement of, you know, "I don't give a bleep about what you think. I'm a Jesus freak and I'm proud of it." I think the song and the record did so well because so many people finally had a song and a platform to say: "Yeah, we are freaks and we're proud of it! You might be a snowboard freak or you might be a football freak, but we're Jesus freaks, among other things."

Is there anything troubling about the idea of a Christian rock celebrity? Is there a problem of the star becoming more important than the message?

Tait: Oh, no question. It's a never-ending battle with a Christian pop musician or whatever you want to call us. There was an article one time in *CCM* magazine that John Fischer wrote—"Christian rock, Blessing or Curse?"—and I thought to myself, that's so appropriate, because as Christians we're called to be servants, we're called to give the glory back to God, to use whatever we have in life to point people to the ultimate leader, servant, messenger, Christ. So, you're up on stage, you're just right, you're singing cool, and you got your cool clothes on. And let's face it, sometimes you get caught up in that crap. And it can ruin you if you're not careful. So there is a constant battle to stop, listen, reevaluate, and say, "Okay, here's why I'm doing this.... I'm not Seal, I'm not Sting. I have a deeper purpose and that purpose will get lost if I indulge myself."

Do you feel that Contemporary Christian music has lost of some the fervor and the confrontational quality it had 30 years ago?

McKeehan: I feel like there are some people who still have that fervor and there are others who are definitely making music for the marketplace. They're making music for fellow believers, people who believe the way they do and who therefore will buy their music. Other people are very confrontational in the way that they write, and they're talking more or less to people who don't believe the way that they do. I have no problem with either of those. For me, I think when dc Talk puts out a song, my goal is to make the kind of art that the whole world stands up and notices. But at the same time, I know many times the whole world won't take notice and that people who believe the way I do will automatically connect with my music.

Do you feel that you've reached secular audiences with your message?

Tait: No question. I know we haven't sold six million records in the Christian market alone. I'm always the recognizable one because I have dreads and I'm always wearing something kind of crazy, so people will stop me and talk with me. It's always cool to hear non-churchgoers buy the record, 'cause their friends turn them onto it. They just think it's cool music.

Have you encountered any barriers in getting your message to a wider audience?

Tait: Well, MTV is the biggest, probably, and I'll have to hold back some of my anger on that one. They used to have a campaign that said, "Free Your Mind." They didn't free their mind much when it came to dc Talk.

Was there a particular video they refused to air?

Tait: Oh, it wasn't a particular video. It was the whole concept of dc Talk. Our platform is our Christian belief and you know they never gave Courtney Love or Tina Turner a hard time about being Buddhist.

You've had conversations with people at MTV and radio programmers about this?

McKeehan: Oh, yeah, definitely, we've had conversations about some of that. And I know what the Virgin promotion team was up against in many instances. It's like you can sneak one by the goalie, but next time he's going to catch it. I think Jars of Clay's "Flood" saw mainstream success and then they tried to follow it up, but everybody had learned that they came from this [Christian] marketplace. Dc Talk had a Top 30 [secular] single with "Just Between You and Me" in 1997, and I think with the second single, the DJs started going, "Wait, wait, this group's from the Christian market." Hey, I'm not here to whine about it. My job is to make music that I'm passionate about. And I believe if I focus on my art, sooner or later, if it's excellent, the world will notice.

Are there myths about Christian bands that you'd like to dispel?

Tait: Yeah, the biggest myth is that because we're Christians we can't be incredible musicians. After all, if I may be cocky for a second (but you can print this), the closer we get to the Creator the more creative we should get. In all practicality, we're probably more equipped to be the creative juice of the jewel than anybody else. Back in the Renaissance, the Christians ran things.

Do you think there is a true Christian pop subculture? Does it reinforce the idea that Christians are something different and separate?

McKeehan: Yes, it does. And I wish it didn't exist. I wish that the music that is connecting with people would rise to the top, barring all politics. I think that it's important that we don't alienate ourselves from the mainstream system of music.

Tait: There is definitely a healthy Christian pop subculture, and no, it's not good that we should be off on our own because, if I may get spiritual for a moment here, the great commission is to get out into the world. We don't want to create this little undergrowth, this little world of our own. If we're ostracized, how are we going to reach the people that we're supposed to be proselytizing?

Was that always a goal of dc Talk's?

Tait: Yes, for sure, no question. We grew up in Christian homes, we grew up with Christian beliefs and in Christian schools. And so for us, it's natural. We don't think about being Christian musicians, or writing a song about God. It's like, He's the center of our lives, so whenever I write a song,

I'm not going to write a song about getting down with some chick, because that's not what's on my mind. Do those thoughts cross my mind sometimes? Yes, I struggle with those things, because I'm a human being. I'm a male, I'm just like any other guy. But at the same time, I'm being called to be holy, to be Christ-like, in all the ways that He put forth.

How close is black and white Christian music these days? Are they very distinct?

Tait: Toby and I have had long talks on tour buses and planes about this; it's a situation we don't understand. It's gotten better, with groups like Anointed and Out of Eden, even Kirk Franklin coming from a gospel side for the most part. He started to bridge the gap a bit. It's just a mind-set, I think. Blacks are more traditional in their faith and their music's a little bit more traditional—conservative, if you will. It's mostly always, "Jesus, Jesus, God, God, Christ, Christ" in the song. And with Contemporary Christian style, a lot of blacks, a lot of my friends and parents, look at it like it's worldly because it's not keeping near the cross. It's not hymnology.

What do you say when you get those opinions?

Tait: You know what I say to people like that? My God is bigger than all of that. Who am I to say God is only this or that? You can't put God in a box.

How does your audience break down? Is it racially mixed?

Tait: There are more whites than blacks. I wish there were more blacks, but that's just the way it goes. All I can do is keep praying for those people and trying to reach out to them, because it's a mentality. It's a traditional, set-in-stone mentality. This is what you do. You're black, you eat watermelon, you eat fried chicken, you play basketball. You're white, you play golf, you're a member of the country club.

Does it come down to that some black music fans think dc Talk sounds too "white" for their taste?

Tait: I don't know, because we've done R&B, we've done rock, we've done hip-hop.... If we were in the mainstream world, maybe we'd have more sales to black people. I don't know. But for what we do, the whole Contemporary Christian music market is mostly well-heeled white masses.

So it's more of a denominational breakdown than a racial one?

Tait: Oh yeah. I'd agree with that, for sure.

Do you regard dc Talk as a form of ministry?

Tait: Oh, no question. What we do, definitely. We like to think that.

Not all Christian bands would necessarily say that, although a lot of them do.

Tait: You can get caught in words, though. Words like "ministry" make people think, "Oh, wait a second, they're preaching at us."

Well, you may define the term differently than someone else would.

Tait: Yeah. Freakin' Marilyn Manson, he has a ministry.

You think so?

Tait: You better believe he does. Read his lyrics.... I think he definitely has a purpose in his lyrics—to affect people.

Few pop artists take responsibility for what they say—obviously, you do.

Tait: Well, those people live in denial. *Anybody* with masses looking to them, following them, buying their records, whether they admit it or not, they're role models. Some don't admit it because they're bags of lint. They're "breath and britches," my dad would call them. But anybody on a platform is a role model, because kids are watching them. You're a punk if you won't admit it.

You don't stop being a role model when you get off the stage. Is that hard for you?

Tait: Oh, of course it's hard. It's very difficult. There are days when I just go, you know, man, I just don't feel like being that.... But even if I weren't a Christian, even if I was just a morally good guy, it would be a struggle.

McKeehan: We've always set out to be honest about our shortcomings. In early Christian music, it seemed that everybody looked so perfect up there. Everybody on that stage sure looked like they had it together. I'm not saying that they said that, but it sure looked like they did. For us, it was like, "Man, we're struggling to stay on this narrow road and not fall into some crazy temptation." So being vulnerable with the audience and letting them know about our struggles had a lot to do with us connecting with people. I think people always appreciate and are drawn to honesty.

Are there songs of yours that express this?

McKeehan: Oh yeah, like "What If I Stumble," "The Hard Way," "Fearless," "Supernatural," "Jesus Freak"—if you listen closely to most of our songs, you'll find that. They're sort of a confession that we're struggling with our relationships with each other, with our relationship with God. And I think it's sort of a testimonial to the fact that we depend on God's grace.

How do you view the experience of an artist like Michael English [who confessed to an extra-marital affair in 1994]? Is he a bad guy? Has he failed?

Tait: He fell. He's a Christian. And he's still forgiven. I mean, look at Jim Bakker—same thing. What do you say? Those two made mistakes. Their platforms will forever be affected [by] it and people will lose faith in them. But you know, Christians aren't perfect, we're just forgiven. We can move forward, but the consequences are there. The Jim Bakkers of our world and Mike English, they live with the consequences of their sins. And that is enough punishment on this earth, especially with the cynical society we live in today. That's enough right there to make you wish you could go back to being a child and have a second shot at it.

If something like that happened to you, would your audience forgive you and stay with you?

McKeehan: I think ultimately they would. There might be some offense taken initially and I think there needs to be respect for the platform that we hold. I think there's responsibility that comes with any platform. I don't want to be a poor example to people. I need to think about that when I take the stage and when I speak from the stage and when I write a song. Just put that all together and you've got my answer.

For more on dc Talk, see page 155.

MATT ODMARK

(guitarist, Jars of Clay)

In 1995, Jars of Clay burst upon both the Christian and secular music worlds with "Flood," a surprising crossover radio hit. Their moodily tuneful brand of folk/pop was very much in step with the alternative rock sounds of the mid-1990s. Jars of Clay offered more than just the hip flavor of the moment, though—there was a convincing idealism and idiosyncratic songwriting

Matt Odmark
Photo by Michael Wilson

approach to these four young Midwesterners that was definitely their own.

Formed at Greenville College in Illinois, the band—singer Dan Haseltine, guitarist Matt Odmark, bassist Stephen Mason, and keyboardist Charlie Lowell—earned a double-platinum album for its self-titled first CD. Subsequent albums—1997's Much Afraid, 1999's If I Left the Zoo, and 2002's The Eleventh Hour—have displayed both creative growth and a commitment to God-centered songwriting.

Like other Christian groups that have enjoyed secular success, Jars of Clay has faced the challenge of reaching out to a larger secular audience while retaining the loyalty of its core base of believers. Desiring to step outside the familiar confines of the Christian "zoo," yet feeling some unease about the mainstream entertainment world, the band's career path will be an interesting one to follow in years ahead.

Is there greater scrutiny given to Christian bands than to secular ones?

MO: Sure. You kind of carry the banner of being a Christian band regardless of where you are, whether you're just playing for youth groups or in the more mainstream music arena. It can be a tough spot to be in…. We've found ourselves in all sorts of areas of crossfire, where we were doing things that were getting blown out of proportion or misunderstood.

Can you give any examples?

MO: Well, we did some touring in clubs early on, which was a pretty radical concept…. Most Christian bands weren't performing or intentionally touring in bars regularly. We were one of the first groups to do that in a while. A lot of people initially took that to mean that we must not care about being Christians anymore, [like] we would rather endorse rock'n'roll and alcohol and all the kind of vices that come along with it…. For us, we really felt like in those kinds of bar environments we had a chance to connect in an intimate way with people that would've never heard our message any other way. For us it was a tremendous opportunity, not only career-wise, but as far as how it fit into the ideology of what we were doing. But there's all sorts of room for misinterpretation and you can't explain to every single person exactly what you're doing and why you're doing it.

Has *If I Left the Zoo* received more or less attention than *Much Afraid* in the secular market?

MO: In the secular market, I would say they've received about the same. And the story's not over yet for *If I Left the Zoo*; there are still some singles left to go.

But…there haven't been a lot of bones thrown at us from that side of the marketplace. We've been struggling through what that means in the last year. And what it's meant for us is that we're really trying to nurture the audience that we do have, which is primarily a Christian church audience. We spent a good two years focusing on mainstream opportunities that maybe haven't been there, at the expense of nurturing and building the audience that has been there….

Was "Flood" more or less a fluke crossover hit? Have you consciously tried to duplicate the process that led to that single?

MO: You could call it a fluke. It was a song that had legs all by itself. Our mainstream distributor wanted to press a single and release it.

That was Silvertone/BMG, right?

MO: I think so, yeah. So almost without even trying it really took off and had us running catch-up for a good year or so after. That was a tremendous gift and something that we never anticipated. And we loved all the opportunities that that song gave us. We loved being a Christian band that got to play in festivals alongside artists like Joan Osborne and Seal and whatnot. We thought that was a great thing for not only our band but for Christian music in general. We've really tried to continue to write records that we feel like would give us more opportunities to do that. We've just been waiting around for one of those records, one of those songs, to really, really connect again.

Does the phrase "If I Left the Zoo" have to do with moving out into the larger secular world?

MO: To some degree—the title has several different dimensions of meaning. We just liked the playful idea of asking, "Is the grass going to be really greener someplace else?" I liked the self-doubt of thinking, "We're going to try and do something that's a little uncomfortable for us, that's going to stretch us into a place that's different for us." Musically, that's what that record was about.

Did you receive any criticism for possibly watering down your Christian message? Have you ever dealt with that?

MO: Somewhat. We do get some criticism on lyrics. There are a lot of people that feel like if you're not literally quoting Scripture or just rewording it in a more practical or clear way, then it has no place being called Christian [music]. And I think although that might be helpful in terms of delineating and categorizing music, it's not very artistic. The job of the artist isn't really to write textbooks on religion. That's another person's job. We're not really interested in writing songs that

are textbooks on theology. We're interested in putting music to what we believe and to the gospel in a way that makes people feel it and believe it, in a way that a textbook can't always do. I think we're comfortable with the risk that that requires us to take.

I know that there are a lot of people who do really connect with what we're trying to do. And I think that's ultimately why most people listen to music. They're longing to connect in that deeper, more poetic way with the meaning behind life.

Have you been treated differently from secular bands by the mainstream music business?

MO: Yeah, definitely. Even when we were at our most successful in the mainstream world we ran into a kind of prejudice or stereotype. There are stations to this day that refuse to play the song "Flood" and they made it clear [why]: "You guys are a Christian band and we don't play that kind of music." It had nothing to do with, "We don't like your song," or anything like that. It really was about the spiritual identity of the band.

That's a kind of bigotry, isn't it?

MO: It sort of is in a way, because you can go, "Oh gosh, you play this Sting single and he believes in more Eastern religions or he has this certain spiritual identity, but his music is not treated that way." Those artists may be very evangelistic in their music, but they're not going to get treated the same way a "Christian" band is. For a band like us, it's a very frustrating position to be in.... This is the way the industry works—there's this genre of music that's been cocreated by both the record industry at large and a Christian music industry that says, "We're this separate music genre." They've positioned themselves in a way to make it easy for the mainstream world to look at them and go, "They're just a bunch of weirdos making pretty lame music."

What about the stereotype of Christian music?

MO: Yeah, there's sort of a stereotype that Christian music is usually anything but cutting edge, and it's cheesy, and doesn't have that much to offer musically. And the Christian music industry has been pretty comfortable saying, "We're separate." I think on both sides of the fence there have been people who've lived that way for 20 years and have been comfortable to work things that way.

Do you think these barriers have been coming down a little in recent years?

MO: Yes, but there's a long way to go. Take for example an artist like Sixpence None the Richer, a great band that's been around a long time and is really long overdue for the kind of success that they're now seeing. And so I'm super happy to see people finally get to hear their music and hear what a great band they are. But the thing that seems peculiar to me is, here's a band that had one of the biggest songs of 1999 ["Kiss Me"]—they should've been repeatedly on the cover of just about every major media magazine in the country. Yet nobody even knows what they look like, as far as I can tell.... [They're] a real band that's come out of nowhere, that's great, that's got an attractive girl singer, all these kind of marketable aspects. And yet they're sort of the anonymous band of 1999.

What would you attribute that to, if anything?

MO: I attribute that to the fact that there's still some resistance, especially by major media publications like *Rolling Stone* and *Spin*. There's resistance to a Christian band being something that they need to concern themselves with.... I think you're dealing with probably one of the most liberal segments of the media, the arts and entertainment segment, which is historically anti-Christian. I don't think I'm saying anything too shocking by saying they're liberal. You just have the simple fact that they see it as uncool. For some reason Britney Spears is a lot more cool to them then a legitimate band with legitimate music that happens to be Christian. And they're in the business of shaping our culture's concept of what's cool.

Do you have to deal with interview questions like "How can a Christian band be cool?" and "Can you rock out if you're a Christian?" How do you deal with that?

MO: How do we deal with those questions? I think we just answer them honestly. We love rock music and we think we're a great band. And we think we get away with being a great band without having to engage in all these self-destructive habits. In fact, we really found a peace in who we are in God that allows us to be a much better band than we could be in any other way. But really, the much bigger question to me is, do they really realize how corporate most music has become? Most of the big rock stars are playing golf on the weekends. But because we're Christian, they want to think we're these moralist freaks.

Your band has a tour pastor named Michael Guido. How does that become part of your road experience?

MO: When we're gone [on tour], it'll be for the better part of two and a half months. It uproots us from our normal community and support system. Community's a very important thing for anybody, but especially for us. As Christians, anything we can do to keep connected to a sense of community is key. Having our own pastor is one of the ways that we can do that. It really breaks down to someone that's there to challenge us with a balanced perspective on who we are and what we're doing and what it's all about—which is something that's really easy to lose the longer you're away from home.

It's difficult to imagine a secular rock band bringing someone along to put life in perspective. The idea is to imagine yourself as larger than life.

MO: It's because we have a totally different perspective on who we are and why we do what we do. As Christians, we really understand the megalomaniac rock god thing as really just ending in death and destruction. And none of us want that. You only have to watch [VH-1's] *Behind the Music* two to three weeks in a row to watch how pathetically the same every story is. So for us, we love music but we don't love being a rock band enough to let it destroy us and everything we hold dear.

How do you wrestle with that, especially when "Flood" was doing so well?

MO: We wrestled with it a lot. When "Flood" was big, we were phenomenally busy…. We would go for months without seeing home or without seeing a familiar face, other than just the five of us in the band. It took a couple of years to recover from it. And then the even more difficult thing was to go through two records without seeing the same sort of success. And then you go, "Does this mean we suck now, does this mean we're doing it wrong? Does this mean that God doesn't like us anymore?" Whatever the questions might be, you need some sort of framework to work those things out and most artists don't have that. The only way most artists have to deal with it is to bury those questions and sort of anesthetize the pain, and maybe they'll survive it and maybe they won't.

Where would you like to see Jars of Clay in a couple of years?

MO: I would like to see us make even more serious and more radical inroads into mainstream music. I feel like we're in really an exciting musical time right now, because I parallel it with the last two decades. At the beginning of each decade you have this sort of stale feeling in music, which I feel like is right where we are now. We have all this corporate manufactured music—the beginning of the 1980s and the beginning of the '90s felt the same way. And all of a sudden a band like Nirvana or U2 just rises to the top and redefines everything. I'm ready for that to happen. I would love Jars of Clay to be the band that helped define music for the next 10 years.

That's not just in the Christian sphere, but across the board?

MO: That's across the board. And I don't know if that's an egotistic place to be, but that's why we make music. It's not just to be pretty good. We want it to be great. So I hope to see the music stretch bigger and broader and see the band touch people in a more significant way. I'm really looking forward to the next three or four years to see what happens in that vein. I think it's as much our job to do as anyone else's.

For more on Jars of Clay, see page 182.

PETER FURLER

(singer/drummer, the Newsboys)

Since their 1988 recording debut, the Newsboys' eclectic 1960s and '70s–influenced pop/rock sound has been a mainstay of Christian radio. The band was cofounded by Peter Furler and John James in their native Australia—since the pair's arrival in United States in 1987, a series of American bandmates have rounded out the group.

From the start, the combo had a zany streak of humor, refined further when Steve Taylor became their lyricist/producer in the early 1990s. A playfully positive attitude infused such hits as "Not Ashamed,""Spirit Thing," and especially "Shine," the band's anthem. The Newsboys developed their ability to make fun of American cultural excess and still keep the focus on God.

The group had become a big concert draw and was hitting the gold album sales mark when James decided to bow out as lead singer in 1997. Taking the front man's spot, Furler kept the momentum going on the soulful CD Love Liberty Disco (1999). The Newsboys went on to release a "best of" CD, Shine: The Hits, in 2000 and an all new album, Thrive, in 2002.

What is the Christian music scene like in Australia?

PF: Australia to me always seemed more cut and dried, more black and white. If you call yourself a Christian in Australia, usually there's a consequence to it. Over here [in the United States], you've got "In God We Trust" on the dollar bill, so it's not such a big issue to be a Christian.

Peter Furler
Photo by Allen Clark

In Australia, it's not like that. If you want to confess your faith, it's gotta be there.

Did you play secular venues when you started out?

PF: We played regular pubs. It wasn't always great—there was one time the guy who owned the pub stopped the show and threw us out.

Because you were Christians?

PF: Yeah. The audience was all half-drunk, so they didn't care…. It was good for us as a band, because it's how we cut our teeth. I think even today we have a fear of the crowd, a fear of rejection. Because over there, you'd get a beer bottle in your head in a second, even if you were doing a good job.

What's your relationship with your current audience like?

PF: I really feel that our part in this industry is to put into song what we've gone through. And what we've gone through, especially in the last couple of years, has been a wave of love. We encourage our fans [to see] that it's not about the T-shirts with the Christian slogans on them, it's not about the sticker on the car, it's not even about the way to lure people to a Christian concert. I don't believe Christian music will change the world—obviously, it can have an effect on people's lives. But I feel our job is to encourage fans to go back to the gospel for what it's really about: looking after the orphans and the widows and the poor, and loving one another so that the world outside knows that we are His disciples.

Does the American interconnection between Christianity and commerce bother you?

PF: I struggle with it, because we're a band that's sold a lot of records now. It's not like it used to be—we used to ride around in a van and eat 7-Eleven burgers. Obviously, a lot has changed. It's just a matter of knowing your own heart.

Is there a danger in being idolized by your fans?

PF: I'm not saying that it doesn't happen. I've never wanted someone's autograph in my life, so I probably walk around in a bubble—I don't understand it. We get fans cheering for us, but it's never been something I've struggled with. I don't walk on stage every night feeling great about myself. I know my limitations. I'm not the best singer in the world—in fact, I'm far from it. So when I go out, I'm hoping I'll at least keep everyone happy.

In early 2000, there was some controversy about the band wearing eye makeup in its publicity photos—did that catch you by surprise?

PF: You know, I was at a time of life when I didn't think anything was going to catch me by surprise. So, no, it didn't. It's hard to describe—I think it was me struggling with insecurities, maybe hiding behind that. It was [around the time of] the second record without John James, the old lead singer. I'd just come off a tour where every night I walked out on stage and I had this feeling like everyone was thinking, "He's not the singer! Where's John?" I was really insecure about it.

How did that connect with wearing makeup and the criticism you received?

PF: You get caught in this scene of trying to become something you're not. You read about all these great front men of rock-'n'roll who become something else when they go on stage, and maybe I got caught up in that…. I wasn't putting on certain clothes and eye makeup to go out and get glory, I was doing it to hide from certain things. But that's a form of selfishness. God wants me to be broken. He wants me to walk out there busted and that's when He can work.

Does it make sense to you that people were disturbed by that?

PF: Yeah, 'cause I'm disturbed by it now. I think it sends out a signal that we have to be like the world to make a difference in the world. And that's just so untrue. If you want to make a difference in the world, look at what Christ did. He made the hugest difference and He didn't need anything.

Who do you think your audience is? Is it 90 percent Christian?

PF: I would say, sadly, that it's 90 percent. That's the whole subculture thing. I get a bit annoyed at the end of the show—I might say, "Are there any believers, any Christians here?" And every hand goes up. It annoys me—I feel like a lot of our show is really directed toward the church more so than just toward the lost.

Have you had much secular success?

PF: The most effect we've had on the outside world has been on the *Love Liberty Disco* tour [in 2000]. We called it the "Dome Tour"—we took this 3,000-seat inflatable building with us from city to city, and we'd erect them in a mall car park or wherever there was a piece of asphalt. So people would just come along and check our shows out. That happened a lot.

Have you run into prejudice against Christian artists when you've tried to get into the mainstream?

PF: I have, but I think I understand it. I think our songs are very radio-friendly, and obviously Christian stations play them to death. I think certain songs, like "Entertaining Angels," would've had a shot at being mainstream songs. The problem we've run into is not that our music isn't up to scratch—if it wasn't, it wouldn't sell anything. What we've run into is that we have too much baggage. We've sold too many records. The radio programmers all know who we are—"Oh, the Newsboys, they're that Christian band." So when we turn up on the desk, it's not really prejudice. They're just being businesspeople. And it wouldn't be wise to have us on this station, because all of a sudden it was like they're promoting some belief. It's kind of like the school prayer thing.

Is that real? Would people really object if it went out over the airwaves?

PF: I doubt it. Not in this country. But if I were a radio station promoter and if I weren't a believer, I'd definitely shy away from it just to be safe. The point is, you've got lots of other choices. You've got hundreds of bands putting out stuff every week.

On the other hand, are we hearing watered-down, lightweight music on Christian radio these days?

PF: There's two dangers. One danger is that you don't mention [God] enough, and the other danger is that you're mentioning Him too much to get airplay. So it works both ways. But the one thing I love about Christian music is that it has to connect to people. In mainstream music, you can have a hit about nothing. You can have just a hook or a beat with a guy grunting. But in Christian music, the spirit's gotta connect.

Is the bedrock of your touring playing in churches?

PF: The reason we took this building with us [on the "Dome Tour"] was the fact of all were welcome. 'Cause even if you're gonna play at the Methodist church or Baptist church, a lot of times other people won't come. It's sad, but that's the way it is. So to combat that, as soon as we could we moved out of churches. We're not against bands doing it—I might end up playing churches the rest of my life. Right now, while we can, we're not.

It comes down to straight finances, too. It costs us five times as much to play an arena than to play at a 10,000-seat church, even though they seat the same amount of people. But it's worth it. That way, we're playing in the real world and hopefully we're being a light, as opposed to being hidden in some church.

Where do you think the Newsboys will be artistically and career-wise in a couple of years?

PF: Hopefully, artistically and otherwise, we won't be thinking about it too much. There'll be less of ourselves. I've been listening to our [greatest] hits CD, and I think I've finally figured out what our sound is. But you got to be careful not to think about it too hard. If you think about yourself too much, we grow and He shrinks.

For more on the Newsboys, see page 205.

CHARLIE PEACOCK

Singer/songwriter/producer/author Charlie Peacock has established himself as one of Christian music's most prolific artists and provocative commentators. Originally based in Sacramento, he released his first album, Lie Down in the Grass, *on the Exit label in 1984. This effort was indicative of Peacock's penchant for Third World rhythms and thoughtful, Christian-based lyrics. By 1989, he had relocated to Nashville and begun a highly successful production career, going on to work with such notables as Avalon, Margaret Becker, Audio Adrenaline, Twila Paris, and Out of the Grey, among others. His own recording career flourished as well, yielding such hits as "Almost Threw It All Away" and "In the Light." Not content to adhere to Christian music's conventions, he tested the genre's limits with albums like the sensuous* Love Life *(1991). Peacock sought to promote a broader approach to Christian-based creativity with the Art House, a study series held at his home from 1991 to 1996. He also attempted to put his ideas into practice by founding re:think, a record label affiliated with Sparrow.* Crossroads, *his 1999 book, criticized the Christian music industry for its insularity and artistic narrowness. Peacock spent much of 2000 and 2001 working toward a master's degree at Covenant Theological Seminary in St. Louis, Missouri.*

Charlie Peacock
Photo by Michael Wilson

Do you see a trend toward setting up a protected, separate culture among evangelical Christians?

CP: Yes, very much so. I think that's still indicative of the church in America, particularly among evangelicals, where there's a Christian version of everything and that kind of cocooning effect.

How do your ideas work with that?

CP: In my book, I try to describe the notion that the Christian life is not constituted of the stuff of abandoning culture, of abandoning the earth. It's actually about a stewardship, a caretaking role, and that involves the everywhere and everything of life. I really tried to paint a different picture for folks, particularly one where Contemporary Christian music would not be the end-all answer to what it means to be faithful to God through music.

Do you feel comfortable with the term "Contemporary Christian music"? Is that the kind of music you make?

CP: No, I've never felt that at all. My whole involvement with Contemporary Christian music and the effect that the label has on people is so contrary to who I am as a human being, as a disciple of Jesus, and an artist. It could not be more contrary.

But a lot of people have seen you as a leader in this musical category....

CP: Yeah, because you're sort of at the mercy of the conventions that the people vote for.

Does the audience define what Christian music is?

CP: Yeah, very much so. All you have to do is examine the way that Christian radio stations function to find out how much the audience controls what actually makes it on the air. It would be different if they were selling advertisements. But the fact that they function mostly due to listener support means that when they [the listeners] vote [by supporting the station financially], they really vote with their dollars. It really is that kind of consumer that ends up defining the music because they're the ones in a sense who dictate what is or isn't a Christian lyric.

Were you ever discouraged from saying certain things by your record company?

CP: The only time was back in 1991 or '92, when I did this *Love Life* album. Sparrow told me when I delivered the album that they were very unsure [whether] they could put the album out or not. It had to do with singing about human sexuality. This was where my theology came up against this big machine and its theology and one of us had to give. The album had a song on it called "Kiss Me Like a Woman, Love Me Like a Man," which in any other context would've been, "Yeah? So what's the problem?" What they ended up doing was talking to [evangelical author and lecturer] Josh McDowell, a voice of authority in youth ministry, and he gave his blessing to it. So they were courageous enough to put it out. It didn't do tremendously well, and they got a lot of product sent back with people saying things like, "When Charlie Peacock starts making Christian music again we'll start selling it." There were stores that sold it and [Amy Grant's] *Heart in Motion* sort of under the counter, like a PG-13 thing. But that was a silly time; there's been a lot of progress since then. People now expect that Christians can sing about relationships.

Are there still real barriers facing a Christian artist trying to make it in the secular world?

CP: When we first started running experiments back in the early 1980s, when Amy Grant was making her first forays into [the secular market], I think there was still some genuine prejudice against a person who professed to be a Christian. I think that the last 15 or 20 years have brought about such pluralism in the culture, though, and a respect for your right to spirituality, that now that's not so much the problem. I think what we—the people in a position of power within Contemporary Christian music—have done is really shot ourselves in the foot by creating a genre of Contemporary Christian music. Basically, it fences the music in on its own.... People like the Gospel Music Association are becoming like trade associations, building a brand. And I think those kinds of folks really differ from the artists for the most part. The artists are not into building a brand. You see that same kind of tension in every sphere of the music business.

Did Christian music change after the early Jesus Music days?

CP: Yeah, I think that it did become [formulaic], very much so. The consistent thing that you have is the co-opting of style. There are very few artists who can claim to be making an original statement or even an innovative statement. Everybody knows that part of what we're doing here is co-opting current styles and putting so-called Christian lyrics to them.

That's part of the way the music is marketed to youth pastors. I don't know if you've sussed that element out, but it's a very integral part of the dissemination of the music across America. It goes back to the very beginning, when they did the youth musicals—they [the musicals] were essentially marketed to choir directors, and through the choir directors they would reach the choir, and then the congregation, and so forth. As a strategy, it was pretty smart. Today, a certain portion of marketing goes toward youth pastors, because these people are often the caretakers of youth at a church setting and music is obviously involved. There was the notion early on that this would give the youth pastors a tool. Say you've got a young person who comes in, and they're listening to music where either you or the parent discern that the lyric is not good for them—you'll be able to offer this Christian alternative. That whole idea of the Christian alternative to the world became the basic [reason] for which the music was constructed.

You imply in your book that perhaps these Contemporary Christian labels shouldn't exist at all. If that happened, what would become of the artists?

CP: They would return to their communities. They would be regional artists; some of them would remain national artists. The churches would care for them if they have vital ministries that were important—by that I mean that they would invite them to speak and play their music. They [the artists] don't need the infrastructure of the record company. There's plenty of infrastructure out there for independent artists and they'd be able to get their CDs made and shipped where they needed to go. What they'd be losing is their participation in the radio and distribution network. I think that would be real healthy for a lot of artists.

The other thing is, the artists who are really competitive in terms of the pop market would have the opportunity to go head-to-head with the rest of their competitors.... There [would be] nothing to keep artists from integrating with the church around the world and still be involved on a mainstream record label.

Do you feel that any sort of pop music genre is appropriate for Christian expression?

CP: No, I don't think so. This has been what I think is one of the fallacies that the church has embraced, especially this Contemporary Christian music culture—that the form is neutral. I think that this is completely opposite to the way that culture runs. Often enough, the medium has become the message, and there's a lot of power in that. There are lots of things...out there that...would be in opposition to Christianity or incongruent with your message. You might feel foolish co-opting that for the cause of Christ.

I make those kinds of choices as an artist. I don't just look around and say, "Gosh, everything's up for grabs." I think we can make mistakes as artists and we don't realize that the things we bring into our own work aren't necessarily neutral. When Bruce Springsteen wrote "Born in the U.S.A.," do you think he ever thought there would be a bunch of Republicans that would want to co-opt it for their campaign? What he was trying to say about the Vietnam War, people took as American nationalism. That's just one example of how you have to be wise with what you're saying and what forms you use.

What do you feel your responsibility is to your audience?

CP: I feel like my particular role and responsibility is not the same as another artist's. I'm not saying this is the way an artist should be. But I do feel that my role is like a scout that goes ahead of the wagon train. I take the lay of the land and come back and say, "safe ahead," or "take cover," and provide commentary on the journey. That both happens in the lyric and how the music is constructed. That's the model of artistry I'm comfortable with.

Who were your models in this?

CP: Miles Davis, very much. I've always thought [well of] the idea that one could remain very active inside the music, in and out of popularity, being willing to make mistakes in public and able to grow as an artist.

For more on Charlie Peacock, see page 220.

REBECCA ST. JAMES

A native of Australia, singer/songwriter Rebecca St. James Smallbone began her recording career at age 16 with the release of her self-titled debut CD in 1994. She quickly earned a large following through her fervently Christian message and well-crafted, dance-oriented sound. As much an evangelist as a musical performer, she advocates a firmly moral lifestyle through her recordings and in concert. Sexual abstinence before marriage is a particularly important cause for her. What is remarkable about St. James's music is its visceral power—such albums as God *(1996) and* Pray *(1998) have a primal energy to them that reaches the body as well as the spirit. Though her audience is made up largely of committed Christian youth, she has gained some notice in the mainstream.* Pray *received a Grammy Award for best rock gospel album. She is also the author of several popular devotional books.*

Did you grow up intending to be an entertainer?

RS: No, not really. It wasn't this big, huge dream. Even though it was a natural part of my life, it was actually hard for me to get up in front of other teens because I'd be intimidated by them, or by adults that had a lot more life experience than me. And here I was, this little girl getting up on the stage. So if I was going to do it, it had to be for some reason other than that I just wanted to get up there. It became my passion for God that drove me up there, because I really felt in my heart that this is what He was leading me to do.

Were your mom and dad always supportive of your desire to do this?

Rebecca St. James
Photo by Kristin Barlowe

RS: Not hugely at first, because they knew the ins and outs. My dad was a Christian concert promoter in Australia. He and my mom knew that it was hard to keep perspective, especially for a young person, when everybody's telling you you're great. They knew the challenges of it—the good, the bad, and the ugly. They were a little unsure about their 13-year-old daughter getting involved in music. I mean, we're talking about 10 years ago now. And they've been there, they've walked me through it. My dad has always said, "Be careful not to believe your own publicity. Don't take it too seriously. Remember you're a servant, not a star."

When did you start writing lyrics?

RS: Actually about the same time. I was probably 12 [or] 13 when I first started writing lyrics. I wrote a song about my brother at school—"A Little Bit of Love," a song that ended up going on my first album. I found him crying at school one day because he felt like he didn't have any friends. He had just started school. And I gave him a hug and he ran off and played after that and he was fine, and that little bit of love went such a long, long way, 'cause afterwards he wanted to spend more time with his big sister. So, that little story gave me that inspiration for a song. My first one.

How do you see the role that you've grown into? Do you think of yourself as a minister first, or as a creative artist?

RS: I do see myself as a minister first. Because, like I explained to you earlier, if I hadn't felt called to this and that God had given me the platform to do it, I wouldn't be singing. So, it's really because of the message that I sing. I definitely value the creative part as well—the music gives me that expressive way of sharing the message. It serves as a vessel.

Your albums have been very rock and dance/pop oriented. Do you think the music itself has a spiritual quality to it, apart from the words?

RS: What I pray for in my albums is that the music carries that power and that you feel something, something that is linking with the lyrics to be doubly powerful. It can't be just the lyrics on their own that hold that power—the music has to carry it as well. It's both of them to me.

Are you ever concerned that your music is too sensual or too carnal, especially rhythmically?

RS: No, no. I think sometimes you've got to be a little bit careful vocally. Sometimes I do whispers or speaking parts and you've got to be careful and make sure that it's not wandering into that sensual land. But with my music, with the drumbeats or anything like that, I never worry about it being more harmful than good.

Do you see yourself in a leadership role?

RS: Yeah.

Is that hard for you?

RS: I think it was, especially at first—and as a female especially. I'm definitely no kind of feminist—I'm probably more the other way in just believing the Bible, that God put men oftentimes in leadership for a reason. But I think as a woman I find it a bit of a struggle at times being the strong one. And I think I need to remind myself that I'm part of a team. My dad is my manager and that helps a lot, so I can really rely a lot on his leadership and his wisdom. And you know, I have a bandleader that I can rely on and I have guys that I work with, producers and players and stuff like that. And so whenever I do feel overwhelmed, like, "Oh, I'm the leader here," I think that God wants to remind me to rely more on Him and also to rely on the other people in my team. Sometimes I get overwhelmed, but most of the time I actually don't mind it, because I've grown up my whole life being the oldest sister, kind of needing to be the responsible one. So it actually feels like a pretty natural role.

How careful are you in what you say in your lyrics and onstage?

RS: I'm very careful. Some people would criticize me to a fault that I'm too careful, but I don't believe that I am. I was reading in the Bible the other day where it says that "It's better for a man to put a stone around his neck on a chain and throw himself to the bottom of the sea than to cause one of the little children to stumble." I'm just very aware of the impact and the power of music—Christian music—but also of what you share from the stage…. At times I'm intimidated by that responsibility. I have little kids that come up to me after a concert and they'll say, "You know, I fall asleep at night listening to your music." So they're getting these messages put in their heads and I want to make sure that it's something that's of God, not just something that I feel on a specific day to write about.

You speak out at your concerts against consumerism and getting too caught up in fashion. Is that a problem in the Christian music world?

RS: I probably don't talk about it in concert so much, but I had a song on my first album called "We Don't Need It," which talks about [how] you can have the money, the fame, you can have all these things, but we don't need it, because God has given us everything we need and that's really not what life is about. I definitely think that in Christian music it's a battle, because you do have to look good for your photo shoots, you have to look good for your concert performances. People have a certain expectation of how you should look, both record companies and the audience. I don't think the audience minds as much as we think they do, but the record labels and industry people definitely have a certain picture of how you need to be, and I feel the pressure at times that there would be disappointment if I didn't try and live up to that. It's a bit of a contradiction in a way, because the whole Christian message is more about what is in the heart. I'm trying to remind myself, "Rebecca, focus on being beautiful in your heart and not so much on the outside, because the beauty of the heart is what is lasting, but the outside is going to fade. You're going to get old. It's not eternal."

Is it a good or bad thing for Christian music to be isolated from the mainstream?

RS: That is the big debate: Should it be separated, why is it separated, all of that. But I just wonder if it will always be isolated because of its message, because it's offensive to people. Christian music challenges people's lifestyles, it challenges how you're living. Even to the Christians, sometimes that can be challenging. We're not always living how we should be.... I think the awareness of Christian music and the quality of Christian music is going up and up all the time, which is great. And I'm glad about that because it means more people are listening. But I wonder if there will always be some isolation.

Are there a lot of misconceptions about what Christian music is?

RS: Yeah. I think a lot of mainstream people think that Christian music is this southern, gospel, tap-your-toe, old-style, white-haired, clap-along kind of music. And it's totally not that way. Christian music has everything from reggae to rock, from AC [Adult Contemporary] to heavy metal. It's got every kind of format that there is, pretty much. And I think a lot of people don't understand that, that it's a legitimate genre on its own.

Do you think about reaching a larger audience? And if so, would that mean that you would do something different than what you do now?

RS: I do think about that, but I'm unsure that that's what God's called me to do. I've always kind of said that if God wanted my songs to be on secular radio, great. But you know, I'm not going to purposely water down my message to achieve that. I'm trying to be faithful to creating music that's glorifying to Him.... I think that's my plan of attack. You know, I'm open to it being played on secular radio. It's not like "Oh no, that would *pain* me!" I'm definitely not like that.

You don't feel that you can perform mainstream pop songs and still help spread your faith just by letting people know you're a Christian?

RS: No, not really. Part of the reason I'm passionate about being bold is because my generation has been messed around with so much. They're just sick of things being hidden. They want the truth and they want you to be up-front about it. I'm a Christian, I love God, [and] I'm not ashamed to say it. I'm not saying that because other people are approaching it differently that they're doing it wrong. Because I feel like people have different callings. But I feel that for me, personally, God has called me to be very bold and up-front about who I am and what I believe.

You're very open in what you say on stage about your personal life. Does that get uncomfortable at times?

RS: Yeah, well, what I am mostly up-front about is my commitment to abstinence, to waiting for sex. I tell people every night that I'm going to wait until after I'm married and that I'm a virgin. It's not really uncomfortable, actually. I think it would be more uncomfortable telling people this person to person. Every now and then at concerts I'll get a little "Heh, heh," a little snicker here or there, but very, very rarely. I've been talking about this for something like four years now. And most of the time I get applauded.

Who do you admire in music? Who do you listen to?

RS: I mainly listen to Christian music— dc Talk and Jars of Clay and Third Day. I've enjoyed Jennifer Knapp recently, and there's a new group called Earthsuit that's fabulous. And this comes back to the whole responsibility thing. Some people think I'm crazy in this way, but when I get asked this kind of question in an interview, I want to mainly recommend Christian music because it's what is going to build people up in their faith.

I really rely a lot on my producers to know what's going on out there, what's current, and then try to explore something new and something fresh. So part of [the reason] why I don't listen to a whole lot of secular music is my sense of responsibility, but part of it too is that I know how strongly I'm influenced by things. I want to protect my own ears so that I am coming up with something that's creative and different.

Is that also true with respect to TV and films?

RS: Yes, because I know how strongly we're all influenced by things. I'm at the stage now with movies that unless it's been recommended to me by a trusted friend, I'm not going to see it. Because I find a lot of what's being put out today to be pretty offensive. The boundaries aren't drawn in a very godly way in a lot of movies, so I'm actually very careful.

If so much of secular pop culture is unhealthy, do you try to dissuade your producers and video directors from exposing themselves to it?

RS: A guy that I worked with a lot, [ForeFront Records cofounder] Eddie DeGarmo, his whole philosophy was, "I don't like watching the TV, but I watch it to keep up with everything." And I may not have spoken out against it, but I probably would have given him a few funny looks.... I think he knows that I might not necessarily agree with that, for me. I don't know. I don't think I have actually challenged it in other people, but I think they know where I stand. And so I think even my own stance might be challenging to them. I think our lives speak so much more than our words. It seems like words are so cheap today because so much of what people speak is hogwash. They're not really backing it up. But people hopefully will see my life and see that I'm attempting to lead a radical Christian life. And hopefully that will speak even more than my words.

I've noticed you've used the word "radical" in a few of the interviews that I've read. What does it mean to live a radical Christian life?

RS: Radical is nonconformist, not conforming to the way things are done by everybody else. I heard a phrase a while back that said, "Even a dead fish can go with the flow." And it's so true. Somebody that's radical is not going with the flow, is not doing it because everybody else is doing it. They're attempting to make a stand for something else. And the radical Christian life is just going against the flow, going God's way.

What would greater success in your work mean to you? More records sold? More people at your concerts? Or something beyond that?

RS: I think hearing the stories of God moving and God using this for His glory. So I suppose hearing more stories of God moving would be greater success. To me, success personally is being faithful to what God is calling me to do.

For more on Rebecca St. James, see page 235.

MICHAEL ROE

(singer/guitarist, The 77s)

One of Contemporary Christian music's most enduring cult bands, the 77s are known for their quirky, eclectic sound and soul-bearing lyrics. By any standard—secular or Christian—this Sacramento-based group has released a series of highly impressive albums that, unfortunately, never quite reached the audience they've deserved. The band's closest brush with mainstream success came with its self-titled third album, released by Island Records in 1987. Despite glowing reviews and active touring, the 77s failed to crack the secular big time. From there, they signed with Word Records, releasing two of their best albums before going the independent route. It may be the band's fate to be always caught between the secular and Christian music worlds, fitting into neither comfortably. Fortunately, the 77s have carved out their own career niche, sustained by a devoted fan base and the respect of their Christian alternative-rock peers. Michael Roe's vocals, guitar work, and songwriting have been constants in the group since its beginnings. The current line-up—Roe, bassist Mark Harmon, and drummer Bruce Spencer—came together in the mid-1990s. A Golden Field of Radioactive Crows (2001) showed that the 77s have kept their raucous pop/rock edge and finely honed sense of humor intact after two decades of music-making.

Michael Roe
Photo by Chris Knight

How did the 77s get started?

MR: When the group was first put together it was made up of individuals attending a church—Warehouse Ministries in Sacramento. I started going there in 1979, but that church had been operational [since] the mid-1970s. It was attractive to a lot of hippie types—art-driven people, all kinds of people that didn't fit into a regular church. By the time I came around they had a fully functional group of artists on staff who were doing all kinds of interesting artistic outreaches to the community at large. When I came on the scene they thought, this is a good opportunity to create something like a rock'n'roll band that could play out at schools and places around town and advertise what was happening at this church. But what they ended up with was far more than they bargained for, because the group we ended up putting together was quite explosive and dramatic and wilder than what was happening at the church. But they loved it, because it reminded them of their hellfire preaching from the old days. It was just screaming over a bunch of raucous guitars. That's how the pastor saw it at the time—it reminded him of when he was young, which was a window for me into how a lot of preachers see what they do. What they're doing is just as much rock'n'roll as Elvis Presley.

Did the motivation behind the band's existence change over time?

MR: Yes, because after about four years of being the church's mascot band, we started getting a few more opportunities professionally. We had artistic pretensions for affecting the culture, not just the community. It was a wonderful notion, a bit naïve perhaps. We were ill equipped to do anything like that, but we tried.

Did you see your band as a ministry? Do you feel comfortable calling it one?

MR: It depends upon which era you're talking about. When we were really pushing hard to get a big-time secular record deal, it made us uncomfortable to think of it as a ministry. Now that I've had to rethink and reprocess all of this for many, many years, I don't have any trouble calling what I do everything from being a song-and-dance man to a ministry to anything in between. It's a ministry, it's entertainment, it's about everything I can think of.

Why does the term "ministry" apply to what you do?

MR: Because ministry implies service and servanthood. There's no question that we are serving people with this music. We were writing from a Christian world view…. We had no idea what would happen when the records went out there. All we could go by was what people told us after they bought them. The effect was everything from amusing to profound.

What would be an example of the profound side?

MR: I wrote a song about abortion ["You're a Pretty Baby" on *All Fall Down*] and I had women send me photographs of the babies they didn't abort after hearing the song. There were people going through divorces or broken relationships or illnesses or various kinds of problems and they reported that this was the only record that kept them hanging on or gave them the courage to be a Christian in a world full of people who judge them. I think the number one message that has been there throughout the records has been, "Be yourself. Find who it is you are." I think we represented that individuality.

Were you ever concerned that your message wasn't being clearly understood?

MR: No, because I think that's the beauty of art—it has the ability to transform without there necessarily being a direct or a specific message. I always thought rock'n'roll was more fun when you didn't sing the words out clearly. A lot of times people got things totally different from what we intended, or read spiritual meaning into something that had no meaning whatsoever. That's my favorite— that's part of what the person brings. That's why people get healed at services held by charlatans. I know people who have found God by listening to "Stairway to Heaven," just by focusing on those lyrics that are redemptive in their own way.

What have been the positives and negatives of working within the Christian music field?

MR: We've had some good times, because we're treated like family. Business-wise, to be quite candid, it's a colossal pain in the ass. I can't say it better. You get taken advantage of more because you're part of the family. You show up and you get paid in an offering rather than the money you were supposed to be paid by contract because, "Bless the Lord, brother, we don't have enough.... Here's ten dollars and some burritos and a tank of gas." It becomes quite comical after a while—you learn to accept that there's going to be a lot of nonprofessional situations. But then again, this happens in the "real world" as well. I've felt the same amount of buffoonery everywhere. It's just that in the church world it's funkier and funnier.

Is there anything about rock music that's antithetical to a Christian message?

MR: That's a real good question—it has to do with the kind of rock'n'roll you're doing. Because rock'n'roll is such a huge sponge, that term can mean everything from electronica to old classic rock and shoe-gazing mumbling [a style of British alternative rock]. I think the more elements of sensuality and flesh that your style embodies, the harder it is to rid yourself or cleanse yourself of it. You almost have to make it part of the message by either being ironic with it and…playing it off in a sort of mocking way, or by just blazing ahead and ignoring that aspect of it.

How did your band deal with this?

MR: Fortunately, our church was so encouraging, the fruit of what we were doing was so positive, that we got away with an awful lot of wild stuff that even I wouldn't do today—mostly because I grew out of it.

You had some trouble with Word Records about one of your songs, "Dave's Blues" [on *Drowning with Land in Sight*]….

MR: We'd said "kicked my ass" [in the song] and the record company turned it backwards. That song was about Dave [Leonhardt], our previous guitarist, who was struggling with Hodgkin's disease at the time. I was trying to come up with a lyric that was angry enough to describe what was happening. I felt that was the phrase to use, and the record company didn't like it.

Are those sorts of things still major issues at Christian record labels?

MR: Oh, yeah. There are certain rules— I was told that the rule is "no tits, no ass, nothing about sex that's explicit." In America, sex is the number one taboo,

and yet our number one obsession. Whereas in Europe, people would laugh at this sort of thing.

Do you think there is any basis for the argument that the drum rhythms in rock music are inherently pagan or demonic?

MR: Drumming has spiritual power, and not all rock'n'roll is based on such rhythms. But I think the spirit behind the music is more important than the drumming itself. I don't think there are any drumming cadences that are consigned to the devil. That's just not the way things are. The devil uses things that the Christians leave lying around. So therefore, if everything is ours and we're not using those rhythms, then certainly they're going to be used elsewhere.

Has your band ever been afraid of falling into heresy?

MR: I'm sure a lot of our songs are not theologically sound. But our excuse for that is, well, it's just rock'n'roll after all. I wouldn't say they were unsound, [though] they may have not been theologically complete…. My job isn't to evangelize people into liking Christian rock…. My job is to make a living and hopefully draw people to Christ in the process—and lots of other things.

Do you feel you're connecting on a spiritual level with your current audience?

MR: Absolutely. The feedback has been 100 percent. In fact, the content is even more important than it was, because it's not part of some spoon-feeding process. It's more of an intimate relationship between artist and consumer. As you continue to reflect each other back and forth over the years, you get a picture of the kind of person who listens to your music and what they're going through.

Can you describe that picture?

MR: Believe it or not, a great deal of our audience is incredibly straight, in the sense that they don't come from a rock'n'roll point of view. They're not all a bunch of crazy weirdos, although we get those. Most of these people are family oriented, they hold down jobs, they dress conservatively. But they have problems that are common to everyone, and sometimes they [the problems] don't stay in the closet like they'd like them to. That's why they reach out for us so much. It could be some secret sin or some other strange problem. A lot of these people come from broken relationships or are going through them, stuff like that. A lot our songs deal with that because I've been through a lot of that stuff.

These could be Christians who have some issues with their upbringing....

MR: Absolutely. It's the hypocrisy and the narrowness. I have my own story to tell.

My parents were strong Christians but stifled me in a lot of fundamental ways. I daresay it damaged me really good— I came out of my family as messed up as any person from a non-Christian point of view, perhaps more so. But I don't regret it, I just accept it as part of the human race.

Has this been addressed in your music over the years?

MR: Yeah, it has. I think it permeates everything we do to some degree. The band is sort of one big walking, screaming statement against the boring upbringing of our parents.

Any examples of songs for people who have struggled with this?

MR: Probably a song called "I Could Laugh" [on *The 77s*]. It's a long Velvet Underground–style acoustic piece, kind of a tone poem with me rambling on about how "Momma don't understand/ She wants to hold my hand night and day"—that kind of thing. Then it drifts on through this guy's life, the people he's hurt along the way. It's quite a piece. I think that song has struck a chord with a lot of people because it's very honest about the kinds of things you think about late at night when you're up late worrying about your life. And in the end, it talks about how I've still got to face God—I could laugh, but it's not funny. I've had a lot of people come up and say that it really hit them, especially the part about Mom not understanding. It's a symbol for parental misunderstanding overall, and that kind of begins that long road you go down oftentimes, or use as an excuse. I know I did—I didn't have one [an excuse], but it seemed like the best one going.

What allowed you to overcome that and return to the faith you were raised in without bitterness?

MR: God came to me personally and specifically. I could not have escaped that or pulled myself out. It was very definitely a divine act of coming to me, rather than me trying to work my way out of it.

This was the experience that caused you to go to the Warehouse Ministries church?

MR: Oh, yeah. It was a turning point. And I'd always feared things like that. I grew up in the Assemblies of God Church, where you had this idea that you're going to be sitting in church one day and suddenly the spirit of God will call you to the ministry in some faraway land. You live in constant fear of hearing that call. And yeah, it happens.

Was leading a rock band the equivalent of accepting that call to ministry?

MR: Well, I certainly didn't want to look at it like that. When the call came, I imagined myself in a suit with a very bad, ugly tie, leading people down a healing line like Oral Roberts. And I thought, "Find yourself some other chump—I am scramming." That whole picture was so repugnant to me. I couldn't relate to it, I didn't want it, I thought it was stupid. Well, I believe what God had planned for me was quite different from that. If anything, it was the opposite of that, and yet achieved the same effect with different people in a different way for different reasons.

Any advice you'd have for Christian musicians who are attempting to reach a larger audience than their local audience?

MR: I would just say, make sure of your calling. Make sure you know what you're doing and why you're doing it. Stay close to God—that's the number one thing. If you get away, you can mess yourself up and mess a lot of other people up. It's not something to play with. It's more serious than if you just want to start a rock'n'roll band. I've pretended that it hasn't been serious, and the longer I go, the more serious it gets.

Any thoughts about setting up young Christian musicians in the roles of teachers and ministers?

MR: It's very wrong, because no novice should be in a position of authority like that until they're prepared, and here we have a 17-year-old girl with a voice and we put her up on stage singing Christian songs, and she wields authority like a dull knife. And it's unfortunate—this girl's still growing, she's going to make mistakes, she's not an elder, she's just a kid. And yet she's singing these heavy truths that have this heavy effect. So yes, it is a problem. And the whole Christian star-making machinery I think is absurd.

I think we've mimicked the world in that way and allowed ourselves to be worshipped like gods.

That's not what your band has wanted?

MR: No, we've eschewed that as much as possible. I'm the reluctant messiah [laughs].

For more on the 77s, see page 238.

JACI VELASQUEZ

Texas-born Jaci Velasquez is one of the brightest young stars in Christian music. While still in her teens, she released her debut album Heavenly Place (1996), which introduced her appealing mix of pop and Latin sounds. This CD went on to earn her a GMA Dove Award and reach gold certification, an impressive accomplishment for a 16-year-old. A fiery live performer as well as an impressive recording artist, she was signed to Sony Discos for the secular Latin market in 1999. That year, her single "Legar a Ti" became the first recording by a Christian music artist to top the Latin charts. Velasquez has been able to build a career in two markets thanks to her vivacious style and polished singing abilities. She tends to sing about her faith with a hint of sensuality, favoring language with a romantic ring. Her 2000 album Crystal Clear further developed her blend of festive rhythms and uplifting messages.

Do you feel you're singing mostly to people who are believers?

JV: When I was solely in the English market, I got a lot of letters from people saying that they'd never listened to Christian music before and their friends said, "You've got to check this out." And they suddenly said, "This is good. This is Christian music, okay." And they actually went to church, because, well, it can't be all bad then. And they got saved. So I know for a fact that it's making a difference. It's really important to me to have that happen. And now in the Latin market, my life's been more of a testimony. I tend to be a little more conservative in the Latin market than in the Christian market, even in the way I dress, the way I act,

Jaci Velasquez
Photo by Thunder Image Group

everything. I become a little more reserved in the Latin market, because I know for a fact that I'm the only person they might have to look at as a testimony for who Christ is. In the Christian market, I just have fun—I'm comfortable. It's easy, because everyone's a Christian. I kind of feel like I'm leading two separate lives in some instances.

Have you been surprised at how you've been received in the Latin market?

JV: It has surprised me, because I didn't think I'd be really successful in it. I thought I would just sell to the Latin Christian people. I didn't think the Latin mainstream buyers would really support me. I don't know—it's just been like one big roller-coaster ride for me, and I try to do the right thing in it all.

Did you ever aspire to be a secular singer when you were growing up?

JV: No. It was very normal to do Christian music within my family. I sang with my parents since I was nine years old, traveled and sang in different churches every-where.... When I started recording my Latin record, I was obviously asked to sing secular songs, and in some instances I do have some love songs on my record. I've gotten a lot of flack about that, because I wasn't just singing about my faith. A lot of people were a little weird or upset about it. But I had to be true to

who I was. Even on my first and second albums, I didn't just sing about my faith. I sang about who I was to my family, what friends are about, what relationships are about—for me, anyway, and my 16-year-old view of it [laughs]. I've been blessed to do shows in front of people who would never set foot in a church.

Are you ever afraid of putting too much sensuality into the way you sing about God?

JV: Ever since I was a little girl, I've always had people in the studio tell me to watch myself so that I didn't sound too sexy. But it finally came to the point where it was like, "I sing the way I sing." And I think that's partially why there has been success with what I do, because my tone is what it is—it's low and it's airy. I've gotten letters about it and about the outfits that I wear, stuff like that. But I'm only 20 years old—I'm not supposed to dress or act old.

There are a lot of opinions about how a Christian artist should sing or dress....

JV: Obviously, you can't compromise who you are. You can't go, "Oh, I'm gonna wear this, because if Britney [Spears] can do it, why can't I?" I mean, I'm not an idiot, but I know that I'm only 20 years old and I want to reach the girls that are my age. I don't want to suddenly be like a deity, something unreachable, unattain-able. I'm very normal. I just happen to have an evening job that requires me to be on stage and sing every night.

Is what you do more of a ministry than a form of entertainment? How do you combine the two?

JV: That's always controversial. Some people feel that it should only be a ministry. How in the world can it only be a ministry? Whenever there's money, a lot of people involved, and a pedestal, it's about business as well. There's a business to everything we do in life. But I was talking to my brother and mom last night, and I go, okay, people try to bring God into everything, into making a deal with somebody: "Lord, please let this deal happen, 'cause it will enlarge my company." Do you think God really cares that your company gets larger? He has too much to worry about! I believe in what I do—there is a ministry side to it. And there's an entertainment and a business side. I'm not going to fool myself and be little miss perfect and say, oh, it's all about just praising the Lord all the time. That's what it *should* be, but it's not always about that.

I was talking to Rebecca St. James about how a singer can be exalted on stage, especially a Christian singer. There's a danger of the messenger being confused with the message....

JV: I totally agree with that. I mean, I'm not perfect. It's really hard to live out

everything you're trying to be about. I don't do a very good job at it. I mean, Rebecca makes me look like Satan. She's perfect—you know what I mean. I'm not trying to over-spiritualize everything, but I definitely would say that I fail. I mess up all the time in life, in my spiritual walk, in my personal life, in my artistry life. It's easy to confuse everything and put Christian artists on pedestals and think they should live lives above reproach. You try, you do everything within your power to do it, but when it comes down to life and the real world, I'm only human.

Do you think your audience expects a certain degree of perfection from you?

JV: I think they expect a certain amount of perfection. I had a grandmother walk up to me the other day—she goes, "Whatever you do, don't do anything wrong." I go, "Huh?" She says, "Please just do everything that you're supposed to, because my granddaughter looks up to you so much." I went, "Hello! Thanks a lot! That's a lot of pressure." You know, that's not fair. But that's the life I've bargained for, and I have to live my life as close to Christ's way as possible. That's okay. But I'm not going to lie to myself and say that if I'm not perfect, then I don't deserve to do what I do.

Do you feel comfortable listening to secular pop records?

JV: That's always an issue, and I'll probably get in trouble for telling you this, because the politically correct answer would be to say that I'm very selective on what I listen to. But truthfully, I am an artist and I find creativity and beauty in all genres of music. So for me, I love when I can respect a melody line from an amazing song. That's what being in the music business is all about—when you can appreciate everything. But I also listen to a lot of Christian music.

Is there a chance that you might make a record mainly for the mainstream?

JV: There have been so many talks about it and a lot of offers to do it. I've thought about it. I don't know that I will—I haven't made a choice to do it right now. I think it would be really hard to water down who I am.... They'd have to take me the way I am or not at all.

For more on Jaci Velasquez, see page 261.

A-Z ENCYCLOPEDIA

A

ADAM AGAIN
Formed mid-1980s in Southern California

A much-admired Christian cult band, Adam Again enjoyed a fervent following despite a lack of airplay or hit records. This alternative rock/R&B group achieved even greater legendary status following the death of its cofounder, singer/keyboardist/guitarist Gene Eugene, in 2000. Though its album output was comparatively small, Adam Again's impact was considerable, particularly on other Christian rock artists.

Born in Fort Frances, Ontario, on April 6, 1961, Gene Andrusco—known as "Gene Eugene" onstage—first pursued a career as a television actor, appearing on such shows as *Bewitched* and *Cannon*. It was only in the mid-1980s that he reconnected with teenage bandmates Greg Lawless (guitar) and Paul Valadez (bass) to launch a serious recording project. Also part of the group at the start were singer Riki Michelle (Eugene's wife) and saxophonist Dan Michaels. Adam Again's debut album, *In a New World of Time*, was released independently in 1986; its tracks married dance grooves to thoughtful lyrics. *Ten Songs by Adam Again*, released in 1988 on the Word-distributed Broken label, reached a larger audience. This effort was more cohesive than the first, with Eugene's lyrics showing a sharp-edged

social consciousness in tracks like "Tree House." The band expanded to a 10-piece ensemble for tours during this time.

Homeboys (1990) was a departure, emphasizing aggressive funk/rock arrangements and moody, poetic lyrics. The band added a live drummer (Jon Knox) for the first time and allowed greater room for Eugene's and Lawless's searing guitar flights. The tough-minded yet spiritually tinged lyrics of this album matched the rough edges of the music. Eugene's caustic, plaintive vocals (somewhat reminiscent of REM's Michael Stipe) were especially strong on the title track and a cover of Marvin Gaye's "Inner City Blues." Moving to their own Brainstorm label, Adam Again delivered an even stronger album with 1992's *Dig*. The melancholy tone of its songs reflected Eugene and Michelle's disintegrating marriage. Despite its bleak surface, *Dig* has moments of grandeur and inspiration, especially in its stripped-down title track. "Hopeless, Etc." and "World Wide" are among its other high points, railing against inner demons and social injustice. Though its Christian references are understated, *Dig* is as profound a statement of spiritual longing as any rock album of its era.

Adam Again returned to deliver a final album, *Perfecta*, in 1995. While overshadowed somewhat by *Dig*, this song collection contained such potent tracks as "Don't Cry" and "What's Your Name." Never a prolific songwriter on his own, Eugene spent much of the 1990s cowriting with or producing albums for a host of important Christian pop and rock artists, including **Jon Gibson, Randy Stonehill, Joy Electric,** Tourniquet, and Plankeye. He was especially important in working with acts on Tooth & Nail Records, a key independent Christian rock label. Eugene also moonlighted as a member of **the Lost Dogs** and the Swirling Eddies.

In March 2000, Eugene passed away of natural causes at his Huntington Beach, California, studio. *A Tribute to Gene Eugene* documented a concert in his honor at the 2000 Cornerstone Festival, featuring performances by **Michael Knott** and members of **the Choir, the 77s,** and **Over the Rhine.** This CD package also included an acoustic solo album by Greg Lawless, *Prayers and Lowsongs.* In 2001, KMG Records released an Adam Again compilation, *Worldwide Favorites.*

Amazingly, Gene Eugene and Adam Again never scored a hit single on Christian radio or earned a GMA Dove Award nomination. Neither did they have any real impact on the secular rock marketplace. This band's sometimes disturbing, often profoundly moving body of work awaits wider discovery.

In a New World of Time
   (independent release, 1986)
Ten Songs by Adam Again (Broken, 1988)
Homeboys (Broken, 1990)
Dig (Brainstorm, 1992)
Perfecta (Brainstorm, 1995)
Homeboys/Dig (KMG compilation, 2000)
Worldwide Favorites (KMG compilation, 2001)

AGAPE
Formed 1968 in Southern California

True Jesus Music pioneers, Agape broke ground for later Christian rock acts to follow. Considered too loud and crude for gospel radio in the early 1970s, the group reached its audiences mainly as a live act. The band's spiritual fervor was matched by its throbbing blues-rock sound, tempered in its final phase by jazz influences.

Agape was formed after singer/guitarist Fred Caban had a conversion experience at a coffeehouse in Huntington Beach, California, in 1968. Taking their name from the Greek word for "divine love," Caban and bandmates Lonnie Campbell (bass) and Mike Jungman (drums) performed at such Christian youth venues as the Salt Company Coffeehouse in Hollywood. John Peckhart replaced Campbell prior to sessions for Agape's debut album, *Gospel Hard Rock.* Released in 1971, the LP was considerably rawer than most of the early Christian rock of its time. The band comes across on this disc as heavily Jimi Hendrix–influenced, with touches of San Francisco psychedelia and Grand Funk Railroad thrown in. The lyrics are straightforward sermons for Christ, the music surprisingly sensual and catchy at times.

After replacing Peckhart on bass with Richard Greenburg and adding Jim Hess on keyboards, Agape recorded 1972's *Victims of Tradition.* Like the first album, this effort was a limited pressing and received little airplay. *Victim of Tradition* showed noticeable growth on the band's part—the melodies were better defined and the music effectively added funk rhythms and jazzy piano lines. Such tracks as "Wouldn't It Be a Drag" and "Change of Heart" presented the group's messages of sin and redemption in steamy blues/rock settings. Caban proved an inventive guitarist, unleashing flashy riffs to punctuate his altar calls.

Making little headway in its attempts to reach a larger audience, Agape called it quits at the end of 1974. The group's recordings slipped into obscurity until the small Tucson-based Hidden Vision label reissued them more than 20 years later. In addition to the two studio albums, Hidden Vision also brought out *The Problem Is Sin*, a compilation of live and unreleased recordings. An Agape reunion album was said to be in the works in 2000.

Gospel Hard Rock (independent release, 1971; Hidden Vision, 1995)

Victims of Tradition (independent release, 1972; Hidden Vision, 1995)

Live (independent release, 1973; Hidden Vision, 1996)

ALL SAVED FREAK BAND
Formed 1968 in Cleveland, Ohio

This bizarre early Jesus Music band achieved a measure of local fame around the Midwest in the late 1960s and early '70s. Amateurish at times but touched with moments of inspiration, the All Saved Freak Band adhered to a cultish doomsday doctrine that separated it from most of its fellow Christian music pioneers. Beyond the group's oddness, it deserves to be remembered for its intriguing blend of blues, rock, folk, and classical elements.

The mastermind behind the group was the Reverend Larry Hill, who broke away from the Assemblies of God in 1965 to become an independent street evangelist and radio broadcaster in Cleveland. Given to prophetic visions, Hill founded the Church of the Risen Christ and predicted a devastating war between the United States and China that would lead to the end of the world. To help advance these beliefs, he formed a rock band with musician Joe Markko, initially named Preacher and the Witness. This group became a more serious venture when it recruited Glenn Schwartz, former lead guitarist with the James Gang and Pacific Gas & Electric. Changing its name to the All Saved Freak Band, the group added sisters Pam and Kim Massmann, who brought with them a classical influence.

The All Saved Freak Band weathered the loss of several members in a 1971 auto accident and relocated to a communal home base in rural Ohio. Hill's prophesies grew increasingly conspiratorial, accusing the Roman Catholic Church and the Soviet Union of being in on the plot to destroy America. Finally, after years of recording and touring, the group released its first album, *My Poor*

Generation, on its independent Rock the World label in 1973. A fairly subdued, even genteel work, the record compensated for its rambling lyrics with the Massmann sisters' sweetly folksy vocals and chamber music–style arrangements. The band released a pair of albums three years later: *For Christians, Elves & Lovers,* a largely acoustic, classically influenced excursion, and *Brainwashed,* which veered more toward the blues/rock for which guitarist Schwartz was noted.

Meanwhile, the Church of the Risen Christ had devolved into a survivalist cult, with Hill exercising dictatorial control over his followers. His increasingly apocalyptic view of the world is reflected on the All Saved Freak Band's last album, *Sower.* A compilation of recordings made during the 1970s, it finally appeared on the ominously named War Again label in 1980. The strangest and most disturbing of the band's albums, *Sower* benefits from singer Joe Markko's soulful vocals and some imaginatively progressive, rock-flavored arrangements. *Sower*'s centerpiece is "Prince of the International Kaleidoscope," a bitter attack on the Rockefellers, the Jesuits, the John Birch Society, and other villains in Hill's cosmology. By the time *Sower* was released, the All Saved Freak Band had broken up and most of Hill's followers had scattered.

For all its uneven songwriting and questionable theology, the All Saved Freak Band makes for compelling listening even today. Hidden Vision Records began reissuing the group's albums in the late 1990s.

My Poor Generation (Rock the World, 1973; Hidden Vision, 1998)

For Christians, Elves & Lovers (Rock the World, 1976; Hidden Vision, 2002)

Brainwashed (Rock the World, 1976; Hidden Vision, 2000)

Sower (War Again, 1980; Hidden Vision, 2000)

ALLIES
Formed 1984
in San Bernardino, California

A melodic rock band with a military motif, Allies was formed by refugees from earlier Christian groups. Lead singer **Bob Carlisle,** guitarist Randy Thomas, and keyboardist Sam Scott had all been members of Psalm 150, a Southern California group active in the early 1970s. After Thomas completed a seven-year stint as leader of the Sweet Comfort Band, he reconnected with Carlisle and Scott and, adding bassist Matthew Chapman and drummer Jim Erickson, launched Allies. Signed to Light Records, the group quickly found an audience for its muscular, anthemic sound. A 1985 self-titled debut album benefited from the production touch of ex-Kansas singer John and brother Dino Elefante. Allies' themes of personal struggle and triumph—evident in such early singles as "Surrender" and "Don't Run Away"—were underscored by army surplus costuming the group wore in concert. Carlisle, for instance, sported fatigues and a gun belt while performing.

Virtues, the band's second album, continued in a similar hard-but-tuneful vein. Moving over to the DaySpring label, Allies released its third LP, *Shoulder to Shoulder,* in 1987; this LP added an R&B influence to its sonic mix. The chief stock-in-trade of the band continued to be soaring, if somewhat overblown, power ballads, reminiscent of Kansas, Triumph, REO Speedwagon, and similar outfits. Allies returned to the sound of its first two albums with *Long Way from Paradise* (1989) and continued to score Christian radio hits like "All Day, All Night" and "Trust in God." By 1992, though, the band had run out of steam and decided to disband. Carlisle went on to a successful solo career, while Thomas founded the duo Identical Strangers with singer Andy Denton.

Allies (Light, 1985)
Virtues (Light, 1986)
Shoulder to Shoulder (Light, 1987)
Long Way from Paradise (DaySpring, 1989)
The River (DaySpring, 1990)
Man with a Mission (DaySpring, 1992)

MAIA AMADA
Born c. 1959 in Scarsdale, New York

Raised in an artistically inclined family, Amada began singing as a child and earned notice at age 14 as a cast member of the Broadway show *The Me Nobody Knows.* A year later, she joined a band that included drummer/songwriter Alan Pugielli, who went on to become her husband and musical collaborator. Her singing skills were further refined by college training in opera and jazz. A stint singing advertising jingles (Internal Revenue Service, Ju-Ju Jeans, Coca-Cola) helped pay the bills as she worked toward a recording career.

In 1980, Amada and her husband embraced Christianity and dedicated their music to their faith. *Maia Amada,* her 1992 debut album, presented her as a self-assured R&B/pop vocalist with an upbeat, spiritual message. The album yielded three Christian radio hits, "Love Never Fails," "Love Is for Always," and "There's a Place." Switching labels, Amada released *Faith Remains* on Intersound, containing the singles "Second Chances" and "Love's the Key." She toured extensively in support of these releases, winning favorable notice for her deep-toned, supple vocal stylings.

In 1995, Amada took part in the sessions for *Sisters: The Story Goes On,* a multi-artist project that also included **Ashley Cleveland, Kathy Troccoli,** Crystal Lewis, and other female Christian singers. After a long hiatus from record-making, she released her 1999 CD *Out of the Ashes* independently. A Christmas album appeared two years later.

Maia Amada (DaySpring, 1992)
Faith Remains (Intersound, 1994)
Out of the Ashes (independent release, 1999)
Scarlet Ribbons (independent release, 2001)

CAROLYN ARENDS
Born 1968 in Vancouver, British Columbia

Singer/songwriter Carolyn Arends appeared on the Contemporary Christian scene as a fresh, folksy voice during the mid-1990s. While her hits grew scarcer toward the end of the decade, she has continued to release albums and has branched off into authorship as well.

A native of British Columbia, Arends has played piano and guitar and written songs since childhood. After initially studying biochemistry and later earning a degree in psychology, she decided to pursue a career in music. With encouragement from writer/artist/producer **Mark Heard,** she recorded rough demos of her material and landed a songwriting contract with Bensen Publishing. **Susan Ashton, Kim Boyce,** and **Lisa Bevill** were among the artists who recorded her songs, and Christian country artist Michael James won a GMA Dove Award for his version of Arends's "Love Is."

Signing with Reunion as a recording artist, Arends debuted with *I Can Hear You* in 1995. The album's largely acoustic sound underscored her intimate focus as a songwriter. Two tracks—"The Power of Love" and "I Can Hear You"—received much Christian radio airplay. Arends toured churches and smaller secular venues in support of the release, then went on to record *Feel Free* (1997). A bit more rock-oriented than her first effort, this album's standout tracks included "Do What You Do," a song inspired by the Dr. Seuss book *Oh, the Places You'll Go. This Much I Understand* was released in 1999, followed by 2000's *Seize the Day and Other Stories,* a compilation CD combining previously released and newly recorded tracks.

Arends parted company with Reunion following the release of *Seize the Day.* A year later, she resurfaced on the Signpost label with *Travelers,* an all-acoustic album of new material (along with a cover of **T-Bone Burnett**'s "River of Love"). She has continued to tour actively in the United States and Canada. Her side projects include a collection of inspirational stories, *Living the Questions: Making Sense of the Mess and Mystery of Life,* published by Harvest House in 2000. Applying biblical teachings to everyday difficulties, the book echoes themes found in Arends's work as an artist and songwriter.

I Can Hear You (Reunion, 1995)
Feel Free (Reunion, 1997)
This Much I Understand (Reunion, 1999)
Seize the Day and Other Stories (Reunion, 2000)
Travelers (Signpost, 2001)

SUSAN ASHTON
Born July 17, 1967, in Houston, Texas

Walking the line between country and pop, Susan Ashton released a series of popular Christian albums before making a leap into the secular market. Her sweet, smooth vocal style has been compared to country's Suzy

Bogguss and folk's Shawn Colvin, while her albums' songs and production approach have placed her on the more adventuresome side of Adult Contemporary.

Ashton was born Susan Rae Hill; she later adopted her mother's maiden name to avoid confusion with singer/songwriter **Kim Hill.** She began her career at age 18 as a background singer for Wayne Watson and **Dallas Holm.** Two years later, she signed a recording contract with Sparrow Records and, in 1991, released her debut album *Wakened by the Wind.* A well-realized first effort, the album introduced Ashton as a thoughtful, intelligent artist and was quickly embraced by Christian music fandom. Producer Wayne Kirkpatrick cowrote much of the album's material, including the singles "Down on My Knees," "Benediction," and "In Amazing Grace Land"; he remained a guiding presence throughout her years with Sparrow. Over the course of her next several releases, Ashton began to develop as a writer, though she would always record more outside material than her own originals. "Walk on By" and "Remember Not" were among her better mid-'90s singles. On her final Sparrow album, 1996's *A Distant Call,* she recorded with such notables as **Amy Grant,** Alison Krauss, and Sheryl Crow (who cowrote the single "All Kinds of People").

In 1994, Ashton toured Europe as Garth Brooks's opening act. The secular market beckoned and, in 1999, she released her Capitol debut as a country artist, *Closer.* She

was reportedly recording a second album for the label in 2001.

Wakened by the Wind (Sparrow, 1991)
Angels of Mercy (Sparrow, 1992)
Susan Ashton (Sparrow, 1993)
Along This Road (with Ashton/Becker/Dante)
    (Sparrow, 1994)
So Far: The Best of Susan Ashton
    (Sparrow, 1995)
A Distant Call (Sparrow, 1996)
Closer (Capitol, 1999)

AUDIO ADRENALINE
Formed 1991 in Grayson, Kentucky

Like its ForeFront labelmates **dc Talk,** Audio Adrenaline moves adeptly between modern pop genres while maintaining a focus on evangelical lyrics. The five-member group puts across its message with a cheeky sense of humor that winks at cultural fads and human foibles. Despite the band's seeming potential to cross over into secular music, it appears content to address the concerns of its Christian audience.

Audio Adrenaline was formed by singer Mark Stuart, singer/guitarist Barry Blair, and keyboardist Bob Herdman while they attended Kentucky Christian College in Grayson, Kentucky. At the time, the three were education and ministry majors, studying to be teachers and youth pastors. Originally intended as a summer ministry project, the fledgling group received assistance from the college as a way of attracting potential students. Adding bassist Will McGinnis and drummer Brian Hayes, Audio Adrenaline performed at Christian youth gatherings across the Midwest and earned a strong following. By the end of 1991, the band members had left college and signed a record deal with ForeFront. Their self-titled debut album yielded the singles "My God" and "DC-10," both rooted in punk/speed metal sounds.

Don't Censor Me (1993), the band's second album, was a major creative and commercial advance. Produced in part by the Gotee Brothers (which included **dc Talk**'s Toby McKeehan), the album's tracks had a vibrant, playful sound reminiscent of Crowded House and similar mid-1980s secular bands. Among its standout songs was "Big House," a buoyant, quirky track that stressed Christian love and acceptance of all peoples; released as a single, it earned a GMA Dove Award nomination and found its way into church services. Other cuts, like "Jesus and the California Kid" and "Scum Sweetheart," expressed a fundamentalist viewpoint while having fun with classic rock and modern hip-hop sounds. *Don't Censor Me* went on to sell more than 300,000 copies.

In 1994, drummer Hayes was replaced by former Geoff Moore & the Distance member Greg Harrington (who, in turn, was later replaced by Ben Cissel). After releasing *Live Bootleg* in 1995, the band returned a year later with a new studio album, *BloOm*. More sedate than previous releases, *BloOm* contained the much-played

single "Never Gonna Be as Big as Jesus" and went on to earn gold certification. Audio Adrenaline raised its energy level for its next effort, *Some Kind of Zombie* (1997). The title track was partly inspired by singer Stuart's childhood, spent in Haiti with missionary parents. The album tapped into an array of techno and hip-hop sounds and reached into the secular realm for a cover of the 1973 Edgar Winter Group hit "Free Ride." In conjunction with the album, the band released a book, *Some Kind of Journey: On the Road with Audio Adrenaline— 7 Days, 7 Issues, 7 Souls.* Modeled somewhat on the MTV programs *Real Life* and *Road Rules,* the book profiled seven young people and their struggles with moral issues.

Underdog, the band's 1999 release, was another fast-paced pastiche of '90s rock and R&B styles. The single "Get Down" was a catchy call for devotion, while "Jesus Movement" updated the blissful sentiments of 1970s artists like **Phil Keaggy** and **Love Song** in a contemporary context. The acoustic folk/pop number "Houseplant Song" was a satiric look at the anti-rock diatribes published by Bob Larson and other evangelical authors in earlier decades. By the time the band's *Hit Parade* compilation appeared in 2001, it had sold more than a million records. A self-produced album, *Lift,* was released in 2001.

Audio Adrenaline (ForeFront, 1992)
Don't Censor Me (ForeFront, 1993)
Live Bootleg (ForeFront, 1995)

BloOm (ForeFront, 1996)
Some Kind of Zombie (ForeFront, 1997)
Underdog (ForeFront, 1999)
Hit Parade (ForeFront, 2001)
Lift (ForeFront, 2001)

AVALON
Formed 1995 in Nashville, Tennessee

Avalon's harmony-centered sound has invited comparisons with everyone from ABBA to Destiny's Child. The band's high-gloss brand of R&B/pop quickly secured its place in the upper ranks of Christian artists. The stylishly wholesome image projected by this Nashville-based quartet matches the comfortable, engaging quality of their recordings.

Sparrow Records producer Norman Sinclair assembled Avalon as a vehicle for ministry as well as music. Two of the singers chosen, Jody McBrayer and Janna Potter (now Janna Long), had been members of the veteran Christian group Truth. Also brought on board were Michael Passons (a solo Christian performer) and Nikki Hassman. The group took its name from the legendary island paradise found by King Arthur after searching for the Holy Grail. Not long after coming together, Avalon was added to the roster of the Young Messiah tour, a multi-artist concert package organized by Sinclair. The band did well enough to merit the recording of a self-titled debut CD, released by Sparrow

in 1996. *Avalon* benefited from **Charlie Peacock**'s deft production, which emphasized close harmonies amidst bright R&B-slanted arrangements. "Give It Up" and "This Love" were among the tracks that received extensive airplay. Another cut, "Let It Be Forever," was a celebration of a couple's Christian love that displayed Avalon's ability to reach a wide audience.

The group's fortunes took off in earnest with the release of 1997's *A Maze of Grace.* The album featured the stirring number "Testify to Love," which went on to become (according to industry publication *CCM Update*) the longest-running number one Adult Contemporary single in the history of Christian music. Its popularity prompted country singer Wynonna Judd to record it for inclusion on the *Touched by an Angel* soundtrack CD. "Testify to Love" helped boost *A Maze of Grace* to the gold sales level. The song also won a 1999 GMA Dove Award, as did another *A Maze of Grace* track, the inspirational hit "Adonai." (The group had won a Dove Award the previous year for best new artist as well.)

In 1998, Hassman signed a solo recording deal with Sony Records and left the group. After reviewing some 100 audition tapes and failing to find a replacement, the group found Cherie Paliotta, thanks to a referral from its backup band. She joined the group in time to participate in the recording of *In a Different Light* (1999). Produced by Brown Bannister (the man behind the early success of **Amy Grant,** among many others),

In a Different Light kept the group's momentum on an upward swing, earning them a second gold album. "Can't Live a Day" and "Take You at Your Word" were among the hit singles from this release. During this period, Avalon kept busy with a 200 shows-per-year touring schedule and appearances on both secular and Christian television.

Joy, a Christmas album, followed in 2000. *Oxygen* came next in 2001—this Bannister-produced song collection had a number of high points, including the sleek "By Heart, by Soul" (featuring guest vocalist Aaron Neville) and the moody title track (originally recorded by secular rock band Mr. Mister with different lyrics). "The Glory," *Oxygen*'s first single, added a touch more rock to the band's sound and promised to bring it yet another Christian radio hit.

Avalon (Sparrow, 1996)
A Maze of Grace (Sparrow, 1997)
In a Different Light (Sparrow, 1999)
Joy (Sparrow, 2000)
Oxygen (Sparrow, 2001)

MARGARET BECKER
Born July 17, 1959, in Bayshore, New York

Margaret Becker's music has evolved considerably since her first album was released

in 1987. Recently, her writing and performing approach has moved away from explicit Christian advocacy, earning her a degree of criticism from her older fans. Still, she remains a respected figure in the Contemporary Christian music world and enjoys a faithful following.

Becker was born on Long Island, New York, of first-generation German and Irish parents. She studied violin as a child, then switched to guitar and began writing songs. By age 16, she was singing in local jazz clubs and dreaming of becoming a cabaret performer in New York. While attending James Madison University in Virginia, she embraced evangelical Christianity, a decision that redirected her musical career. After a number of secular publishers rejected her spiritually tinged songs, she moved to Nashville in 1985 and found acceptance in the Contemporary Christian music community.

Signing a song publishing deal with Sparrow, Becker placed tunes with **Steve Camp** ("One on One"), **Sandi Patty** ("Exalt Thy Name"), and **Steven Curtis Chapman** ("Wait"). She gained further exposure as a background singer with **Rick Cua**'s touring group. Her debut album, *Never for Nothing*, was released by Sparrow in 1987 and was both a critical and popular success. The LP emphasized rock power ballads reminiscent of Heart, Patty Smyth, and other mid-1980s secular acts. Becker's vocals on such tunes as the anthemic "Fight for God" and the introspective

"Never for Nothing" were soaring and passionate, if strident at times.

Later albums on Sparrow found Becker moving away from guitar-driven pop/rock toward more R&B-influenced sounds. In tandem with producer/cowriter **Charlie Peacock,** her lyrics and arrangements gained nuance and polish. She continued to earn Christian radio airplay and, in 1992, received GMA Dove Awards for both her album *Rock House* and its title track. In 1994, she teamed up with **Susan Ashton** and **Out of the Grey**'s Christine Dente for a well-received trio album, *Along the Road.*

Released in 1995, *Grace* was a particularly strong album, yielding the ultra-catchy "Deep Calling Deep," a number one Christian radio single. Despite her steady success, Becker became frustrated with the music business and took time off following *Grace's* release. This career reevaluation mirrored ongoing spiritual struggles. Her return to her Catholic heritage sparked criticism from some in the evangelical community and even led to protests at a few concerts.

Becker weathered such controversy and returned to recording, releasing *Falling Forward* in 1998 and *What Kind of Love* a year later. The latter album combined hip-hop grooves with strings and semi-acoustic arrangements. The CD's best tracks, including "Friend for Life" and the title number, displayed Becker's increasingly refined, understated vocal approach, a far cry from the melodramatics of her first release. Her lyrics showed greater subtlety

as well, using a Christian perspective as a basis for commentary on the human condition rather than explicit evangelism.

Over the years, Becker has contributed essays to a number of Christian magazines and has authored two books: *With New Eyes* (Harvest House, 1998) and *Growing Up Together,* a collection of stories about siblings (Harvest House, 2000). (For more about Margaret Becker, see pages 51–55.)

Never for Nothing (Sparrow, 1987)
The Reckoning (Sparrow, 1988)
Immigrant's Daughter (Sparrow, 1989)
Simple House (Sparrow, 1991)
Soul (Sparrow, 1993)
Along This Road (with Ashton/Becker/Dente)
  (Sparrow, 1994)
Grace (Sparrow, 1995)
Fiel a Ti (Spanish) (Sparrow, 1995)
Falling Forward (Sparrow, 1998)
What Kind of Love (Sparrow, 1999)

BOB BENNETT
Born March 21, 1955,
in Downey, California

A big, burly man with a wry lyric touch, Bob Bennett is known for his skill at dealing with everyday events from a Christian perspective. His songs tend to be highly personal and often deal with family issues. Though only sporadically successful at reaching large audiences, Bennett continues to enjoy a cult following.

Bennett began playing guitar at age nine and was part of a rock group in high school. By the mid-1970s, he was working as a night-club performer around Southern California. In 1977, he began to explore Christianity through the influence of his roommate Dan Rupple, a member of the Christian comedy duo Isaac Air Freight. Embracing the faith, Bennett began writing Christian songs and, in 1979, released his debut LP, *First Things First*, on Maranatha. Two years later, he released *Matters of the Heart* on the CBS-owned Priority label, yielding the singles "Come and See" and "Mountain Cathedrals." *Matters of the Heart* went on to be chosen as album of the year for 1982 by *CCM* maga-zine. Unfortunately, Priority folded while Bennett was recording a follow-up album.

In 1985, Bennett was back with *Non Fiction*, an LP of small but telling observations about life and faith released by Star Song. That same year, he opened 35 concert dates for **Amy Grant** as a solo acoustic act. The exposure didn't translate into record sales, however, and Bennett asked to be released from his contract. In 1987, he reunited with Rupple to cohost a morning Christian talk program on KBRT radio in Los Angeles. The following year, he contributed three new songs to an Urgent Records compila-tion album of his older recordings, called *Lord of the Past*. Two of these new composi-tions—the title track and "Yours Alone"— became major Christian radio hits. During fall 1990 and spring 1991, he performed on a 70-date tour with **Michael Card**.

Songs From Bright Avenue, a song collection dealing in part with the breakup of Bennett's marriage, was released in 1991. One track, "No Such Thing as Divorce," was featured several times on Dr. Laura Schlessinger's syndicated radio program. In the mid-1990s, he began performing at secular venues around Southern California. His most recent album, 1997's *Small Graces*, was recorded at Michael Card's studio and released on the Myrrh-distributed Covenent Artists label.

First Things First (Maranatha!, 1979)
Matters of the Heart (Priority/CBS, 1981)
Non Fiction (Star Song, 1985)
Lord of the Past: A Compilation (Urgent, 1989)
Songs from Bright Avenue (Urgent, 1991)
Small Graces (Covenant Artists/Myrrh, 1997)

LISA BEVILL
Born 1968 in North Carolina

Over the course of four albums, Lisa Bevill has blended pop, rock, and R&B elements and dealt with a variety of faith-related themes. Growing up in Nashville, she began her career as an in-demand session background singer, contributing to albums by Christian artists (among them **Amy Grant, Michael W. Smith, Carman, Rich Mullins, Petra,** and **Russ Taff**) and country performers (including Wynonna Judd, Reba McEntire, and Vince Gill). She also found work singing advertising jingles for such famous clients as McDonald's, Chevrolet, and Domino's Pizza. Her versatile abilities led to a recording deal with the Sparrow-distributed Vireo label, which released her debut album *My Freedom* in 1992. "Place in the Sun" (cowritten by **Carolyn Arends**) brought her a chart-topping Christian radio hit that same year. Around this time, Bevill became the first female artist spokesperson for True Love Waits, a campaign promoting abstinence before marriage; her single "Chaperone" (cowritten by **dc Talk**'s Toby McKeehan) was included in a CD compilation in support of the cause.

In contrast to the lighter pop of her first album, Bevill's 1994 CD *All Because of You* took a more rock-oriented approach. This **Charlie Peacock**–produced effort included such singles as "No Condemnation" and "Make It Better." She took a softer, more Adult Contemporary approach on her next album, *Love of Heaven* (1996). While touring to support the release, Bevill decided to scale back her career to focus on her family. She left Sparrow by the end of the decade.

Lisa Bevill, released by the independent Ministry Music label in 2000, marked her return to record-making. Featuring her own compositions, the album dealt with her spiritual and artistic growth since her heyday with Sparrow. "How Strong He Is," an R&B number, was among its better tracks.

My Freedom (Vireo, 1992)
All Because of You (Sparrow, 1994)
Love of Heaven (Sparrow, 1996)
Lisa Bevill (Ministry Music, 2000)

BIG TENT REVIVAL
Formed 1994 in Memphis, Tennessee

Drawing upon Middle America's varied musical traditions, Big Tent Revival offered an eclectic amalgam of acoustic rock, blues, country, and traditional gospel during the latter half of the 1990s. As the name indicates, there was a street preacher–like spirit to the band's songs. The Memphis-based quintet's raw, scruffy energy—sometimes obscured by the production of its albums—was one of its strong suits, particularly in concert.

Singer/guitarist Steve Wiggins, guitarist Randy Williams, and drummer Spence Smith formed the nucleus of Big Tent Revival in 1994. A year later, bassist Rick Heil was recruited. The combo soon secured

Big Tent Revival, with lead singer Steve Wiggins (center)
Photo by Scott Greenwalt

a deal with Ardent Records (affiliated with Memphis's legendary Ardent recording studios), which in turn hooked up with ForeFront for Christian market release. Their 1995 debut CD, *Big Tent Revival*, attracted a great deal of attention without much advance hype and contained one of the band's signature tunes, "Two Sets of Joneses," a catchy, acoustic-based number. The album's rootsy sound—replete with accordion and tight vocal harmonies—tread in the same territory as John Mellencamp, Counting Crows, and the folksier side of Tom Petty.

Adding keyboardist David Alan, the band released *Open All Nite* in 1996. Similar in sound to the first album, it featured the provocative track "If Loving God Was a Crime," which touched upon Christian conflicts with government. "Famine or Feast" and "Mend Me" also received much Christian radio airplay. *Amplifier* (1998) opted for a more aggressive rock approach, a direction continued on *Choose Life* (1999). By the time of the latter's release, Steve Dale had replaced Heil as the group's bassist.

Big Tent Revival folded in 2000, releasing its final concert as a live album. *Big Tent Revival Live* is a good summation of the band's virtues, containing such favorites as "What Would Jesus Do" and "Choose Life." The album closed with an a cappella rendition of "O Come Let Us Adore Him," a fitting goodbye statement from a group that always kept its evangelical focus. Front man Wiggins is currently pursuing a solo career.

Big Tent Revival (Ardent/ForeFront, 1995)
Open All Night (Ardent/ForeFront, 1996)
Amplifier (Ardent/ForeFront, 1998)
Choose Life (Ardent/ForeFront, 1999)
Big Tent Revival Live (Ardent/ForeFront, 2001)

KIM BOYCE
Born c. 1961 in Winter Haven, Florida

"Perky" was a word applied to singer Kim Boyce at the start of her recording career. This stemmed in part from the bright, cheerful dance/pop sound of her early albums, aimed mostly at a teenage audience. Her 1950s-style retro-glamour image reinforced the idea that her music was on the light side. Boyce strived for greater maturity as an artist on later albums before making a career move toward inspirational writing and speaking.

Boyce began performing at age eight as part of her family's gospel group, the Melody Three Singers. In 1983, she won the Miss Florida beauty pageant and went on to become a finalist for Miss America. Moving to Nashville, she found work as a background singer for **Carman** and the Joe English Band, among others. Signing with Myrrh Records, she released her debut album, *Kim Boyce*, in 1986 and gained Christian radio exposure with such hits as "Darkened Hearts" and a cover of secular artist Alison Moyet's "Love Resurrection." She received a GMA Dove Award nomination for best new artist in 1988. Boyce actively toured to support her releases and became known for her high-energy, choreography-filled concerts. Her striking looks—reminiscent of Marilyn Monroe in some publicity shots—raised her visibility in the Christian media market further.

After recording four albums for Myrrh, Boyce switched to Warner Alliance in the early 1990s. *Facts of Love,* her first release for the label, found her moving toward a more organic, less techno-driven sound. The songs displayed an increasingly mature perspective on love, marriage, and biblical themes. "Love Has Made the Difference," "Dancin' to the Beat of Your Heart," and "By Faith" were among her Christian radio hits during her years with Warner Alliance. Changing labels again, this time to Diadem, Boyce released *As I Am* in 1997. This Adult Contemporary-slanted offering featured such key songs as the title track and "Amazing Love for Me," a duet about parenthood and sacrifice sung with her husband, musician Gary Koreiba.

In recent years, Boyce has been active as a speaker at Christian inspirational conferences and other events. She's also authored and coauthored a series of books, including *Dreams I'm Dreamin', Beauty to Last a Lifetime,* and *Touched by Kindness.*

Kim Boyce (Myrrh, 1986)
Time and Again (Myrrh, 1988)
Love Is You to Me (Myrrh, 1989)
This I Know (Myrrh, 1991)
Facts of Love (Warner Alliance, 1992)
By Faith (Warner Alliance, 1994)
As I Am (Diadem, 1997)

BRIDE
Formed 1986 in Louisville, Kentucky

Considered the "Christian AC/DC" in some circles, Bride has proved an enduring force on the Christian heavy metal scene. The group's relentless guitar riffing and grinding tempos underscore the stark contrasts drawn in its lyrics between sin and salvation. Enduring lean times and membership changes, Bride has held onto its core audience as it has continued to release albums on a variety of record labels.

Brothers Dale and Troy Thompson (vocals and guitar, respectively) founded the group in Louisville after playing traditional southern gospel music with the Hillview Lads. Recruiting drummer Stephan Rolland and bassist Scott Hall, the Thompsons started a band called Matrix, which toured the Christian rock circuit extensively. After securing a contract with Refuge Records' Pure Metal custom label, Matrix changed its name to Bride and, in 1987, released its debut album, *Show No Mercy.* In this early phase, the band favored makeup and teased hair typical of 1980s heavy metal bands, and its sound had a similar overwrought quality. This began to change after the release of a "best of" collection, *End of an Age,* in 1990. Moving over to Star Song, Bride entered a productive period with a pair of new members, bassist Rick Foley and drummer Jerry McBroom. The band's more refined hard rock direction yielded a series of impressive albums, most notably 1992's

Snakes in the Playground. Dale Thompson came into his own as a raw-throated rock preacher, his messages punctuated by brother Troy's slashing guitar work.

Unlike most hard rockers, Bride managed to receive mainstream Christian radio airplay in the early '90s with such tunes as "Goodbye" and "I Miss the Rain." The group won four GMA Dove Awards during this time, including one for best hard rock album for 1994's *Scarecrow Messiah*. *Shotgun Wedding* (1995) gathered the strongest tracks from Bride's Star Song period, including such signature tunes as "Psychedelic Super Jesus," "Everybody Knows My Name," and "Rattlesnake." That same year, Bride signed with Rugged Records and released *Drop*, an atypically acoustic-oriented record that confused some fans. Jumping to yet another label, Organic Records, the band returned to harder rock on 1997's *The Jesus Experience* and 1998's *Oddities*. The latter album was of particular interest for its diversity and intense hellfire-and-brimstone lyrics. Among its better moments was "Tomorrow Makes No Sense," a merciless self-indictment from a sinner's point of view.

After years of struggle, Bride almost disbanded after *Oddities*. But the Thompson brothers soldiered on, recruiting new bassist Lawrence Bishop and Mike Loy and releasing *Fist Full of Bees* on the new Absolute label in 2001. This release was a welcome return to form and promised better days for the band. Through all the turmoil, the group has continued to tour, winning a particularly strong following in Brazil. Both Dale and Troy Thompson released a variety of side projects during the '90s as well.

Show No Mercy (Refuge/Pure Metal, 1987)
Live to Die (Refuge/Pure Metal, 1988)
Silence Is Madness (Refuge/Pure Metal, 1989)
End of an Age (Star Song, 1990)
Kinetic Faith (Star Song, 1991)
Snakes in the Playground (Star Song, 1992)
Scarecrow Messiah (Star Song, 1994)
Shotgun Wedding (Star Song, 1995)
Drop (Rugged, 1995)
The Jesus Experience (Organic, 1997)
Oddities (Organic, 1998)
Fist Full of Bees (Absolute, 2001)

BURLAP TO CASHMERE
Formed mid-1990s in Brooklyn, New York

The New York–based septet Burlap to Cashmere has reached out to both secular and Christian audiences with its feisty brand of European-flavored folk/rock. Though still at the cult-artist level as of 2000, the group's instrumental prowess and optimistic message showed promise of reaching a wider audience.

Flamenco-style guitar work and Latin rhythms give the band a distinctive sound. Founding members Steven Delopolos (vocals, guitar) and John Philippidis (lead guitar, vocals) draw upon their Greek heritage for inspiration. Their band grew out of a college theater project; over an 18-month period, the pair added second guitarist Mike Ernest, bassist Roby Guarnera, keyboardist Josh Zandman, drummer Teddy Pagano, and percussionist Scott Barksdale. Burlap to Cashmere attracted attention as a New York club act and went on to secure a deal with A&M Records. After the release of a five-song EP, *Live at the Bitter End,* the band made its album debut with *Anybody Out There?* in 1998.

Emphasizing acoustic textures with some synthesizer touches, *Anybody Out There?* captured the energy of the band's self-described "Mediterranean stomp." Such tracks as "Digee Dime" and "Basic Instructions" had the footloose, slightly ragged mood of street musicians performing for spare change. Other songs, such as "Eileen's Song" and "Treasures in Heaven," were more subdued and reflective. Chief songwriter Delopolos brought a yearning, defiantly hopeful outlook to his lyrics. "Skin Is Burning" and the album's title track examine the claims of the human world versus those of the spirit in plain yet poetic terms.

Anybody Out There? got off to a strong start in the mainstream pop sector, helped by the band's 1998 tour with **Jars of Clay.** When A&M faltered, Squint Entertainment rereleased the album for the Christian market.

Live at the Bitter End (A&M, 1997)
Anybody Out There? (A&M/Squint, 1998)

Burlap to Cashmere
Photo by Michael Wilson

T-BONE BURNETT
Born January 14, 1948,
in St. Louis, Missouri

A singer/songwriter/producer of great versatility, Joseph Henry "T-Bone" Burnett was among a handful of Christian rock musicians to gain notice in the early 1980s secular market. His highly eclectic, often mordantly satiric albums attracted critical praise if not strong sales. Burnett may have had his greatest influence as a producer of other artists and as a model of creative independence among his fellow Christian artists.

Active in Texas in the early 1970s, Burnett first gained attention as a key member of Bob Dylan's Rolling Thunder Review tour group in 1975–76. Joining forces with fellow Review members Steven Soles and David Mansfield, he assembled the Alpha

Band, an intriguing folk/rock trio that released three albums on Arista Records. The band's final LP, *Statue Makers of Hollywood* (1978), was the first to fully display Burnett's Christian faith. Such tunes as "Rich Man" and "Mighty Man" castigated human greed and arrogance with an almost Old Testament fervor. These themes would be returned to on Burnett's first solo album, 1980's *Truth Decay*, a rockabilly-slanted effort featuring "Madison Avenue" and other cultural critiques. After a somewhat overblown LP for Warner Brothers, *Proof Through the Night* (1983), he returned to form with the subdued, countrified *T-Bone Burnett*. This 1986 Dot Records LP contains perhaps Burnett's most gracefully written paean to God, "River of Love." Returning to the rock market, he recorded *The Talking Animals* (1998) and *The Criminal Under My Own Hat* (1992) for Columbia. These discs found his disdain for secular modern civilization tempered by a bit of self-criticism. A new album, *The True False Identity*, was reportedly in the works for 2002 release.

Burnett's career as a producer blossomed in the 1980s and early '90s—his clients included **Bruce Cockburn,** Elvis Costello, Roy Orbison, Los Lobos, the Wallflowers, and Counting Crows. His most important collaborator during this time was singer/songwriter **Leslie** (later **Sam**) **Phillips,** whom he went on to marry. Recent work with folk/country artist Gillian Welch and supervision of the soundtrack to the Coen

brothers' film *O, Brother, Where Art Thou?* have boosted his reputation further.

During the 1999 presidential impeachment controversy, Burnett criticized the likes of the Reverend Jerry Falwell and Pat Robertson with the sort of anger he formerly reserved for secular American targets. Always the maverick, he remains a cantankerous voice in the service of Christian music.

WITH THE ALPHA BAND:
Statue Makers of Hollywood (Arista, 1978)
SOLO:
Truth Decay (Takoma, 1980)
Proof Through the Night
(Warner Brothers, 1983)
T-Bone Burnett (Dot, 1986)
The Talking Animals (Columbia, 1988)
The Criminal Under My Own Hat
(Columbia, 1992)

CAEDMON'S CALL
Formed 1992 in Ft. Worth, Texas

Among the best of Contemporary Christian music's new crop of folk/rock bands, Caedmon's Call matches its thoughtful lyrics with an affable, acoustic-based sound. The lighter side of REM's early recordings are a useful reference point; a palette of 1960s rock references and southern poetic touches are common to both groups. Over the course of two major label releases, the Texas-based sextet built its college-circuit following into solid success in the Christian market and growing recognition in secular musical circles.

Caedmon's Call traces its origins to 1991, when singer/guitarist Cliff Young began writing songs with Aaron Tate while the two attended Texas Christian University in Ft. Worth. Moving to Houston the following year, Young launched the group after recruiting singer/ guitarist Derek Webb, drummer Todd Bragg, and singer Danielle Glenn. (Though he declined to join, Tate continued to cowrite material with Young for the band.) Bassist Aric Nitzberg, percussionist Garett Buell, and keyboardist Randy Holsapple (later replaced by Josh Moore) completed the initial lineup. The band's name derives from Caedmon (d. 680), the first English Christian poet.

The band actively toured the college circuit and self-released a pair of albums, 1994's *My Calm/Your Storm* and 1995's *Just Don't Want Coffee*. The group quickly attracted attention and, in 1996, was named as one of the top 50 unsigned bands in the United States by *Musician* magazine. With the help of singer Wayne Watson, it secured a deal with Warner Alliance and released a self-titled album in 1997. *Caedmon's Call* yielded a string of chart-topping Christian radio hits—including "Lead of Love," "Hope to Carry On," "Coming Home," and "This World"—and eventually earned a GMA Dove Award for modern rock/alternative album of the year. Much favorable comment was generated for the band in both the Christian and secular press. Unfortunately, Warner Alliance experienced difficulties during this period and folded before Caedmon's Call could release another album. Despite album sales of more than 250,000, the band ran into financial problems and struggled to continue as a live act.

The situation improved when the group signed with Essential Records, which released its *40 Acres* album in 1999. Tunefully expressing themes of faith and forgiveness, the album utilized banjo, accordion, tabla drums, and Mellotron in singles such as "There You Go," "Thankful," "Where I Began," and "Shifting Sand," which filled the Christian airwaves. *Long Line of Leavers,*

Caedmon's Call. Left to right: Todd Bragg, Danielle Glenn, Garett Buell, Derek Webb, Josh Moore, and Cliff Young
Photo by Michael Wilson

released in 2000, took the band's eclecticism still further, delving into 1940s-style jazz and Brazilian rhythms. The following year saw the release of *In the Company of Angels,* an album of worship songs.

Caedmon's Call has become known for its exceptionally loyal, mostly college-age audience. The group's fans often travel hundreds of miles to see them perform, inviting comparisons to the Grateful Dead's devoted "Deadheads." In 1997, the band formed Caedmon's Guild, an organization for its followers that has sponsored an annual weekend retreat and songwriting contest. Young's interest in new talent led him to start Watershed Records (distributed by Essential), which has released albums by singer/songwriters Bebo Norman and Andrew Peterson.

My Calm/Your Storm
    (independent release, 1994)
Just Don't Want Coffee
    (independent release, 1995)
Caedmon's Call (Warner Alliance, 1997)
40 Acres (Essential, 1999)
Long Line of Leavers (Essential, 2000)
In the Company of Angels (Essential, 2001)

THE CALL
Formed 1979 in Santa Cruz, California

Something of an American counterpart to U2, the Call gained critical favor during the 1980s and early '90s for its stirring brand of modern rock. Rather than preaching on specific points of dogma, the band applied its Christian beliefs to grand themes of human struggle and justice. After dissolving in the early '90s, the original members of the group resumed recording and touring by the end of the decade.

The baritone vocals and gospel-influenced songwriting of Michael Been defined the Call's sound from its beginning. His early musical involvements included playing bass on **2nd Chapter of Acts'** classic "Easter Song" in 1974. Five years later, Been formed Motion Pictures with drummer Scott Musick, guitarist Tom Ferrier, and bassist Gregg Freeman. Performing around Northern California, the group changed its name to the Call and secured a deal with Mercury Records. Augmenting the lineup was Garth Hudson, renowned keyboardist with the Band, one of the Call's chief influences.

The Call's three albums for Mercury set the pattern for later releases—the songs were dark-tinged calls for moral regeneration, colored by ringing guitars and swirling keyboard textures. "The Walls Came Down," a scathing attack on corporate power from 1983's *Modern Romans,* is the best-known tune from the band's Mercury period. In 1985, the group added Jim Goodwin on keyboards and saw Been taking over the bassist's slot after Freeman's departure. The theme of man's relationship with God became ever more explicit in the Call's songs as it switched to the Elektra label. "Everywhere I Go" and "I Still Believe," both found on the 1986 LP *Reconciled,* were passionate declarations of faith set to surging rock tracks. The latter song became the band's only major Christian radio hit and was later covered by singer **Russ Taff** as well.

Another change in record companies—this time to MCA—brought the Call renewed success with its 1989 CD *Let the Day Begin.* The title track—a fervent prayer on behalf of working men and women—became an MTV hit and later served as Al Gore's 2000 presidential campaign theme song. After 1990's *Red Moon,* the group went on an extended hiatus. Been recorded a 1995 solo album (*On the Verge of a Nervous Breakthrough*) with the assistance of his old bandmates. Finally, in 1998, the Call reassembled to release *To Heaven and Back* on the small Fingerprint label.

The Call's Michael Been
Photo by Chris Knight

Several anthologies of the band have appeared; *The Best of the Call,* released by Warner Resound, is the most comprehensive.

The Call (Mercury, 1982)
Modern Romans (Mercury, 1983)
Scenes Beyond Dreams (1984, Mercury)
Reconciled (Elektra, 1986)
Into the Woods (Elektra, 1987)
Let the Day Begin (MCA, 1989)
Red Moon (MCA, 1990)
The Best of the Call (Warner Resound, 1997)
To Heaven and Back (Fingerprint, 1998)

STEVE CAMP
Born April 13, 1955, in Wheaton, Illinois

"I want to run a mission a yard from the gates of Hell," Steve Camp sang in his biggest Christian radio hit, "Run to the Battle." This expression of defiant faith sums up the essence of his recorded output over a two-decade span. Never shy about his beliefs, Camp has devoted his recording career to extolling fundamentalist Christianity in plainspoken terms. Disheartened with trends in the Christian music world, he took on the roles of pastor and evangelist during the 1990s.

A committed Christian since boyhood, Camp was inspired by the musical side of the Jesus movement during the early 1970s. He made contact with Christian rock pioneer **Larry Norman,** who helped shape his songwriting and career direction. Studies in music composition and theory at Chicago's Roosevelt University also aided his development. In 1975, Camp released his first recording, a secular-market single on Mums/CBS. Rather than pursue this direction further, however, he decided to move into Christian pop music and went on to sign with Myrrh Records. *Sayin' It with Love,* his first album with the label, was released in 1978.

Camp enjoyed several Christian radio hits during the late '70s and early '80s, beginning with "Gather in His Name." His most significant release, though, was the aforementioned "Run to the Battle," a single that topped the Christian charts for 16 weeks in 1984. (The song went on to become a hit for a second time when Camp rerecorded it in 1990.) Moving over to Sparrow Records, he continued to write anthems to rouse the faithful. Musically, his records were steeped in the pumped-up, slightly brittle pop/rock sounds typified by Phil Collins, Richard Marx, and similar 1980s secular hitmakers. The 1987 singles "Foolish Things" and "One on One" were typical of the upbeat fare he recorded during this period. Camp recorded with both Nashville-based Christian musicians and top Los Angeles session players, lending his strictly biblical lyrics an appealing sonic sheen.

By the early '90s, Camp had become concerned over the increasing secular ownership of Christian music labels. He likewise worried that the music's basic message was becoming watered down as its market expanded. After a long association with

Sparrow, he signed with Warner Alliance and recorded a pair of albums with noted producer Michael Omartian. His 1993 album *Takin' Heaven by Storm* yielded his last big Christian radio hit, "I'm Committed to You," a celebration of lasting love. Not long after, though, Camp decided to bow out of the commercial side of Christian music in favor of full-time ministry.

In 1999, Camp released *Abandoned to God,* his first album in five years. By then, he had become a pastor at Grace Community Church in Sun Valley, California; he subsequently moved his ministry to Nashville. Today, he combines performing and preaching in what he terms "concert crusades." Camp continues to speak out against negative trends in Christian music as a controversial but still respected voice of experience.

Sayin' It with Love (Myrrh, 1978)
Start Believin' (Myrrh, 1980)
For Every Man (Myrrh, 1981)
It's a Dying World (Myrrh, 1982)
Fire and Ice (Myrrh, 1983)
Shake Me to Wake Me (Sparrow, 1984)
One on One (Sparrow, 1986)
After God's Own Heart (Sparrow, 1987)
Justice (Sparrow, 1989)
Consider the Cost (Sparrow, 1991)
Takin' Heaven by Storm
    (Warner Alliance, 1993)
Mercy in the Wilderness
    (Warner Alliance, 1994)
Abandoned to God (Ministry Music, 1999)

MICHAEL CARD
Born April 11, 1957,
in Madison, Tennessee

It's been Michael Card's career mission to interpret and dramatize Scripture in folk/pop song form. His lyrics examine the nuances of biblical stories and, though he has an eye for dramatic detail, he never strays far from the basic text. Perhaps best known for writing the **Amy Grant** hit "El Shaddai," Card has released albums steadily over the past two decades and has established himself as an author of Christian books for adults and children as well.

Card's pursuit of songwriting and performing was something of an accident. The grandson of a Baptist preacher, he earned a master's degree in biblical studies from Western Kentucky University (where he also taught physics and astronomy in a master's program). While still a college student, he began writing songs on Christian themes at the request of his pastor. This grew into a full-time endeavor and led to a recording contract with Milk & Honey Records. *First Light*, his 1981 debut LP, established him as an unusually literate singer/songwriter with high theological standards. Card particularly distinguished himself in depicting the life of Jesus, touching upon this theme in such early hits as "Love Crucified Arose" and "This Must Be the Lamb."

In 1982, Amy Grant included Card's song "El Shaddai" ("God Almighty" in Hebrew) on her *Age to Age* album. A modern-day hymn in praise of the Creator, "El Shaddai" went on to win a GMA Dove Award for song of the year and to become one of Contemporary Christian music's best-loved songs. It served to raise Card's profile as an artist further as he entered a long and productive relationship with Sparrow Records. Among his better-known 1980s releases was *The Final Word*, which received a Dove Award for best praise and worship album in 1988. This LP contained "Joy in the Journey," a celebration of the Christian life that became one of Card's standards. In 1989 he released a children's music album, *Sleep Sound in Jesus*, which went on to earn gold certification.

As a singer, Card has often been compared with secular artist Dan Fogelberg. His melodies have both folk and classical shadings, dressed up with rock guitar and drums on some albums. During the 1990s, he began to favor Irish folk instrumentation, including hand drums and uilleann pipes. If the musical settings changed, the focus of Card's lyrics remained the Bible (particularly the New Testament). Highlights of this period are 1994's *Poiema*, which included a musical prayer for Northern Ireland, "The Greening of Belfast," and 1997's *Unveiled Hope*, a musical examination of the Book of Revelation. By the end of the decade, Card had sold more than two million albums.

In addition to his active recording and performing career, Card has established himself as a popular Christian author. His published works have included children's books (*Sleep Sound in Jesus*, 1989), poetry collections (*Close Your Eyes So You Can See*, 1996), and devotionals (*Parable of Joy*, 1995).

First Light (Milk & Honey, 1981)
Legacy (Milk & Honey, 1983)
Known by the Scars (Sparrow, 1983)
Scandalon (Sparrow, 1985)
The Final Word (Sparrow, 1987)
Present Reality (Sparrow, 1988)
Sleep Sound in Jesus (Sparrow, 1989)
The Way of Wisdom (Sparrow, 1990)
Come to the Cradle (Sparrow, 1993)
Poiema (Sparrow, 1994)
Close Your Eyes So You Can See
    (Myrrh, 1996)
Unveiled Hope (Myrrh, 1997)
Starkindler (Myrrh, 1998)
Soul Anchor (Myrrh, 2000)

BOB CARLISLE
Born September 29, 1956
in Los Angeles, California

Known for his years as lead singer with the band **Allies,** singer/songwriter Bob Carlisle successfully launched himself as a solo artist in the early 1990s. He might well have remained largely unknown outside of Contemporary Christian music if it hadn't been for his 1997 song "Butterfly Kisses," a crossover country/pop hit of phenomenal proportions. This unabashedly sentimental expression of a father's love for his daughter made Carlisle a mainstream media celebrity and encouraged him to record further celebrations of family life from a Christian perspective.

Raised in Santa Ana, California (a suburb south of Los Angeles), Carlisle began learning guitar at age seven. His father, who sold acoustic instruments, encouraged his son by letting him sit in with such famous musician friends as guitarist Doc Watson and dobro player Tut Taylor. Besides this country influence, he was also absorbing the R&B sounds of the 1960s, particularly artists like Otis Redding and James Brown. By his teenage years, Carlisle had become involved with the local Jesus Music scene, performing with the group Good News. He next joined Psalm 150, which also included his future songwriting partner Randy Thomas. The band recorded an album but failed to become a commercial success. The early 1980s found Carlisle active around Los Angeles as a background singer, lending his voice to albums by Barry Manilow, REO Speedwagon, and Mötley Crüe, among others. He also worked regularly as a performer at a local nightclub called Rosie's.

Feeling out of touch with God, Carlisle walked out of his club gig and sought a new direction. Opportunity arrived via his old friend Randy Thomas, who recruited him for the band Allies, which went on to become a popular recording and touring act. When Allies finally disbanded in 1992, Carlisle signed with Sparrow as a solo act and quickly gained favor on Christian radio with such singles as "Getting Stronger" and "Giving You the Rest of My Life." On his own, he toned down some of the rock bombast of his Allies days in favor of pop balladry with a classic R&B undercurrent. After the release of his second solo album, *The Hope of a Man*, Carlisle switched to Diadem Records and resolved to write songs of a more personal nature. Among these was "Butterfly Kisses," originally written for his daughter, Megan. Though he was reluctant to record it, Diadem recognized the song's potential and included it on Carlisle's first album for the label, *Shades of Grace*.

"Butterfly Kisses" struck a chord with listeners beyond the confines of Christian music, receiving airplay on secular country and pop stations after its release as a single. As interest in the song grew, the secular label Jive Records repackaged *Shades of Grace* as *Butterfly Kisses*; this version of the CD sold some two million copies. An appearance by Carlisle on Oprah Winfrey's television show helped to boost sales further. "Butterfly Kisses" led to several book tie-in projects and encouraged Carlisle to write a song for his son, Evan, called "A Father's Love." A follow-up Diadem release, *Butterfly Kisses & Bedtime Prayers*, was devoted to songs for and about children.

Carlisle went on to resume his career as a primarily Christian market artist, releasing *Nothing but the Truth* in 2000. This album featured such originals as the

Bob Carlisle
Photo by Allen Clark

poignant "After All" and "Forgiveness," as well as cover tunes, including Todd Rundgren's "Love Is the Answer." That same year, Carlisle appeared on the soundtrack album for the popular Christian film *Left Behind*. He kept his soul singer credentials intact by performing with Christian singer **Bryan Duncan** as the Self-Righteous Brothers.

Bob Carlisle (Sparrow, 1993)
The Hope of a Man (Sparrow, 1994)
Shades of Grace (Diadem, 1996;
    rereleased as Butterfly Kisses, Jive, 1997)
Ballads of Bob Carlisle (Sony, 1997)
Stories from the Heart (Benson, 1998)
Butterfly Kisses & Bedtime Prayers
    (Diadem, 2000)
Nothing but the Truth (Diadem, 2000)

CARMAN
Born January 19, 1956,
in Trenton, New Jersey

One of Contemporary Christian music's most enduringly popular artists, Carman Dominic Lucciardello has produced a body of work so diverse as to be unclassifiable. Since the early 1980s, he has tapped into almost every pop music trend imaginable, from rockabilly and doo-wop to techno-dance and hip-hop. Derided by some Christian music critics as superficial and gimmicky, Carman's music seems first and foremost a tool for evangelism. By the late 1990s, he had earned eight gold albums and had branched out into publishing, video, and film ventures as well.

Carman began his career as a night-club performer in New Jersey. While in the process of moving to Las Vegas, he converted to Christianity after attending a concert by gospel singer Andre Crouce. Gospel trio leader Bill Gaither was among those who recognized Carman's talents and urged him to apply them to ministry. His debut album, *Carman* (later retitled *Some-o-Dat*), was released by the short-lived CBS Christian label Priority in 1982.

The esssentials of Carman's basic style are all present on his first LP, though less refined than in later efforts. Carman employs his lounge-honed vocal stylings and some-what broad sense of humor in the service of the Lord, invoking memories of late-period Elvis Presley in spots. His use of Vegas shtick to exalt Christ in songs like "Overcoming Child" and "Washed in the Blood" seems to border on camp. Carman's humor, though, is strategically employed and not intended to undermine his message. Such tracks as "Some-o-Dat" and "God, God, God" are comedy routines that are at once goofy and deadly serious in examining spiritual issues.

Carman's albums showed greater song-writing and production finesse as time went on. *The Champion,* released by Myrrh Records in 1985, earned him a chart-topping Christian radio single with its dramatic title track. His ministry grew hand in hand with his recording career, and his free concerts combined lavish showmanship with fervent revivalism. *Carman Live… Radically Saved!* (Benson, 1988) documents his high-voltage, over-the-top performing style. In song after song, Carman describes the ongoing warfare between God and Satan and extols his audiences to stand boldly against the enemy. "No Way, We Are Not Ashamed,"a 1988 single, was typical in its expression of defiance against the forces of disbelief. Carman could also use comedy as a weapon—"A Witch's Invitation," an extended sermon/skit from 1992's *Revival in the Land,* was played for laughs even as it denounced New Age–style occult dabbling.

It seems as if there has been no musical genre that Carman has not incorporated into his sound. Rockabilly ("Holdin' On"), Latin ("Now's the Time"), early '60s teenage pop ("Sunday School Rock"), country-rock ("Let the Fire Fall"), and spy movie soundtrack themes ("Mission") are only a few of the sonic side trips he took during the '90s. He had a special fondness for rap and hip-hop, as evidenced on his 1993 single "Who's in the House." At times, Carman's efforts to sound current have appeared awkward and forced. Still, his sheer audacity in tackling any style shows chutzpah, if nothing else.

Never part of Nashville's Christian music establishment, Carman's success has transcended the need for radio hits or favorable reviews. Unlike many artists, he has never shied away from explicit evangelism, and established Carman Ministries as a nonprofit organization parallel to his recording career. Seamlessly blending entertainment and religion, he drew enormous crowds during the 1990s, performing to a record-breaking 71,000 people at a Dallas concert in 1994. His video collections have also been strong sellers in the Christian market. *The Heart of a Champion* (2001) marked his motion picture debut, casting him as a boxer forced to choose between ministry and the ring. A two-CD "best of" collection was released by Sparrow in conjunction with the film.

In addition to all of the above, Carman has recorded a number of CDs and videos for children. Among them is *Yo! Kidz! 2: The Armor of God*, which earned gold certification and a GMA Dove Award for children's music album of the year in 1995.

Carman (Priority, 1982; rereleased as Some-o-Dat, Myrrh, 1992)
Sunday's on the Way (Priority, 1983)
Comin' on Strong (Myrrh, 1984)
The Champion (Myrrh, 1985)
A Long Time Ago...in a Land Called Bethlehem (Benson, 1986)
Carman Live...Radically Saved! (Benson, 1988)
Addicted to Jesus (Benson, 1991)
Yo!Kidz! (Word, 1992)
Revival in the Land (Benson, 1992)
The Absolute Best (Sparrow, 1993)
The Standard (Sparrow, 1993)
Yo! Kidz! 2: The Armor of God (Word, 1994)
R.I.O.T. (Righteous Invasion of Truth) (Sparrow, 1995)
I Surrender All: 30 Classic Hymns (Sparrow, 1997)
Mission 3:16 (Sparrow, 1988)
Passion for Praise (Sparrow, 1999)
Heart of a Champion (Sparrow, 2000)

ERIC CHAMPION
Born 1970 in Daytona Beach, Florida

Youthful R&B/pop artist Eric Champion scored a healthy run of Christian radio hits in the early 1990s. His sleek, dance-floor-friendly sound was akin to that of the Jets, Glenn Medeiros, and similar late '80s teenage pop stars. Lyrically, Champion touched upon such themes as homelessness, nuclear warfare, and rampant materialism, matching his socially conscious messages to infectious synthesizer-driven tracks.

Champion came to a Christian music career naturally, having been a part of his family's traveling music ministry since childhood. In 1986, he moved to Columbus, Georgia, and began experimenting with synthesizers and sequencers. He started writing songs as well, placing material with Area Code, Mike Eldred, Truth, and other Christian acts. A demo tape sent to artist/producer Chris Christian's Home Sweet Home Records led to a deal with Myrrh/Word. At age 19, he broke onto the Christian radio charts with "We Are the Young," a generational call to arms that heralded similar singles to come.

Such tunes as "Friends in High Places," "Generation of Right," and "What You're Looking For" brought Champion further hits in the early '90s. *Save the World* (1992) contained his biggest Christian radio single, "The Answer," a celebratory declaration of faith that mixed rap and gospel elements. In 1994, he released *Vertical Reality*, a concept album with a science-fiction storyline. Against a techno-pop backdrop, Champion sang about a future society in which a mind-dominating government computer tries to eliminate belief in God. "Touch" and "Endless" from this album extended Champion's streak of hit singles.

In 1996, Champion moved to Essential Records and adopted a more organic sound. *Transformation*, his label debut, was mostly recorded live and de-emphasized computer-generated tracks in favor of guitar-oriented rock. The themes of its songs—including the singles "Dress Me Up" and "Life Form"—dealt with change and the search for a closer relationship with Christ. *Natural* (1998) marked a partial return to his earlier synthesizer-based approach, though rock touches were still present. Champion's fondness for up-to-date topics was evidenced in songs like "Hacker's Prayer," which declared, "I can feel Your love download on me."

Champion withdrew from the spotlight after *Natural*'s release. As of 2001, he was reportedly teaching at a music school in Florida.

Eric Champion (Myrrh, 1990)
Revolution (Myrrh, 1991)
Hot Christmas (Myrrh, 1992)
Save the World (Myrrh, 1992)
Vertical Reality (Myrrh, 1994)
Transformation (Essential, 1996)
Natural (Essential, 1998)

GARY CHAPMAN
Born August 19, 1957,
in Waurika, Oklahoma

During his two decades-plus career in music, Gary Chapman has been active as a recording artist, hit songwriter, television host, and Nashville event emcee. He received the most attention, though, as the husband of **Amy Grant** from 1982 to 1999. After their breakup, Chapman worked to reestablish himself as an artist in the Contemporary Christian market.

Chapman spent most of his childhood in DeLeon, Texas, where his father, T. W. Chapman, served as minister. A guitar player since his preteens, he landed his first professional gig backing up the Dowlings, a traditional gospel group. But it was as a songwriter that Chapman first gained renown. This led to further touring with the Rambos (featuring gospel matriarch Dottie Rambo), an experience that helped him develop as a songwriter. By the late 1970s, he was living in Nashville and writing material for country artists. One early Chapman effort, "Finally," became a number one country single for T. G. Sheppard in 1982. He also had material recorded by such gospel artists as Jamie Owens-Collins, the Blackwood Brothers, and Rusty Goodman.

In 1979, Chapman placed his tune "Father's Eyes" with Amy Grant. The song—a sensitive number that touched upon both parental and divine love—became a Christian music standard and earned him a GMA Dove Award as songwriter of the year in 1981. That same year, he made his debut as an artist with the release of *Sincerely Yours* by Lamb & Lion in 1981. Though this album and its follow-up, 1982's *Happenin' Live,* didn't yield any major singles for Chapman, they did raise his profile as a songwriter.

For better or worse, it was Chapman's romance and marriage to Grant that truly boosted him into the limelight. The success of "Father's Eyes" led to an opening slot on Grant's 1980 tour, which in turn led to a closer personal relationship. The two were married in 1982; Chapman spent much of the next several years serving as Grant's tour bandleader. When Chapman finally resumed recording in 1987, he aimed for acceptance as a mainstream country artist. While his *Everyday Man* album (1987) didn't crack the secular market, it did reaffirm his status as a Christian artist. He toured with secular artists Bruce Hornsby and the Range in support of the album. After another long gap, he released *The Light Inside* in 1994. This album featured several Christian radio hits, including one written by Grant, "Where Do I Go?"

During the mid-'90s, Chapman diversified his career to include hosting The Nashville Network's *Prime Time Country* and the syndicated Christian radio program *CCM Countdown.* He also hosted numerous live events around Nashville, inaugurating the Sam's Place gospel music series at the famed Ryman Auditorium. He continued to release albums and won airplay with such singles as "Floodgates of Love," "Back Where I Started," and "Written in the Scars." He won a pair of GMA Dove Awards in 1996, including one for male vocalist of the year.

Chapman faced trying times in 1999. His unraveling marriage to Grant finally led to divorce in June. That same year, he released his final album for Reunion Records, *Outside,* which received lukewarm reviews. By the following year, his stints with *Prime Time Country* and *CCM Countdown* had come to an end. Bouncing back, he remarried in 2000 and resumed writing and recording. His 2001 self-released CD, *Circles & Seasons,* was a highly personal song collection. "He Thinks I Hung the Moon" (written for his son Matt) and "Like I Love You Now" (for his new bride, Jennifer) were among its highlights.

Sincerely Yours (Lamb & Lion, 1981)
Happenin' Live (Lamb & Lion, 1982)
Everyday Man (Reunion, 1987)
The Light Inside (Reunion, 1994)
Shelter (Reunion, 1996)
The Early Years (Lamb & Lion, 1997)
This Gift (Reunion, 1997)
Outside (Reunion, 1999)
Circles & Seasons (independent release, 2001)
Best of Gary Chapman—After God's Own
    Heart (Reunion, 2002)

STEVEN CURTIS CHAPMAN
**Born November 21, 1962,
in Paducah, Kentucky**

A Christian music star from his very first single, Steven Curtis Chapman continues to be one of the genre's most influential artists. He's managed to adapt to changing musical tastes without straining for effect or compromising his spiritual focus. There's always been a touch of small-town folksiness and naïveté in his work, even as his albums have grown glossier and more eclectic. Chapman manages to deal with big themes in commonplace ways, portraying himself as a fallible "ordinary guy" trying to lead a Christian life amidst the distractions and heartaches of modern-day America.

Chapman gained early inspiration from his father, who owned a music store and wrote songs. By the time he went off to college to study medicine in Indiana, he was already an adept guitarist and piano player. The urge to pursue music proved strong and in 1981 he left his studies to move to Nashville. Chapman honed his craft as a songwriter while working as a singer at Opryland Theme Park. His tunes were eventually recorded by such artists as **Sandi Patty,** the Imperials, and Glen Campbell. Signing with Sparrow Records, he released his debut album, *First Hand,* in 1987. A more countrified effort than his later work, this song collection yielded an immediate hit single with "Weak Days." It proved the first of a nearly unbroken chain of Christian radio hits extending into the present day.

In many ways, the artistic growth of Contemporary Christian music throughout the late 1980s and '90s can be traced in Chapman's releases. *Real Life Conversations* (1988) found him toughening his sound a bit, building more complex arrangements around his acoustic guitar work. *For the Sake of the Call* (1990) edged even closer to mainstream rock, adding impact to such uplifting anthems as its title track. Orchestral touches lent further drama to *The Great Adventure* (1992), an album that veered between wide-screen rock numbers (such

C

as the title song) and down-home sketches of Christian love and faith ("That's Paradise). *Heaven in the Real World* (1994) had an even greater emphasis on rock instrumentation, resulting in two of his biggest singles, the title track and "King of the Jungle." Through all of this stylistic evolution, Chapman never lost his sense of identity— he remained the same unflamboyant storyteller and extoller of the Lord no matter what the musical setting.

Signs of Life (1996) yielded the single "Lord of the Dance," a blues-tinged testimonial to faith that brought him yet another massive Christian radio hit. In 1998, Chapman received mainstream attention when his song "I Will Not Go Quietly" appeared on the soundtrack to the 1998 film *The Apostle.* The following year, he released *Speechless,* one of his best-realized albums. The album's title track—cowritten with Christian artist Geoff Moore—was a particularly effective invocation of God's majesty. Another key song was "With Hope," inspired by the December 1997 high school shootings in Paducah, Chapman's hometown. *Declaration* (2001) continued in a similar direction, combining propulsive pop/rock with uplifting lyrics in songs like "Live Out Loud" and "No Greater Love."

Chapman has often cited theological writings as catalysts for his music—authors Oswald Chambers, Charles Spurgeon, and Dietrich Bonhoeffer are among those whose ideas have inspired him. Together with Pastor Scotty Smith, he cowrote a book of his own, *Speechless: In Awe of the Power of God's Disruptive Grace* (Zondervan Publishing, 1999).

Most of Chapman's albums from *For the Sake of the Call* onwards have gone gold; two have gone platinum. He has won a record-setting 44 GMA Dove Awards, as well as four Grammys (most recently for *Speechless*). (For more about Steven Curtis Chapman, see pages 56–62.)

First Hand (Sparrow, 1987)
Real Life Conversations (Sparrow, 1988)
More to This Life (Sparrow, 1989)
For the Sake of the Call (Sparrow, 1990)
The Great Adventure (Sparrow, 1992)
The Live Adventure (Sparrow, 1993)
Heaven in the Real World (Sparrow, 1994)
The Music of Christmas (Sparrow, 1995)
Signs of Life (Sparrow, 1996)
Greatest Hits (Sparrow, 1997)
Speechless (Sparrow, 1999)
Declaration (Sparrow, 2001)

THE CHOIR
Formed 1984 in Los Angeles, California

Surviving sonic changes and temporary breakups, the Choir has maintained its reputation as an innovative alternative Christian rock band. The group's atmospheric sound and darkly poetic lyrics paved the way for 1990s groups like **Third Day** and Sonicflood, among others.

The Choir. Left to right: Robin Spurs, Derri Daugherty, Dan Michaels, and Steve Hindalong
Photo by Chris Knight

Singer/guitarist Derri Daugherty and drummer Steve Hindalong formed the core of the group in 1984. Both had experience playing in secular bands; Daugherty had also been a member of televangelist Dwight Thompson's background group. Influenced both by British secular rock groups like the Cure and such Christian rockers as **Daniel Amos,** the duo added bassist Mike Sauerbray and became Youth Choir. The two albums they released under this name—*Voices in Shadows* and *Shades of Grey*—served as rough sketches for more mature efforts to follow. Tim Chandler—a bandmate of Daugherty's from the Dwight Thompson days—replaced Sauerbray on bass in 1986.

Becoming simply the Choir, the group signed with Myrrh and released the **Charlie Peacock**–produced *Diamonds and Rain* in 1986. Highlights of this album included "Render Love" and "Black Cloud," songs that combined a bruised idealism with a sense of musical drama. Lyricist Hindalong's expressions of angst and yearning combined well with Daugherty's distorted, effects-laden guitar lines. This approach was more fully fleshed out on 1987's *Chase the Kangaroo,* a self-produced album containing both Christian radio hits like "When the Morning Comes" and such heartfelt album tracks as "Sad Face." Chandler turned over the bassist's duties to Robin Spurs, who took part in the sessions for *Wide-Eyed Wonder* (1989). Lyricon/saxophone player Dan Michaels joined as well, adding a keyboard-like texture to the band's sound. The rapturous title track and the confessional "Someone to Hold on To" were among *Wide Eyed Wonder*'s standout tracks.

In its own left-of-center way, the Choir was pioneering a form of modern worship music that combined unabashed reverence with surging washes of otherworldly sound. *Circle Slide* (1990) surrounded such expressions of faith as "Merciful Eyes" and "Restore My Soul" with a spacey sort of pop/rock that was definitely ahead of its time. Leaving Myrrh's roster, the band fragmented for a time. Daugherty moved from Southern California to Nashville in 1993, opened his own Neverland Recording Studios, and took on production projects. Hindalong released his acclaimed *At the Foot of the Cross,* a worship album recorded with Daugherty and other players, in 1992.

Daugherty and Hindalong had hopes of crossing the Choir over into the mainstream. Efforts to secure a secular record label deal fell through, though, and they bided their time with an independent release, *Kissers and Killers*, in 1993. Edging back into the Christian market, they licensed the release of their next album, *Speckled Bird*, to R.E.X. in 1994. The band—once again including Tim Chandler on bass—returned to themes of spiritual struggle and awakening on tracks like "Gripped" and the title song. Moving over to Tattoo Records, it released *Free Flying Soul* (1996), an extension of what *Speckled Bird* had achieved. This album proved among the group's most popular, going on to win a GMA Dove Award for modern/alternative rock album of the year.

Following the release of 1997's *Let It Fly*, the Choir went into hibernation as a recording act. Daugherty continued to produce and engineer for other bands and was active as a member of **the Lost Dogs**. Hindalong also took on production work and played percussion on Christian music sessions. Michaels put in a stint as an A&R man for Tattoo and ventured into Web design, while Chandler worked with **Daniel Amos** and other artists. Continuing interest from old fans helped prompt the Choir to regroup once again and release *Flap Your Wings* as an independent project in 2000.

Also in 2000, *City on a Hill: Songs of Worship and Praise*, a multi-artist worship album produced by Hindalong, was released by Essential Records. A successor to *At the Foot of the Cross*, it featured songs cowritten by Hindalong and performed by the Choir, **Sixpence None the Richer, Jars of Clay, Caedmon's Call, Third Day,** and other artists. The album was well received by critics and consumers alike and won a GMA Dove Award for special event album of the year. A follow-up release, *At the Foot of the Cross: Sing Alleluia*, appeared in early 2002.

AS YOUTH CHOIR:
Voices in Shadows (Broken, 1985)
Shades of Grey (Shadow, 1986)
AS THE CHOIR:
Diamonds and Rain (Myrrh, 1986)
Chase the Kangaroo (Myrrh, 1987)
Wide-Eyed Wonder (Myrrh, 1989)
Circle Slide (Myrrh, 1990)
Kissers and Killers (ICCD, 1993)
Speckled Bird (R.E.X., 1994)
Love Songs & Prayers (Myrrh, 1995)
Free Flying Soul (Tattoo, 1996)
Let It Fly (Tattoo, 1997)
Flap Your Wings (independent release, 2000)

CHRISTAFARI
Formed 1989 in Los Angeles, California

Reggae—generally identified with Rastafarianism—has been transformed by Christafari into a vehicle for the teachings of Jesus. Surviving a split in its ranks in the mid-1990s, the Nashville-based group has held onto its core following and continued to spread the gospel to both Christian and non-Christian reggae fans.

Christafari was founded in 1989 by singer Mark Mohr (a.k.a. Tanosback) while attending Biola University in the Los Angeles area. Mohr had gone through a period of drug and gang involvement during his teenage years, becoming a committed Christian at age 17. Previously an adherent of Rastafarianism, he decided to express his newfound faith through reggae. He cofounded Christafari (a Greek phrase for "Christ bearer") with singer/keyboardist James Pach (a.k.a. Jaibo Culture) and singer Erick Sundin (a.k.a. Earth Man). The group spent time working on both its music and its preaching, working hard to be seen as a legitimate reggae band and not merely a Christian novelty. Christafari's musical blend combines traditional roots-reggae with more contemporary dance-hall touches, emphasizing talking and chanting.

The band's debut, *Reggae Worship Vol. 1*, appeared on the Frontline label in 1993. Switching to Gotee, Christafari released *Soul Fire* in 1994, an album which received mainstream distribution through Sony. The band's live show—a lively mix of Jamaican rhythms and Christian exhortations—began to win favorable notice on the reggae concert circuit. In 1996, *Valley of Decision* further displayed the group's versatility and tight musicianship. By this time, the band had grown to include key-boardist Marky Rage, bassist Johnny Guerro, guitarist Bill Kasper, and drummer Ken Yarnes. Mohr's wife Vanessa had also become an integral part of the group, serving as singer/dancer/choreographer. "Selah," "Give a Little Love," "Valley of Decision," and "Surrender" were among the group's mid-'90s Christian radio hits.

In 1997, Christafari suffered a schism when Sundin, Rage, Guerro, Kasper, and Yarnes launched their own group, Temple Yard. The Mohrs and Pach carried on as Christafari, touring with new support players and forming their own record label, Lion of Zion. Increasingly active overseas, the band performed in Canada, Guatemala, Kenya, Uganda, Suriname, and Guyana, among other far-flung points. Christafari was almost as busy on the recording front, releasing four albums between 1999 and 2000.

In addition to leading Christafari, Mohr now serves as a pastor at Sanctuary, a ministry in the Nashville area. He also spearheads Jamaica for Jesus, a Christian missionary organization.

Reggae Worship Vol. 1 (Frontline, 1993)
Soul Fire (Gotee, 1994)
Valley of Decision (Gotee, 1996)
Word Sound & Power (Lion of Zion, 1999)
DUB Sound & Power (Lion of Zion, 1999)
Reggae Worship (Lion of Zion, 2000)
Palabra Sonido y Poder (Lion of Zion, 2000)
Dancehall Baptism Chapter One
   (Lion of Zion, 2000)

ASHLEY CLEVELAND

*Born February 2, 1957,
in Knoxville, Tennessee*

First and foremost, Ashley Cleveland is known for her stirring, black-gospel influenced voice. Gutsy yet graceful, her singing style has gained nuance and control over the years. While her primary exposure as a recording artist has been in Christian music, Cleveland also has a devoted following as a live performer among secular rock and country fans in the Nashville area.

An East Tennessee native, Cleveland's earliest musical influences were hymns she heard in her local Presbyterian church. Moving with her family to San Francisco during her teenage years, she learned guitar and decided to pursue a music career. She eventually settled in Nashville, where she built a reputation as an in-demand background singer and guitarist (working with such notables as Emmylou Harris, John Hiatt, and Etta James) and toured the college circuit as a solo artist. Her participation in a recording project with the Memphis Horns led to a secular record deal with Atlantic. *Big Town*, her debut album, presented her as an R&B/rock belter with mixed results. The sheer vocal power she displayed on this effort invited comparisons with Aretha Franklin, or perhaps a more focused Janis Joplin. On the minus side was the fair-to-middling material (which downplayed her Christian beliefs) and the lack of subtlety overall.

When *Big Town* failed to find a large audience, Cleveland left Atlantic and signed with a Christian label, Reunion. Her next album, 1993's *Bus Named Desire,* was a marked improvement. Pulling back the throttle a bit, Cleveland here displays more interpretive finesse. When she does let go, the results are galvanizing, particularly on "I'm Not Made That Way" and "Better You Get Ready," which also featured blistering guitar work by her husband, Kenny Greenberg. *Bus Named Desire* earned Cleveland a GMA Dove Award nomination for artist of the year, though it didn't yield a Christian radio hit. She fared better with "Where Do I Go?," a 1994 duet with **Gary Chapman**.

Lesson In Love (1995) was produced in a similar vein as *Bus Named Desire,* successfully rocking up gospel-rooted material without de-sanctifying it. Cleveland did well on Christian radio with the title track (displaying her softer side) and the funkified praise number "He Is." Another highpoint was "Revive Us Again," a classic hymn reworked with a deep south R&B swagger. After *Lesson in Love,* Cleveland and Greenberg founded their own label, 204 Records (affiliated with Cadence Communications). *You Are There,* featuring live concert recordings and acoustic studio performances, appeared on this label in 1998. On this release, Cleveland offers a batch of previously recorded songs and fresh material, including a fiery cover of the Rolling Stones' "Gimme Shelter," in appealingly intimate settings. A new album is expected from her some time in 2002.

Big Town (Atlantic, 1991)
Bus Named Desire (Reunion, 1993)
Lesson of Love (Reunion, 1995)
You Are There (204/Cadence, 1998)

BRUCE COCKBURN
Born May 27, 1945, in Ottawa, Canada

Bruce Cockburn is a distinctly different sort of Christian singer/songwriter. For most of his 30-plus years in music, his work has reflected a God-centered world-view, touching upon both the glories of Christ and the sufferings of mankind. An exceptionally adept guitarist, he has added Third World influences to his Anglo-Celtic folk roots. He has stood apart from the Contemporary Christian music industry, making faith-based music very much on his own terms.

Born in Ottawa, Ontario, Cockburn spent time as a street musician in Europe before studying composition at Boston's Berklee School of Music. His self-titled debut LP appeared in 1970. While his first half-dozen releases were popular in his native country, they went largely unheard in the United States. Coincidentally or not, Cockburn's artistic growth coincided with his embrace of Christianity in the early 1970s. The first overt glimmers of his faith appeared on 1972's *Sunwheel Dance* and

became steadily more pronounced as time went on. Several of his early Christian-influenced songs—particularly the haunting "Dialogue with the Devil"—remain among the strongest in his catalog.

Cockburn's spiritual outlook on these early '70s albums was expansive, celebrating the physical majesty of Creation as a manifestation of God's love. By the time he released *In the Falling Dark* (1976), he had developed a jazz/folk/hybrid that was flexible enough to support his intricate, Jack Kerouac–like lyrics. Flashing chains of images lent "Silver Wheels" a cinematic quality, while the hymn-like "Lord of the Starfields" glows with quiet reverence. While these songs lack some of the world perspective of his later work, they capture the spark of spiritual discovery that Cockburn felt at the time. The live album *Circles in the Stream* (1977) provides a good summation of the first chapter of his career.

Signing with Millennium Records in the United States, Cockburn released his land-mark *Dancing in the Dragon's Jaws* album in 1979. His painterly lyrics were never more vivid than here—each song is a landscape delineated with heavenly fire. The playing is playful but tight, veering into jazzy filigree without excess. *Dancing* yielded Cockburn's first American hit single, the genial "Wondering Where the Lions Are." Other tracks, though, have more resonance, among them "Creation Dream" and "Northern Lights." "Let me be a little of your breath/I want to be a particle of your light," Cockburn sings in "Hills of Morning," as lovely a prayer for unity with God as can be found in Christian pop music.

After *Dancing,* Cockburn downplayed his mystical side in favor of scathing social commentaries. From 1980's *Humans* onward, he applied his Christian sense of justice to a host of issues, especially political oppression and the environment. A 1983 trip to Latin America resulted in "If I Had a Rocket Launcher" and similar critiques of American foreign policy. Some of the acoustic delicacy of his music was put aside in favor of more aggressive synthesized sounds. Cockburn's Christian sense of justice was evident in his attacks on the powerful and his defense of the downtrodden, though explicit references to God were few during this period.

Nothing but a Burning Light (1991) marked a return to the more open faith of his 1970s work. Produced by **T-Bone Burnett,** this album had a rough-hewn rootsiness to its sound and boasted such worshipful songs as "Great Big Love" and "Cry of a Tiny Babe" (the latter a retelling of the nativity story). In 1993 he released *Christmas,* featuring his renditions of holiday songs and hymns from French-Canadian and Native American sources as well as familiar tunes like "It Came Upon a Midnight Clear." If Cockburn was still clearly a Christian, his outlook had changed since his younger days—songs like "Strange Waters" (from *The Charity of Night,* 1996) fused the spiritual awe of his '70s songs with the political outrage of his later albums. His activism (particularly on behalf of the environment and war victims) and his faith continue to influence his music in complex, compelling ways.

Those new to Cockburn's music might wish to seek out *Resume* (a 1981 "best of" collection) or *Waiting for a Miracle* (a 1987 sampler of his Canadian singles). Also worth tracking down are his early True North albums, rereleased on CD by Sony in the 1990s. (For more about Bruce Cockburn, see pages 63–67.)

Sunwheel Dance (Epic/True North, 1972)
Night Vision (True North, 1973)
Salt, Sun & Time (True North, 1974)
Joy Will Find a Way (True North, 1975)
In the Falling Dark (True North/Island, 1976)
Circles in the Stream (True North/Island, 1977)
Further Adventures of Bruce Cockburn
    (True North/Island, 1978)
Dancing in the Dragon's Jaws
    (Millennium, 1979)
Humans (Millennium, 1980)
Resume (Millennium, 1981)
Inner City Front (Millennium, 1981)
Stealing Fire (Gold Mountain, 1984)
Waiting for a Miracle (Gold Mountain, 1987)
Nothing but a Burning Light (Columbia, 1991)
Christmas (Columbia, 1993)
Dart to the Heart (Columbia, 1994)
The Charity of Night (Rykodisc, 1996)
Breakfast in New Orleans, Dinner in
    Timbuktu (Rykodisc, 1999)

CREED
Formed 1995 in Tallahassee, Florida

Creed has been *the* great hard-rock success story of the late 1990s and early 2000s. The enormous popularity of this Florida-based foursome is unquestionable—as of mid-2002, its three albums had sold more than 25 million copies worldwide. What is open to debate is whether or not Creed is a "Christian band" in the usual sense of the term. Though its members deny that the group is promoting any particular faith, Christian-derived themes and imagery have been central to its musical identity from the beginning.

Lead singer Scott Stapp (born August 8, 1973, in Orlando, Florida) was raised in a strict Pentecostal household, attending church twice a week and Bible study on Friday nights. Forbidden to listen to rock music and kept home weekend nights under a tight curfew, he grew rebellious and left home at age 17. Moving to Tallahassee, he grew increasingly obsessed with Jim Morrison, dabbling in psychedelic drugs and writing lyrics that drew upon conflicted feelings toward his upbringing. Pre-law studies at Florida State University quickly took a back seat to Stapp's musical ambitions. He began collaborating on songs with guitarist Mark Tremonti (born April 18, 1974), then hooked up with drummer Scott Phillips (born February 22, 1973) and bassist Brian Marshall (born April 24, 1973) to form a band. The newly launched combo began playing around north Florida, forging a sound that mixed the late '80s grunge of Pearl Jam with the '70s hard rock heroics of Led Zeppelin and Bad Company. Stapp emerged as a charismatic front man, making the most of the drama and angst in his Bible-steeped lyrics.

In early 1997, Creed self-released its first album, *My Own Prison* (recorded on a $6,000 budget). The title track received some local airplay, arousing the interest of New York–based Wind-up Records; the label (distributed by BMG) signed the group, remixed the album, and rereleased it in August of that year. "My Own Prison" proved a surprise nationwide hit, establishing the band members on radio and MTV as overnight stars. Creed has hardly had time to look back since.

My Own Prison is an appealing record with a strong sense of honesty about it—rather than cashing in on current trends, the music sounds solid and sincere. Tremonti plays concise, well-honed guitar lines, avoiding grandstanding in favor of telling instrumental phrases. Stapp's sandpaper-rubbed vocals often bring to mind Pearl Jam's Eddie Vedder, sounding both gruff and vulnerable at the same time. It's the lyrics, though, that set this album apart; Stapp's guilt-ridden, self-lacerating examinations of his fears and weaknesses are distinctly his own. Using Christian faith as a backdrop, he plays out personal stories of anguish in such tracks as the title tune, "Illusion," and "Unforgiven." There's no easy peace and salvation offered here. "What's This Life For," for instance, holds out the hope of God's salvation only after unrelieved suffering on Earth. "I'm filthy/ born in my own misery," Stapp sings in "Torn," expressing a view of human sinfulness clearly rooted in fundamentalist belief. For all the fire and brimstone on this album, however, there's no explicit evangelizing. *My Own Prison* doesn't attempt to lead the listener to the Cross, only to capture the conflicts raging within Stapp.

It seems likely that the open-ended quality of the songs on *My Own Prison* helped win Creed its huge audience. The band spoke for millions of young rock fans raised in Christian homes who held onto their faith while wrestling with doubt and temptation. For its part, the group refused to be labeled as a Christian rock act. In interviews, Stapp and Tremonti have stated that their personal "creed" consists of God, family, and their band, in that order. A line was drawn between personal belief and advocacy, however—though all four members acknowledged believing in God, they denied their group made Christian music, per se. If the distinction seems blurry at times, it mirrors the blending of religious and secular identities that countless Americans maintain in their own lives.

My Own Prison went on to sell more than five million copies, scoring hits with its title track, "Torn," "What's This Life For,"

and "One." After intensive touring, Creed came back with 1999's *Human Clay,* another tremendously successful effort. Those looking for earnest spiritual soliloquies in the album were not disappointed—"Higher" (inspired by Stapp's experience with lucid-dreaming), "What If," and "With Arms Wide Open" recaptured the tormented grandeur of the first album. The latter song was a particular standout, a stirring rock anthem written in honor of Stapp's son Jagger. It became the seventh Creed song to top the rock radio charts in the United States, an unprecedented feat.

In August 2000, bassist Marshall left the group, citing "personal and professional differences." Tremonti doubled on bass for the recording of Creed's third album, *Weathered.* Released in 2001, it continued in a similar vein as the first two, with a few added nuances. "Bullets" flashed the group's hard rock credentials, while "Who's Got My Back?" featured a Cherokee chant as an introduction. "My Sacrifice" (yet another chart-topping single) offered an uplifting call for brotherhood in nonsectarian terms.

A true musical phenomenon, Creed's Christian-yet-inclusive themes speak to a vast listenership. Where the band's "creed" leads it artistically and spiritually will be interesting to follow in the years ahead.

My Own Prison (Wind-up/BMG, 1997)
Human Clay (Wind-up/BMG, 1999)
Weathered (Wind-up/BMG, 2001)

CLAY CROSSE
Born 1967 in Memphis, Tennessee

Singer Clay Crosse has been known for rendering inspirational songs with a Memphis soul flavor since his initial hit single, 1994's "I Surrender All." Born Walter Clayton Crossnoe, he began his career as a performer at Memphis's Liberty Land theme park. A demo rendition of the Righteous Brothers' hit "Unchained Melody" helped him secure a deal with Reunion Records. *My Place Is with You*, his 1994 debut CD, defined him as a Scripture-focused, musically polished artist and helped him win a GMA Dove Award for new artist of the year in 1995. Such Christian radio hits as "His Love Is Strong" and "His Love Is Coming Over Me" (both found on his second album, 1995's *Time to Believe*) found him continuing in a similar vein.

Stained Glass (1997) was somewhat of a creative departure for Crosse—such tracks as "Saving the World" (another popular Christian radio single) and "Wicked" added more rock to his sound, while "Sold Out Believer" had a rootsy R&B flavor. Around this time, Crosse experienced a moral crisis that affected both his personal and professional lives. Unhappy with his stage performances, he took a breather from the music business for a time. After a period of spiritual counseling, he returned to the concert stage. His sense of renewal was reflected on his 2000 album, *A Different Man*.

Uplifting worship songs remain Crosse's specialty, as evidenced by the success of "I Will Follow Christ," a GMA Dove Award winner for inspirational song of the year in 2000. The following year saw the release of *Christmas with Clay Crosse*, featuring the singer's renditions of holiday tunes with a Harry Connick, Jr.–like jazz approach.

My Place Is with You (Reunion, 1994)
Time to Believe (Reunion, 1995)
Stained Glass (Reunion, 1997)
I Surrender All: The Collection
   (BMG/Verity, 1999)
A Different Man (BMG/Reunion, 2000)

RICK CUA
Born December 3, 1948,
in Syracuse, New York

Leather jacket–clad Rick Cua sported a hard rocker image at the start of his Christian recording career. Much of his music reflected this image, leaning toward anthemic rockers with big, shout-along choruses. Cua enjoyed a decade's worth of hits before making the transition to music publishing executive.

Hailing from Syracuse, New York, Cua spent his youth playing in local rock groups. He became a Christian in 1977, but continued to play secular music into the following decade. In 1980, he became the bass player for the Outlaws, best known for such secular country/rock hits as "There Goes Another Love Song" and "Hurry

Sundown." Cua played on the band's last Top 40 single, "Ghost Riders in the Sky." While still in the group, he signed a deal with Refuge Records and worked on his solo debut, *KOO-AH*. This album yielded his first (and biggest) Christian radio single, "You Can Still Rock'n'Roll." Leaving the Outlaws in 1983, he turned down an invitation to join the jazz fusion group Spyro Gyra in favoring of pursuing his Christian music career. He moved over to Sparrow and released *You're My Road* in 1985, followed a year later by *Wear Your Colors*. The latter album, produced by fellow artist **Dave Perkins,** was indicative of the thunderous rockers Cua was noted for at that time. From start to finish, *Wear Your Colors* revels in chord-crunching guitars and arena-shaking drums. Songs like "Hungry" and "This Raging Fire" (a Christian radio hit) are statements of spiritual endurance and struggle couched in '80s rock language.

Cua began to soften his rocker stance, recording the ballad "Forever Yours" on his first Reunion album, *Can't Stand Too Tall* (1989). Another track on this album, "For the Love of God," was an autobiographical sketch of a traveling Christian musician that scaled back his heroic persona a bit. Cua continued to receive much Christian radio airplay into the early '90s, faring particularly well with "Dedicated," "Power of the Lord," and "What If?" In 1995, he released his *Times Ten* album on his own independent UCA label. Two years later, he

briefly joined the Christian Celtic band Ceili Rain before accepting a position with Sparrow Music Publishing.

KOO-AH (Refuge, 1982)
No Mystery (Refuge, 1983)
You're My Road (Sparrow, 1985)
Wear Your Colors (Sparrow, 1986)
Can't Stand Too Tall (Reunion, 1989)
The Way Love Is (Reunion, 1992)
Times Ten (UCA, 1995)

THE DAKODA MOTOR COMPANY
Formed early 1990s in La Jolla, California

Relentlessly cheerful, the Dakoda Motor Company harnessed the effervescence of Southern California punk/pop in the service of Christ. The result was two albums for the Christian market that garnered some airplay, then a release pitched toward the secular market that floundered. While the band's lyrics were not theologically deep, its sunny outlook and frisky musical thrust made it highly palatable ear candy.

Guitarist/vocalist Peter King came to the Dakoda Motor Company already a celebrity by virtue of his years as a professional surfer and host of the MTV programs *Sandblast* and *Beach Boys*. He cofounded the band with lead singer Davia Vallesillo in La Jolla, a San Diego beach community; bassist Derik Toy and drummer Chuck Cummins were recruited soon after. After building a local following, they secured a deal with Myrrh Records and recorded *Into the Sun*. Released in 1993, the Dakoda Motor Company's debut album recalls the tuneful power-pop of such 1980s groups as the Go-Go's and the Bangles; at times, Vallesillo even sounds uncannily like Go-Go's singer Belinda Carlisle. The songs on *Into the Son* have an innocence to them that seems rooted both in Christian faith and in the conventions of the band's poppy style. As a guitarist, King sounded well versed in a host of 1960s-era styles, from twanging surf rock riffs to jangling Byrds-like leads. The midtempo "Grey Skies" and the soaring "Freedom" were among the album's tracks that enjoyed Christian airplay.

The Dakoda Motor Company toured with **Petra** and gained favorable notice from both the Christian and secular press. Live, the band delivered a high-energy, fun-filled show, with Vallesillo decked out in her high school cheerleader uniform at some appearances. Adding second guitarist Elliot Chenault, the group released its second album, *Welcome Race Fans*, in 1994. This album had a somewhat heavier guitar sound and some lead vocal turns by King. Its standout tunes included the singles "Truth" and "Stand Up," the latter featuring Vallesillo's bopping rebuke to Satan.

The band took a wrong turn at this juncture, signing with a secular label and distancing itself from the Christian market. In 1995, Vallesillo left the group and was replaced by Melissa Brewer. A year later, *Railroad* appeared on the Holiday/Atlantic label and failed to sustain the Dakoda Motor Company's momentum. Unable to fully establish itself in the secular market and estranged from the Christian music industry, the group broke up. King joined a group called the Surfers, while Toy and Cummins signed on with the Aunt Bettys. Vallesillo surfaced in the late '90s as a Christian singer/songwriter at various California venues.

Into the Sun (Myrrh, 1993)
Welcome Race Fans (Myrrh, 1994)
Railroad (Holiday/Atlantic, 1996)

DANIEL AMOS (DA)
Formed 1974
in Orange County, California

The band Daniel Amos takes its name from two Old Testament prophets, a fitting choice considering the frequently angry (and visionary) pronouncements in lead singer/guitarist Terry Taylor's songs. Progressing through dizzying stylistic changes in its quarter century of existence, the group has managed to survive despite marginal commercial success. Daniel Amos's exceptionally smart, eclectic version of alternative Christian rock has inspired numerous younger bands and retains the support of a worshipful, if limited, fan base.

The group's origins began with Taylor (born May 24, 1950), who was performing with various rock combos around the San Jose area in the mid-1960s. In 1971, he became a Christian and began playing with a Jesus Music trio called Good Shepherd. A year later, he was writing songs and playing with Jubal's Last Band, the direct ancestor of Daniel Amos. Taylor moved down to Costa Mesa, California, to be part of the thriving Christian music scene centered around Calvary Chapel (the nurturing place for **Love Song,** among other groups). By 1974, Taylor and fellow Jubal guitarist Steve Baxter had joined forces with guitarist Jerry Chamberlain and bassist Marty Dieckmeyer to form Daniel Amos. The following year, the roster shifted, with Baxter leaving and keyboardist Mark Cook and drummer Ed McTaggert coming aboard. Signing with Maranatha Records, which was affiliated with Calvary Chapel, they released their self-titled debut album in 1976. This LP— mostly acoustic in a country/ rock vein— gave little indication of the changes to follow.

Shotgun Angel (1977) showed some creative growth, adding Beatles-esque arrangement ideas and touches of synthesizer. Taylor's lyric focus on tracks like "Father's Arms" was reassuringly optimistic. At this point, though, Daniel Amos became caught up in the day's emerging New Wave rock sounds and veered away from the main-stream of late '70s Christian music. The band switched to singer/songwriter **Larry Norman**'s Solid Rock label, recording its seminal *Horrendous Disc* album in 1978. The mellow country moods of previous releases shifted to a harder rock attack and edgier lyrics. Unfortunately, the album remained unreleased until 1981 due to contractual problems between the band and Norman. *Horrendous Disc* met with much critical praise and yielded the Christian radio hit "I Love You #19." The sensibility of this album was way ahead of its time— the dark-tinged angst of tracks like "Hound of Heaven" anticipated the alternative Christian rock sounds that emerged nearly a decade later.

What followed next were a series of ambitious concept albums. *Alarma!* (Newpax, 1981) was a song cycle with science-fiction overtones, jabbing at spiritual blindness and materialism in tunes like "Faces to the Window" and "Colored By." The album's musical settings twitched to jittery New Wave rhythms, accentuating Taylor's sarcastic lyrics. *Doppelganger,* released in 1983, was even more sardonic in tone, skewering soulless modern life in "Hollow Man," "New Car!," and "Real Girls." Daniel Amos toured in support of this album with an elaborate stage show, featuring band members wearing masks with battery-operated lightbulbs in their mouths. This was a far cry from what most Christian rock fans were used to, prompting heckling at some shows. The band pressed on, losing Jerry

Daniel Amos (DA), 1987 lineup. Left to right: Ed McTaggert, Tim Chandler, Greg Flesch, and Terry Taylor
Photo by Brian Tong, *courtesy of DanielAmos.com*

Chamberlain prior to the recording of the third album in its *Alarma!* trilogy, *Vox Humana* (1984). Newly recruited keyboardist Rob Watson helped make this the most synthesizer-oriented Daniel Amos album yet; such tracks as "Home Permanent" and "The Incredible Shrinking Man" mercilessly ridiculed conformity and faddism. "Sanctuary," a sparse, hymn-like ballad, closed the album on a serious note.

Daniel Amos continued to release lyrically challenging, musically inventive albums on a series of labels into the mid-'90s, working past the limitations of techno-rock and back toward a more basic, guitar-oriented approach. Changing its name to DA for a short period, the group released *The Revelation*, featuring the Christian radio hit "Soon," and *Darn Floor, Big Bite*, best known for its abrasive, ominous title track. The band reached a new plateau with 1991's *Kalhoun*, containing such blazing rockers as "If You Want Me To." Taylor had

found his calling as a raw-throated sermon-spouter, leavening his satire with vivid invocations of God's majesty. He hit his stride as a songwriter on *Motorcycle* (1993), reintroducing a country tinge in the luminous "Grace Is the Smell of the Rain." *Bibleland* (1994) was even better, an unflinching look at human weakness and vanity delivered with punk-rock ferocity. Standouts here include the biting title track and the harrowing "Bakersfield." On this and other albums from this period, Taylor chose to prod and disturb his fellow believers rather than offer comforting homilies.

Grasping the whole of Daniel Amos's work isn't easy—besides the albums listed below, there have been Terry Taylor solo releases and band side projects, like the good-humored Swirling Eddies. The compilation CD *Our Personal Favorite World Famous Hits* (KMG, 1998) provides a well-chosen overview of the group's eclectic output. After a five-year hiatus, Daniel Amos released a two-disc CD of new songs, *Mr. Buechner's Dream*, in 2001.

Taylor has also been a member of **the Lost Dogs** since 1992.

Daniel Amos (Maranatha!, 1976)
Shotgun Angel (Maranatha!, 1977)
Horrendous Disc (Solid Rock, 1981)
Alarma! (Newpax, 1981)
Doppelganger (Alarma, 1983)
Vox Humana (Refuge, 1984)
Fearful Symmetry (Frontline, 1986)
The Revelation (Frontline, 1987)

Darn Floor, Big Bite (Frontline, 1987)
Live Bootleg '82 (Stunt, 1990)
Kalhoun (Brainstorm/Stunt, 1991)
Motorcycle (Brainstorm/Word, 1993)
Bibleland (WAL/Word, 1994)
Songs of the Heart (Brainstorm, 1995)
Our Personal Favorite World Famous Hits
 (KMG, 1998)
Mr. Buechner's Dream
(independent release, 2001)

DANIELSON FAMILE
Formed 1994
in New Brunswick, New Jersey

Profoundly weird and impossible to classify, the Danielson Famile exists on Contemporary Christian music's outermost fringes. Lead singer/guitarist Daniel Smith and his four siblings form the core of this unique, avant-garde folk/pop combo. Bafflingly esoteric at times, their mostly-acoustic music has an eerily childlike quality. If nothing else, the Danielson Famile puts to rest the notion that Christian music is inherently bland or conservative.

The group traces its origins to Daniel Smith's senior thesis project at Rutgers University art school. Part of this thesis involved writing a set of songs; these were recorded and eventually released by the independent Tooth and Nail label as the Danielson Famile's first album. At the start, the group consisted of siblings Daniel (guitar), Rachel (flute, keyboards),

Megan (xylophone), and David (drums), along with Chris Palladino (organ). By 1996, 12-year-old Andrew Smith had joined as percussionist.

In 1997, *Tell Another Joke at the Ol' Choppin' Block*, the Famile's second CD, attracted notice from the alternative rock press. The music here is both annoying and fascinating. Singing in a squeaky falsetto, Smith leads his group through commentaries on sex, death, and Christ's transforming blood. Musically, the songs stitch together carnival music, horror movie themes, gospel hymns, and Latin rhythms into odd, often disonant sonic quilts. Glockenspiel, flute, and tinny piano touches add to the mood. "Quest for Thrills" (expressing a love/hate feeling about the human body) and "I Am My Beloved's" (a brooding piece about marriage) are among the highlights in this curious collection.

The Danielson Famile's live shows (often at secular venues) grew to be as provocative

Danielson Famile. Left to right: Andrew, Rachel, Daniel, Elin, Chris, Megan, and David
Photo by Jim & Chuck

as its recordings. The entire group performed in personalized doctors' and nurses' outfits; a stripped-down version of the band featured Daniel Smith playing guitar while standing inside a papier-mâché tree. This sort of quirky playfulness was given free reign on the group's next two albums, *"Tri-Danielson!!" (Alpha)* and *"Tri-Danielson!!" (Omega)*. Daniel Smith sings of childhood fears, adolescent trials, and the need for divine nourishment with a hint of a southern preacher's twang (in falsetto, of course). Taken as a whole, these albums sound like a strange children's pageant at an experimental Pentacostal school. Some tracks are flat-out funny—"Pottymouth," on the *Alpha* album, concerns cussing, bowling, and bad dating habits. For the most part, though, these songs take themselves seriously, at least according to their own aesthetic. The Danielson Famile's Christian message—much of it dealing with the struggle for purity of thought and deed—seems sincere, if highly idiosyncratic.

Fetch the Compass Kids (Secretly Canadian, 2000) traveled still deeper into the peculiar terrain of earlier efforts. Besides touring and recording with the group, Daniel Smith has also released albums by other artists on his own independent label, Sounds Familyre.

A Prayer for Every Hour (Tooth and Nail, 1995)
Tell Another Joke at the Ol' Choppin' Block (Tooth and Nail, 1997)
"Tri-Danielson!!" (Alpha) (Tooth and Nail, 1998)
"Tri-Danielson!!" (Omega) (Tooth and Nail, 1999)
Fetch the Compass Kids (Secretly Canadian, 2000)

DAVID AND THE GIANTS
Formed 1969 in Mississippi

Long-surviving rock band David and the Giants enjoyed a number of Christian radio hits in the 1980s and early '90s. Though they never achieved nationwide fame, the Forest, Mississippi-based band became a regional favorite and released more than a dozen albums on a variety of labels.

The group began its career as a secular group in the late 1960s. Lead singer David Huff and his brothers Randy (keyboards) and Clayborn (bass) formed the band while still in their teens. Completing the roster was drummer Keith Thibodeaux, a child actor best known for playing Little Ricky on *I Love Lucy* and Opie's best friend on *The Andy Griffith Show.* David and the Giants built up a following on the southern club and college circuit, reveling in the excesses of a rock'n'roll lifestyle along the way. By the mid-'70s, they had renounced their self-destructive ways and become Christians. After the temporary departure of David Huff to pursue a solo career, they reformed and toured diligently. Securing a deal with Priority in the early '80s, they gained Christian radio airplay with such singles as "One Less Stone" and "Highway to Heaven." A switch to Myrrh brought the band more hits, including "His Love Lifted Me Up" and "Why." Their music ranged from guitar-fueled rock to amiable country and sensitive ballads. Unifying these elements was a straight-ahead gospel message that conceded little to secular tastes.

By the late '80s, David and the Giants had left Myrrh and established their own label, Giant (distributed by the Benson Company). *Long Time Coming*, released in 1992, spawned two more Christian hits, "Live and Learn" and "Dream On." The band withstood the 1990 departure of Thibodeaux (who formed his own band, Lively Stone) and continued to record into the mid-'90s. David Huff's daughter Kellye and son Lance were members of the group for a time. Eventually, the group folded; Giant Records has remained active, marketing David and the Giants' back catalog and solo albums by David and Kellye Huff.

Under Control (Myrrh, 1985)
Are U Gonna Stand Up (Giant, 1989)
Distant Journey (Giant, 1990)
Long Time Coming (Giant, 1992)
Angels Unaware (Giant, 1995)
Dream (Giant, 1996)

DC TALK
Formed 1988 in Lynchburg, Virginia

Few Contemporary Christian acts have reached the level of success that dc Talk has achieved. This pop/rap/hip-hop/rock trio has sold millions of albums and received considerable attention in the mainstream media. During the 1990s, the group began to perfect its highly accessible sound without losing its Christ-centered message. dc Talk continues to be a standard against which Christian artists are measured.

Toby McKeehan (born October 22, 1964) and Michael Tait (born May 17, 1966) formed the group while attending Virginia's Liberty University (founded by evangelist Jerry Falwell). Their mutual love of music (specifically rap) led them to form DC Talk and the One Way Crew (its original name) in the late 1980s. At the start, the "DC" was a reference to the District of Columbia; record company publicists later asserted that the initials stood for "Decent Christian." The two launched their act by selling copies of a two-song demo, "Christian Rhymes to a Rhythm," door to door. Adding third member Kevin "Max" Smith (born August 17, 1964), they went on to sign with ForeFront Records and relocate to Nashville.

The trio's lack of a fully-developed style made its self-titled debut album, released in 1989, sound more like a rap novelty project than anything else. Still, *DC Talk* sold some 100,000 copies and made the group one to watch. A year later, DC Talk was back with *Nu Thang*, a much more satisfying effort. Here, the group sounds more confident and mature, with McKeehan

Michael Tait (second from right), with current solo group, Tait
Photo by Kristen Barlow

stepping out as a credible rapper. Singing was increasingly emphasized, pointing the way toward the more pop-oriented direction of future albums. The title track and "Talk It Out" (the latter a plea for intergenerational communication) gave DC Talk its first Christian radio hits. The 1991 release of the trio's *Rap, Rock & Soul* video helped boost its popularity further.

DC Talk truly came into its own with 1992's *Free at Last*, a quantum leap forward both artistically and commercially. Keeping on the straight and narrow path has rarely sounded hipper—each track is a lively meld of black and white pop idioms, effortlessly mixing moral lessons and jive patter. While the album works nicely as a whole, certain cuts especially stand out. "That Kinda Girl" is a purity-before-marriage statement with more than a little sensuality in its groove.

The 1973 Doobie Brothers hit "Jesus Is Just Alright" is revamped as a slamming rap/rock track. The funky-but-decent "Socially Acceptable" chides Christians who conform to the world's lax standards. Yielding no less than six high-charting Christian radio singles, *Free at Last* went on to achieve double-platinum sales and win a Grammy Award for best rock gospel album.

Changing the "DC" in its name to lower case, the trio took its time releasing a follow-up album. *Jesus Freak* finally appeared in 1995 and proved to be another pivotal work. Rock elements—especially those with a late 1960s/early '70s flavor—are more prominent this time, interwoven smoothly with hip-hop rhythms and production. The key song here is the title track, an in-your-face anthem of Christian pride that quickly became one of the group's signature tunes. "Jesus Freak" so defined dc Talk's identity that, in hindsight, it overshadowed the abundance of other worthy tracks on the album. Among these was "Just Between You and Me," which crossed over and became a number 29 hit on the secular charts. Such singles as the revelatory "What If I Stumble" and provocative "Colored People" brought the group further Christian radio hits. *Jesus Freak* became dc Talk's second double-platinum album and earned it both Grammy and GMA Dove awards. It also inspired spin-off projects, such as *Jesus Freaks*, a book compiling the deeds of Christian martyrs past and present.

The unexpected level of success reached by *Free at Last* and *Jesus Freak* led to a distribution deal between ForeFront and secular Virgin Records for future dc Talk releases. The group did an extensive North American tour in 1996, documented on its 1997 release *Welcome to the Freak Show: Live in Concert*. Its next studio album, *Supernatural*, arrived in 1998. An almost complete departure from the band's beginnings, the album has a 1990s British pop feel, landing somewhere between Seal and Oasis in sound. The mood is more low-key and thoughtful, less prone to sloganeering. "Consume Me" is an expression of religious passion with a mystical bent. "Godsend" is a silky love song in which the Lord is the divine matchmaker, rather than the subject. The band definitely hasn't gone secular— tracks like "The Truth" and "Into Jesus" aren't far from "Jesus Freak" lyrically. What's new is a more refined, less obvious approach, as evidenced by Smith's spoken word piece "There Is a Treason at Sea." *Supernatural* was seemingly a natural to achieve mainstream popularity; unfortunately, none of its singles became secular hits.

The certified-gold *Supernatural* was followed by *Intermission: The Greatest Hits* in 2000. This "best of" collection gathered together most of the band's best-known songs from *Free at Last* onward, as well as such extras as a cover of **Larry Norman**'s "I Wish We'd All Been Ready." In 2000,

dc Talk contributed a version of Norman Greenbaum's "Spirit in the Sky" to the *Jesus* CBS-TV miniseries soundtrack. Next, the band decided to try its hand at solo projects. These appeared in quick succession in 2001: *Empty* from Tait, *Stereotype Be* from Smith, *Momentum* from McKeehan. *Solo,* a sampler EP featuring tracks from all three albums, was also released. (For more about dc Talk, see pages 68–73.)

DC Talk (ForeFront, 1989)
Nu Thang (FrontFront, 1990)
Free at Last (ForeFront, 1992)
Jesus Freak (ForeFront, 1995)
Welcome to the Freak Show: Live in Concert (ForeFront, 1997)
Supernatural (ForeFront/Virgin, 1998)
Intermission: The Greatest Hits (ForeFront/Virgin, 2000)
Solo (EP) (ForeFront, 2001)

DeGARMO & KEY
Formed 1972 in Memphis, Tennessee

During their 20-plus years together, native Memphis sons Eddie DeGarmo and Dana Key made the journey from a loud'n'heavy blues/rock unit to a radio-friendly, multifaceted pop combo. What remained constant was their commitment to spreading the teachings of Christ without compromise. After a lengthy run of Christian hit singles, the pair separated in the mid-1990s.

The duo could honestly claim a deeply American sound—keyboardist/singer DeGarmo and lead singer/guitarist Key are descendants of Davy Crockett and Francis Scott Key, respectively. Childhood friends, they formed their first band while in sixth grade. During high school, they joined the group Globe, which went on to sign with Hi/London Records in 1972. Earlier that year, DeGarmo and Key had both become Christians, prompting them to leave Globe to pursue faith-based music. Opening a storefront coffeehouse, they put together a three-piece group first dubbed the Christian Band. They also began working for the evangelical organization Youth for Christ, which loaned them money to record a demo tape. Changing their name to DeGarmo & Key, they secured a record deal with Lamb & Lion and released their debut LP *This Time Thru* in 1977. The following year, "Livin' on the Edge of Dyin'" became their first Christian radio hit.

Blues-based rock with a dash of British progressive influence defined the group's sound at the start. DeGarmo's keyboard flourishes brought comparisons with Keith Emerson, while Key unleashed a repertoire of southern rock licks with ease. A changing cast of backup players—including drummers John Hampton and Trent Moxley and bassists Joe Hardy and Ken Porter— rounded out the band during the early to mid-1980s. Such songs as "Nobody Loves Me" (a duet with **Amy Grant**), "Let the

Whole World Sing," and "Alleluia! Christ Is Coming" made the group a familiar presence on Christian radio. *This Ain't Hollywood* (1980) became the first Christian rock album to receive a Grammy nomination for best gospel performance, contemporary or inspirational.

DeGarmo & Key became known for their fierce Christian advocacy. They stirred controversy when the video for their song "Six Six Six" was rejected by MTV in 1984. DeGarmo & Key claimed that religious bias was responsible; MTV ended up placing the video in light rotation after it was reedited. This wasn't their only negative experience with the secular entertainment industry—they later claimed that they were offered an opening slot on a ZZ Top tour if they would refrain from preaching. (They refused.) DeGarmo & Key addressed the MTV squabble and related matters in "We Use the J Word" (from 1993's *Heat It Up*), a defiantly proud statement of faith.

Street Light, released in 1986, was among the duo's most accessible albums. In contrast to their pumped-up Christian rock anthems, the songs here depict characters faced with everyday difficulties. "Every Moment," the album's lead track, is a rousing, upbeat number that became DeGarmo & Key's biggest single. Subsequent albums returned to straightforward preaching, typified by *Heat It Up*'s "God Good/Devil Bad," a Bon Jovi–like shout-along, and "Soldiers of the Cross," a gospel battle cry that became a Christian hit single. Songs in this vein kept flowing forth until the group decided to call it quits in 1995. Their final album, *To Extremes,* rocked harder than most of their output and ended matters on a strong note.

DeGarmo and Key had been involved in side projects while still performing together. In 1987, DeGarmo cofounded ForeFront Records (the future home of **dc Talk** and **Rebecca St. James,** among others) and released a solo album, *Feels Good to Be Forgiven,* a year later. Key released his first solo effort, *The Journey,* in 1990 and went on to record further projects later in the decade. One of his singles, 1991's "Pray for Peace," was used to promote prayer during the Gulf War.

This Time Thru (Lamb & Lion, 1977)
Straight On (Lamb & Lion, 1978)
This Ain't Hollywood (Lamb & Lion, 1980)
No Turning Back/Live (Lamb & Lion, 1982)
Mission of Mercy (PowerDiscs, 1983)
Communication (PowerDiscs, 1984)
*Commander Sozo & the Charge of the Light
    Brigade (PowerDiscs, 1985)*
Street Light (PowerDiscs, 1986)
Street Rock (PowerDiscs, 1987)
D&K (PowerDiscs, 1987)
Rock Solid (PowerDiscs, 1988)
The Pledge (PowerDiscs, 1989)
Go to the Top (Benson, 1991)
Destined to Win (Benson, 1992)
Heat It Up (Benson, 1993)
To Extremes (Benson, 1994)

DELIRIOUS
Formed 1992 in Littlehampton, England

Delirious is among the few British Christian bands to have an impact in the United States, and is credited with helping to reinvent praise music in a modern rock context. Often compared with U2, the quintet has presented itself as worship leaders rather than entertainers, honoring God with guitar-driven rock hymns.

The roots of the group (which sometimes adds a question mark to the end of its name) extend back to the early 1990s, when Martin Smith (singer/guitarist), brother Stewart Smith (drums), and Tim Jupp supplied music for monthly worship events held in the small English coastal town of Littlehampton. This band—which, like the program of events, adopted the name Cutting Edge—wrote plainspoken yet powerful songs to facilitate worship among young believers. With the addition of lead guitarist Stuart Garrard and bassist John Thatcher, the music began to take on a fuller, more dramatic sound. Cutting Edge began to re-create its events in other English locales and to offer tapes of its music. The band took on a more full-time character in 1995, changing its name to Delirious. *Cutting Edge,* a two-CD collection of its initial songs, appeared in 1997. "I Could Sing of Your Love Forever" and "Did You Feel the Mountains Tremble?" were indicative of the sweeping anthemic quality of these early compositions. *Cutting*

Edge eventually earned gold certification in the United States.

Unexpectedly, the band's song "Deeper" went on to top the BBC charts after its release as a single in 1997. Delirious began to stir interest in the States as well, where it was embraced as part of the new wave of praise music. Playing down any pretentions to rock star status, the band appeared at praise events on both sides of the Atlantic, leading thousands of young worshippers in communal devotion to Christ. Almost every song in Delirious's repertoire was addressed to Jesus, expressing reverence and thanks in humble language. If the lyric content remained constant, the band's music grew more refined over its next two albums, *King of Fools* (1998) and *Mezzamorphis* (1999). The key elements were Smith's expressive, at times fragile vocals and Garrard's guitar pyrotechnics.

Glo (2000) advanced Delirious further, bringing in touches of electronica and trip-hop for atmosphere. Tracks like "My Glorious" and "God You're My God" sang hosannas to churning lead guitar lines, while "What Would I Have Done?" glowed with reverence over acoustic slide work. *Glo* demonstrated that praise music can have artistic diversity and nuance while retaining its intense spiritual focus.

Cutting Edge (Sparrow, 1997)
King of Fools (Sparrow, 1998)
Mezzamorphis (Sparrow, 1999)
Glo (Sparrow, 2000)

BRYAN DUNCAN
Born March 16, 1953, in Ogden, Utah

A consummate blue-eyed soul singer, Bryan Duncan has been a Christian music mainstay since the mid-1970s. After a 12-year tenure with the Sweet Comfort Band, he embarked on a solo career that has continued into the present day. Duncan is renowned for his authentic R&B-rooted style, inviting comparisons with James Brown and Smokey Robinson.

The story goes that Duncan was given his first guitar by his minister father, who in turn had received it from a congregation member whose son had committed suicide. During his high school years, Duncan wrote songs and absorbed the influence of such R&B/funk outfits as Sly & The Family Stone. He launched a folk/rock band called Second Timothy while attending college in Florida, then moved to Southern California to take part in the local Jesus Music scene. Duncan performed as a solo act at Calvary Chapel and other Christian venues before joining forces with brothers Kevin and Rick Thompson to form the Sweet Comfort Band in 1972. The band enjoyed a string of successful albums and singles before breaking up in 1984.

Signing with Light Records in 1985, Duncan scored a Christian radio hit on the first try with "Have Yourself Committed," the title track of his first solo album, released in 1985. He brought a sense of sanctified fun to his material, keeping a touch of southern blues and gospel tradition in his contemporary pop songwriting style. Switching to the Modern Art label, he kept up his presence on the Christian airwaves with such mid-'80s singles as "Help Is on the Way," "Every Heart Has an Open Door," and "Paradise." His 1989 album *Strong Medicine* was a particular high point, featuring forays into reggae and rap. *Anonymous Confessions of a Lunatic Friend* (Myrrh, 1990) was another strong effort, featuring both playfully upbeat tunes and from-the-heart balladry. Its single "Ain't No Stoppin' Now" became one of Duncan's biggest Christian hits.

Duncan's work in the mid-'90s grew more confessional and creatively ambitious. The albums *Mercy, Slow Revival,* and *Blue Skies* formed a trilogy dealing with the search and attainment of salvation. Perhaps his most significant release during this time was *Quiet Prayers* (1996), part of the multi-artist *My Utmost for His Highest* series. Duncan's new material for the project, as well as such worship favorites as "El Shaddai" and "I Surrender All," were rendered with finesse and conviction, helping *Quiet Prayers* win a GMA Dove Award in 1997 for inspirational album of the year.

Touring kept Duncan busy during the 1980s and '90s. Annual "Christmas Is Jesus" concert dates with local orchestras and performances with **Bob Carlisle** as the Self-Righteous Brothers were among the highlights. In 2001, he joined forces with his old bandmates to revive the Sweet Comfort Band for a reunion tour.

After a three-year hiatus from album-making, Duncan released *Joyride* on the Diadem label in 2001. Showcasing his feel for blues and jazz as well as R&B, the CD harked back to his first musical loves.

Have Yourself Committed (Light, 1985)
Holy Rollin' (Light, 1986)
Whistlin' in the Dark (Modern Art, 1987)
Strong Medicine (Modern Art, 1989)
Anonymous Confessions of a Lunatic Friend
    (Myrrh, 1990)
Mercy (Myrrh, 1992)
Slow Revival (Myrrh, 1994)
Christmas Is Jesus (Myrrh, 1996)
Quiet Prayers: My Utmost for His Highest
    (Myrrh, 1996)
Blue Skies (Myrrh, 1997)
The Last Time I Was Here (Myrrh, 1998)
Love Takes Time: 17 Bryan Duncan Classics
    (Myrrh, 2000)
Joyride (Diadem, 2001)

EARTHSUIT
Formed c. 1997
in New Orleans, Louisiana

Slightly spacey in sound and mood, Earthsuit became one of Christian music's bands to watch in 2000. The quintet's slippery grooves and enraptured lyrics had a woozy electronica ambiance with a hint of New Orleans funk thrown in. Invitingly danceable and firmly evangelical, the band achieved the hip edge that so many young Christian acts strive for with less success.

Earthsuit developed its genre-hopping sound through live performances at a New Orleans coffeehouse. Founding members Adam LaClave (vocalist) and Paul Meany (keyboardist) maintained the group for a year or so before adding Dave Rumsey (guitar), Roy Mitchell (bass), and David Hutchison (drums). Signed to Sparrow Records in 1999, Earthsuit released its debut album, *Kaleidoscope Superior*, a year later. The title was appropriate—the album's tracks had a swirling feel to them, counterpointing jazzy keyboard lines with hip-hop beats and gentle guitar murmurs. The music's balmy sensuality was tapped to convey a yearning for direct spiritual discovery. "Whitehorse" and "Said the Son to the Shine" offered visions of Christ's presence with a techno-mystical glow. A reggae undercurrent ran through such tracks as "Osmosis Land" and "Sky Flashings," complementing the exalted lyric outlook. Emphasizing the brighter side of the Christian millennial vision, Earthsuit's *Kaleidoscope Superior* was a promising first effort from this forward-thinking quintet.

Kaleidoscope Superior (Sparrow, 2000)

MICHAEL ENGLISH
Born 1962
in Kennansville, North Carolina

In 1994, Contemporary Christian artist Michael English made headlines in the secular press when he confessed to an affair. The scandal overshadowed his impressive accomplishments as a performer and producer; further bad publicity has dogged him since. Beyond his troubles, though, English has earned his place in Christian music both as a gospel singer and an interpreter of contemporary pop/rock material.

Raised in the Pentacostal Church, English was singing hymns from childhood. By age 13, he and his brother Biney were part of a local gospel quartet, the Singing Samaritans. In 1980, he briefly attended barber school before joining the Singing Americans, with whom he toured for two years. His outstanding number with this group was "I Bowed on My Knees and Cried Holy," a powerful showstopper that helped make him famous in the Christian music community. During the mid-'80s, stints with such famed gospel groups as the Goodmans, the Bill Gaither Trio, and the Gaither Vocal Band brought further praise. English battled a debilitating panic disorder even as he pushed himself as a performer. He eventually gained the confidence to attempt a solo career. He secured a deal with Warner Alliance in 1989 and released his debut album two years later.

The *Michael English* album mixed ballads with dance-oriented tunes, providing a tasteful showcase for English's soaring vocals. Christian radio quickly embraced him, sending "Solid as the Rock" to the top of its charts in late 1991. The following year, he won a GMA Dove Award for both new artist and male vocalist of the year (he would win the latter award for two more consecutive years as well). Keeping in touch with his southern gospel roots, he released "In Christ Alone" as a single, which went on to win a Dove for inspirational song of the year in 1993. English's winning streak continued in 1993 with the release of his second album, *Hope,* which received a Dove for pop/contemporary album of the year. Such singles as "Holding Out Hope to You" (another Dove Award–winner), "Save Me," "There Is a Love," and "Message of Mercy" kept him on the Christian airwaves from 1993 into the spring of 1994.

On May 6, 1994—a week after winning five GMA Dove Awards, including artist of the year—English and his record company announced his withdrawal from Christian music because of "mistakes" he had made. Not long after, he publicly confessed to an extramarital affair with Marabeth Jordon, a married singer with the Christian pop group First Call. English returned his Dove awards and Warner Alliance removed him from its artist roster. Many Christian stations dropped his songs from their playlists, incurring the anger of some English fans. As the controversy raged, he accepted a deal for the secular market with Curb Records.

English debuted as a mainstream artist in October 1994 with "Healing," a duet single with country singer Wynonna. The song was included on the soundtrack to the film *Silent Fall* and went on to become the title track to *Healing: The Collection* (Curb, 1995), a compilation album with two newly recorded tracks. *Freedom,* his first all-new album for Curb, appeared in 1996. Though its single "Your Love Amazes Me" became an Adult Contemporary hit, the CD failed to fully establish English as a secular music star. Meanwhile, he continued to work behind the scenes in Christian music as a producer and songwriter, working on albums with such gospel groups as J. D. Sumner and the Stamps, the Gaither Vocal Band, and the Martins. He went on to win a pair of GMA Dove awards as producer of the Martins's 1996 self-titled album and its 1997 album *Wherever You Are.*

After a number of live appearances with the Stamps and on Christian television programs, English reentered Christian music as a recording artist with his 1998 album *Gospel.* His career seemed to be slowly recovering when, in late 2000, he faced charges of illegally obtaining drugs, including the sedative Hydrocone. He eventually spent six weeks in a treatment facility and received three years probation. English discussed his battle with addiction in interviews with the Christian media and won a degree of support. Still, it served to divert attention from the release of his *Heaven to Earth* album in late 2000.

Michael English (Warner Alliance, 1991)
Hope (Warner Alliance, 1993)
Healing: The Collection (Curb, 1995)
Freedom (Curb, 1996)
Gospel (Curb, 1998)
Heaven to Earth (Curb, 2000)

JOHN FISCHER
Born 1947 in Palo Alto, California

Among the first Jesus Music artists to begin recording in the late 1960s, singer/songwriter John Fischer brought a thoughtful, literate touch to his work. After releasing albums for more than 20 years, he shifted his focus to writing books and articles for the Christian media market.

Growing up in the San Francisco Bay area, Fischer's interest in music was shaped by his father, a church music director. By his teenage years, he was playing piano and guitar. His songwriting abilities began to blossom while he attended Wheaton College in Illinois; a year before graduation, he recorded and released his debut album, 1969's *The Cold Cathedral*. Fischer's early work was folk-based and avoided the rock'n'roll stridency of his fellow early

Christian artists. Such tunes as "Way of All Flesh" (from his second album, *Have You Seen Jesus My Lord*) offered straightforward commentaries on life and faith. His music showed a country/rock influence at the start, though jazzier elements would turn up on later efforts.

Back in his native Palo Alto, California, Fischer gained the help of the Peninsula Bible Church in launching the Discovery Arts Guild, an organization that promoted new Christian musical talent. His own performing and recording career continued throughout the 1970s. Among his more notable releases was *Johnny's Cafe* (1979), a song cycle with a Los Angeles jazz/pop feel. Many of its songs—particularly the title track, "Talking Faces," and "Midnight on Main Street"—were vignettes of ordinary life tinged with a Christian overview. In 1983, the title song to his Myrrh Records debut album, *Dark Horse*, earned him the biggest Christian hit single of his career. *Wide Angle*, released in 1992, found him in a provocative mood, bringing a questioning spirit to songs like "Jesus Is the Only Way (but There's More than One Way to Jesus)."

From the late '70s onward, Fischer increasingly wrote for the printed page, contributing a monthly column to *CCM* magazine and authoring books, including *Real Christians (Don't) Dance* and *True Believers (Don't) Ask Why*. He branched out into Christian-themed novels as well, with *Ashes on the Wind*. Still active as a journalist and author, he continues to promote

Christian involvement in mainstream culture and to discourage separatism.

The Cold Cathedral (F.E.L., 1969)
Have You Seen Jesus My Lord (F.E.L., 1970)
Still Life (Light, 1974)
The New Covenant (Light, 1975)
Naphatali (Light, 1976)
Inside (Light, 1978)
Johnny's Cafe (Light, 1979)
Dark Horse (Myrrh, 1983)
Between the Answers (Myrrh, 1985)
Casual Crimes (Myrrh, 1986)
Wide Angle (Enclave, 1992)

FIVE IRON FRENZY
Formed 1995 in Denver, Colorado

Denver's Five Iron Frenzy serves up a zany blend of ska and punk while remaining true to its members' Christian faith. Sometimes silly, sometimes sentimental, the combo has built an international fan base through frequent touring. Its albums have shown creative development, with cheeky humor and expressions of faith remaining constants.

Five Iron Frenzy was launched in the spring of 1995 by Reese Roper (vocals), Scott Kerr (guitar), Micah Ortega (guitar), Keith Hoerig (bass), Andy Verdecchio (drums), Dennis Culp (trombone), and Nathanel "Brad" Durham (trumpet). Saxophonist Leanor "Jeff" Ortega (Micah's cousin) joined shortly thereafter. The group parlayed its Denver-area following into gigs around the country, including a 1995 spot at the famed Cornerstone Festival. From the start, the band attracted both Christian and non-Christian fans by avoiding heavy-handed preaching in favor of a lighter, more comical approach. After self-releasing a seven-inch vinyl record, it secured a contract with the independent Five Minute Walk label and released its CD debut in 1996.

Upbeats and Beatdowns, the group's first album, captured its unfettered goofiness and snappy, horn-accented sound. There were also serious moments, such as "When Zero Meets 15, " which dealt with homelessness. *Our Newest Album Ever!* (1997) showed greater songwriting refinement and more polished arrangements. This growth spurt continued on the 1998 EP *Quantity Is Job 1,* with such idealistic Christian numbers as "That's All Good" and "Dandelions," as well as the wacky mini-opera "These Are Not My Pants." Much like its punk/pop peers **MxPx,** Five Iron Frenzy showed evidence of maturation without losing its manic-but-wholesome edge.

In 1999, Kerr exited the band and was replaced by Sonnie Johnson. Tours took the group to Europe and South Africa over the next several years; the live album *Proof that the Youth Are Revolting* gives an audio glimpse of these ultra-energetic stage shows. *All the Hype that Money Can Buy* (2000) and *Five Iron Frenzy 2: Electric Boogaloo* (2001) were further exercises in ska/punk/pop fun.

Upbeats and Beatdowns
    (Five Minute Walk,1996)
Our Newest Album Ever!
    (Five Minute Walk, 1997)
Quantity Is Job 1 (EP)
    (Five Minute Walk, 1998)
Proof that the Youth Are Revolting
    (Five Minute Walk, 1999)
All the Hype that Money Can Buy
    (Five Minute Walk, 2000)
Five Iron Frenzy 2: Electric Boogaloo
    (Five Minute Walk, 2001)

DON FRANCISCO
Born February 28, 1946,
in Louisville, Kentucky

Don Francisco's special forte is the Christian story-song. Somewhat comparable to **Michael Card** and **Rich Mullins** in his use of biblical lyric themes, he enjoyed his greatest success in 1978 with the hugely popular "He's Alive."

The son of a professor at Louisville's Southern Baptist Theological Seminary, Francisco began playing guitar in his mid-teens. By the early 1970s, he had moved to Los Angeles and found work in a touring cover band. After becoming a committed Christian in 1974, he turned away from secular music and moved to Nashville. He signed with the NewPax label, and in 1976 released his debut album, *Brother of the Son*. The following year he released *Forgiven*, which yielded the now-classic

"He's Alive." A dramatic narrative of Christ's Resurrection as told from the disciple Peter's point of view, the song ranks among the most-played Christian radio singles in the genre's history. "He's Alive" went on to win a GMA Dove Award for song of the year in 1980, with Francisco receiving a Dove for songwriter of the year as well. Other artists who covered the tune include Johnny Cash and Dolly Parton.

Francisco continued to release story-songs that retold Old and New Testament events in contemporary language. He did particularly well in 1980 with "Got to Tell Somebody," an account of Christ's miraculous powers that almost equaled the phenomenal success of "He's Alive." "Adam Where Are You?" and "Too Small a Price" were among his other notable songs in this vein. He stepped away from the narrative format for the country-flavored "Steeple Song," a 1980 single that chided Christians for caring more about their church property than their values. Francisco's performing style—folk-based and with a minimum of show biz slickness—left him increasingly out of the Contemporary Christian mainstream as the '80s wore on. After bowing out of the music business toward the end of the decade, he began recording for the Star Song label in 1991. Among his most significant releases during this period was 1994's *Genesis & Job*, the first in a series of concept albums based on books of the Bible.

Most of Francisco's early albums were out of print by the late 1990s. To help rectify this, he released *He's Alive,* a collection of new versions of his best-known songs, on the independent Progressive Music label in 1997. *Only Love Spoken Here,* an album of all-new material, appeared in 2001.

Brother of the Son (NewPax, 1976)
Forgiven (NewPax, 1977)
Got to Tell Somebody (NewPax, 1979)
The Traveler (NewPax, 1981)
The Live Concert (NewPax, 1982)
Holiness (NewPax, 1984)
One Heart at a Time (Myrrh, 1985)
The Power (Star Song, 1987)
High Praise (Star Song, 1988)
Vision of the Valley (Star Song, 1991)
Come Away (Star Song, 1992)
Genesis & Job (Star Song, 1994)
He's Alive (Progressive Music, 1997)
Beautiful to Me (Shelf Life, 1998)
Only Love Spoken Here (Airlift, 2001)

JON GIBSON
Born January 3, 1962,
in San Francisco, California

Veteran R&B/pop artist Jon Gibson is best known for his sweetly soulful albums from the 1980s and early '90s. His vocal style and songwriting were often reminiscent of Stevie Wonder at the start of his career,

though Gibson developed a more individual sound as time went on.

Gibson was born in San Francisco and raised in San Jose. Inheriting his singing ability from his mother, he won numerous talent contests as a child. He also became caught up in gang activity and was often in trouble with juvenile authorities; he joined the U.S. Army at age 19 to escape a life of crime. After three years of service in Germany, he was honorably discharged. With his father's encouragement, he accepted Christ and began to reflect his faith in his music. In the early 1980s, he was signed to Constellation Records, a secular R&B label, and began to gain wider recognition.

Keyboardist Bill Wolfer produced Gibson's 1983 debut album for Constellation, *Standing on the One.* The album didn't perform well commercially, but the gospel content of its songs helped interest Frontline Records in signing Gibson for the Christian market. Gibson's first release with Frontline, *On the Run* (1986), contained tracks from *Standing on the One* as well as new material. It yielded "God Loves a Broken Heart," which went on to top the Christian singles charts in 1987. Next came 1988's *Change of Heart,* which paired Gibson with a then-obscure rapper named Kirk Burrell (later famous as MC Hammer) on the rap/pop track "The Wall." Other hits from this album included the smoothly tuneful "Friend in You" and a groove-driven cover of the 1984 Michael McDonald/James Ingram hit "Yah Mo Be There." Gibson found a receptive audience for his early Christian albums thanks to a tastefully controlled vocal style and sensitive lyric touch. His understated style of R&B evangelism was akin to the gospel-tinged songwriting of a Curtis Mayfield or Marvin Gaye.

Later albums on Frontline continued in this vein. *Body and Soul* (1989) contained some of Gibson's best work, including the Christian hits "Father, Father," "In the Name of the Lord," and "Everyone Needs the Lord." Stevie Wonder contributed harmonica to Gibson's cover of "Have a Talk with God," a Wonder song originally heard on his *Songs in the Key of Life*. Gibson self-produced his next album, 1990's *Jesus Loves Ya*, featuring the Christian radio hit title track. In 1994, he moved over to the Brainstorm label and released *Love Education*, the source of two more hit singles: "Jesus" and "Someday Paradise."

After a five-year absence, Gibson returned with *The Man Inside* in 1999. Rather than revamp himself for the hip-hop market, he stuck to his old-school soul ways, singing about God's love with mellow aplomb.

Standing on the One (Constellation, 1983)
On the Run (Frontline, 1986)
Change of Heart (Frontline, 1988)
Body and Soul (Frontline, 1989)
Jesus Loves Ya (Frontline, 1990)
The Hits (Frontline, 1991)
Forever Friends (Frontline, 1992)
Love Education (Brainstorm, 1994)
The Man Inside (B-Rite/Word, 1999)

AMY GRANT
Born November 25, 1960,
in Augusta, Georgia

If there is a single central figure in Contemporary Christian music, Amy Grant is it. She became the first artist to cross over from the Christian to the secular airwaves when "Find a Way" reached the mainstream in 1985. Grant won and held onto fans in both markets thanks to her distinctive voice, a knack for choosing good songs (many of which she wrote herself), and an ability to adapt to changing styles. By 2000, she had sold more than 20 million albums. Following her career from teenage Christian idol to mature mass-appeal artist is illustrative of how the Contemporary Christian genre has developed overall.

Grant was born in Augusta, Georgia, and spent most of her childhood in Nashville, the third daughter of Dr. Burton Paine Grant. Though neither of her parents were especially musical, she began to sing at an early age and, by junior high, was playing guitar as well. During her teens, she was drawn away from her Church of Christ upbringing and toward the charismatic movement. In 1973, Grant began to attend services at Nashville's Belmont Church, frequented by musicians, ex-hippies, and other left-of-center types. The church started a coffeehouse, Koinonia, which provided a stage for some of her early performances.

Influenced by such artists as James Taylor and John Denver, Grant wrote her first songs while a student at Nashville's exclusive Harpeth Hall finishing school. At 15, she began working at a local recording studio owned by artist/producer Chris Christian; her duties included sweeping floors and erasing tapes. Christian heard one of Grant's demo tapes and was impressed enough to play it for Word Record executive Stan Moser over the phone. This led to her signing with the label in 1976 and releasing her self-titled debut album on Word's Myrrh label a year later. This fledgling effort was produced by Brown Bannister, a fellow employee at Christian's studio who would take a major role in shaping Grant's career. While lacking the polish of later efforts, the album revealed her as a singer and songwriter of promise and sold respectably. (It eventually earned gold certification.) The track "Old Man's Rubble" became her first Christian radio hit. Grant began to build an audience as a live performer in 1978, flying to shows in between studies at Furman University in Greenville, South Carolina.

My Father's Eyes, Grant's second album, proved an important creative advance. Released in 1979, the LP featured songs by Grant as well as a traditional hymn, "O Sacred Head." The most significant track, though, was "Father's Eyes," written by singer/songwriter **Gary Chapman.** The song's message of Christian love demonstrated in everyday life was a good match for Grant's unaffected vocals. A combination of warmth and restraint became hallmarks of her singing style—her clear-toned, vibrato-free voice conveyed both strength and sweetness. Bannister's production avoided overblown arrangements, favoring tasteful pop/rock with a minimum of orchestration. These elements would be developed further on 1980's *Never Alone,* which yielded the Christian hit "Look What Has Happened to Me."

During this period, Grant's concert excursions grew more ambitious. She appeared as part of the Billy Graham Crusade and opened for the Bill Gaither Trio gospel group during the winter of 1980–81. The next year found Grant on her first national tour, with **DeGarmo & Key.** These performances were documented on her *In Concert* album, which included a collaboration with the duo, "Nobody Loves Me Like You." (A studio version of this song became a Christian hit single in 1981.) Her personal life was equally eventful— she began attending Vanderbilt University in Nashville in 1981 and married Gary Chapman in 1982.

Returning to the studio, Grant recorded 1982's *Age to Age,* with Bannister again at the production helm. This album would prove pivotal in her career, containing some of her best-loved songs. "Sing Your Praise to the Lord," written by **Rich Mullins,** became an instant Christian standard— Grant sang its joyfully worshipful lyrics with reverent passion, surrounded by a

Amy Grant
Photo by Sandra Johnson

classically tinged arrangement. Just as important was "El Shaddai," a **Michael Card**–composed praise song that gave her another hit and went on to win a GMA Dove Award for song of the year. Thanks to these and other tunes, *Age to Age* became the most important album released by a Christian record label in the early 1980s. It received a Dove for best pop/contemporary album and helped Grant win the first of four Doves for artist of the year. The album also brought her considerable attention in the secular market and helped spur interest in other Christian music acts. *Age to Age* would become the first of nine consecutive Grant albums to be certified platinum, the

first Christian album in history to reach that mark.

Next came *A Christmas Album*, containing both holiday standards and original tunes, such as **Michael W. Smith**'s song "Emmanuel," which became a Christian radio hit in early 1984. Later that year came *Straight Ahead*, a song collection with a more rock-oriented sound. Grant's singing had a looser, grittier quality in spots, particularly on the dramatic story-song "Angels" (yet another Christian radio favorite). "It's Not a Song" (cowritten by Chapman) avoided direct religious references, anticipating more successful crossover attempts. The album also contained the sort of stirring declarations of faith that Grant had become known for—tracks like "Thy Word," "Doubly Good to You," and "The Now and the Not Yet," all worthy successors to "El Shaddai."

For some time, Grant's managers Mike Blanton and Dan Harrell had been planning to cross Grant over into the mainstream. They achieved this with *Unguarded*, released to the secular market in 1985 via A&M Records. From her album cover look—bopping and finger-snapping, dressed in a faux leopard-skin coat—to the more aggressive sound of her music, this release signaled a career change for Grant. Her shift away from praise and worship music toward pop material was not as radical as it appeared—Grant had grown up singing secular tunes. If anyone could bring a Christian sensibility to music for the mainstream, it was she. She succeeded to a limited degree with "Find a Way," an upbeat pop/rock single off the album, cowritten with Michael W. Smith, that broke into the secular Top 40. Considered the first real Christian crossover hit, the song used "love" as a substitute word for "God"—an approach Grant would return to in the future. *Unguarded* had a bright, energetic feel, sacrificing some of the intimacy of her earlier albums in favor of a more commercial sound. Follow-up singles like 1986's "Stay for Awhile" and "Love Can Do" edged even farther from Christian content, matching wholesomely romantic lyrics with busy, synthesizer-driven tracks. (Both of these tunes are found on *The Collection,* her 1986 "best of" album.)

Further mainstream projects followed. Grant collaborated with Art Garfunkel on *The Animals Christmas,* a cantata written by Jimmy Webb and released by Columbia in late 1986. In 1987, she topped the secular pop charts with "The Next Time I Fall," a duet with Peter Cetera. By the time she released *Lead Me On* in 1988, Grant was becoming a familiar voice on secular pop radio. The songs on *Lead Me On,* one of her best albums, are mostly Grant originals (written with Chapman and Smith, among others), exploring the roots of her faith and the presence of God in the world. The track "1974" dealt with her first awakening as a Christian, while "Faithless Heart" wrestled with her weaknesses and fears. The socially conscious

"Lead Me On" (a big hit on Christian radio, a lesser one on the secular airwaves) ranks among Grant's best performances— she tears into the lyric with fiery emotion. Bannister's production is more nuanced and less busy here than on *Unguarded. Lead Me On* went a long way toward solidifying Grant's persona as an artist of substance, not merely a token Christian in the alien camp of secular entertainment.

Heart in Motion (1991) dispelled any lingering doubt that Grant was of secular pop-star caliber. Bannister turned over the bulk of the production duties to Keith Thomas, a veteran Christian musician fluent in the pop trends of the time. The result was a meticulously crafted album that's a consistent pleasure to hear. Grant's vocals take on new R&B colorations, adding an intimate, even sensual feel to the tracks. By themselves, the hits from this album— "Baby, Baby," "Every Heartbeat," "That's What Love Is For"—are sunny, spirit-lifting tunes that fit Top 40 radio perfectly. But the ensuing media attention also served to present Grant as a fun-loving, stylish young Christian woman to a huge secular audience. Direct references to God were toned down on some (but not all) tracks. Songs like "Ask Me" and "Hope Set High" allowed her to sing of her love for Jesus in a friendly, inviting manner. If not a clear-cut work of ministry, *Heart in Motion* was nevertheless an important evangelical statement. It became Grant's biggest seller, eventually reaching the five million-unit mark.

After releasing another holiday album, the triple-platinum *Home for Christmas,* she followed up *Heart in Motion* with another mainstream-slanted CD, *House of Love* (1994). The R&B quotient was higher here, with Grant and country star Vince Gill pairing up à la Marvin Gaye and Tammi Terrell on the album's title track. "Oh How the Years Go By" and "Our Love" depict enduring relationships in family-friendly terms, while "Helping Hand" and "Children of the World" offer encouragement to those in need. Joni Mitchell's "Big Yellow Taxi," an unlikely cover choice, gets a pleasing acoustic treatment. *House of Love* lacks some of the fizz and sparkle of *Heart in Motion,* but still fulfills its intentions.

By this point, Grant was thoroughly established as a secular hit-maker, with the freedom to record just about anything she liked. She moved away from glossy dance/pop toward a modern folk/rock sound on 1997's *Behind the Eyes,* surrounding her vocals with acoustic guitars, organ, and scaled-back drums. This approach worked well on lyrically thoughtful tracks like "Take a Little Time," "Leave It All Behind," and "Curious Thing." Grant's vocals have a newfound maturity to them here; musically, the songs hark back to the singer/songwriters she loved in her teens. There's the sense that Grant has no need to prove her Christian fervor to her original audience, nor to strain herself to appeal to secular fans. She sounds comfortable, self-assured, willing to be herself. *Behind the Eyes* sold less well than did her two previous albums, but still earned gold certification. In 1998, it won a Dove for best pop/contemporary album.

Not all of Grant's Christian fan base was happy with the direction she had taken. The songs on *Behind the Eyes* were criticized by the evangelical publication *Christianity Today* for their lack of Christian content. Even more controversy ensued when, in June 1999, Grant and Chapman divorced. The breakup of Christian music's most famous married couple came as a shock to many, though the two had apparently been growing apart for some time. As a result, Grant's music was dropped from some Christian stations for a while. Weathering the storm as best she could, she went on to release her third holiday album, *A Christmas to Remember,* in late 1999. She married Vince Gill in March 2000.

In May 2002, Grant celebrated 25 years in Christian music by releasing *Legacy… Hymns and Faith.* This album, coproduced by Brown Bannister and Vince Gill, featured traditional hymns along with four original songs. Coming on the heels of Michael W. Smith's *Worship* CD and similar praise music projects, *Legacy* made it clear that Grant desired to reclaim her role as a leading Christian artist.

Amy Grant (Myrrh, 1977)
My Father's Eyes (Myrrh, 1979)
Never Alone (Myrrh, 1980)
In Concert (Myrrh, 1981)

In Concert Vol. II (Myrrh, 1982)
Age to Age (Myrrh, 1982)
A Christmas Album (Myrrh, 1983)
Straight Ahead (Myrrh/A&M, 1984)
Unguarded (Myrrh/A&M, 1985)
The Collection (Myrrh/A&M, 1986)
Lead Me On (Myrrh/A&M, 1988)
Heart in Motion (Myrrh/A&M, 1991)
Home for Christmas (Myrrh/A&M, 1992)
House of Love (Myrrh/A&M, 1994)
Behind the Eyes (Myrrh/A&M, 1997)
A Christmas to Remember
    (Myrrh/A&M, 1999)
Legacy…Hymns and Faith
    (Word/A&M, 2002)

KEITH GREEN

Born October 21, 1953,
in Sheepshead Bay, New York;
died July 28, 1982, in Lindale, Texas

"No compromise" was the motto of singer/songwriter Keith Green, one of Contemporary Christian music's most revered exponents. A fervent, sometimes angrily prophetic artist, he became an early critic of commercialism within the Christian music industry. His musical ministry was tragically cut short by a plane crash in 1982, though the soul-bearing spirit behind Green's music continues to inspire the faithful.

From an early age, it seemed certain that Green was destined for a musical career. Born in New York and later moving with his family to the Los Angeles area, he began appearing in stage musicals at age eight. In 1965, he signed a recording deal with Decca Records, which hoped to make him a teen idol; that same year, he became the youngest member of ASCAP. Stardom didn't come, however, and Green drifted into a lifestyle of drugs, sex, and exotic religions. His life began to change in the early '70s, when he met and eventually married songwriter Melody Steiner. Her influence helped lead him to fully embrace Christianity in 1975. Once his faith was certain, Green became involved in a host of Christian music projects, including the 1976 stage musical *Firewind* (cocreated by **John Michael Talbot**). Green joined the band Good News for a time. Most importantly, he began to write songs reflecting his spiritual awakening— among his early efforts was "Your Love Broke Through," cowritten with **Randy Stonehill** and recorded by **Phil Keaggy**, among others.

Green was brash and sincere, both as an artist and as a man. He unambiguously put his music in the service of his faith, founding Last Days Ministries in 1977 to actively spread the gospel. That same year saw the release of his debut album, *For Him Who Has Ears to Hear*, on Sparrow. This LP captured his boisterous singing style (reminiscent at times of Cat Stevens) and piano-based pop/rock tunefulness. "You Put This Love in My Heart," "Because of You," and "Your Love Broke Through" typify the enthusiastic expressions of praise that fill many of his songs. Green's playful side is shown in "No One Believes Me Anymore," sung from the viewpoint of Satan. *For Him Who Has Ears to Hear* sold well and established Green as an influential figure in both music and ministry.

Increasingly, Green sought to shake up the complacency of his fellow believers. His second album, 1978's *No Compromise,* featured "Asleep at the Light," a plea for Christian activism that ranks among his most important songs. Green's performance of this tune is tinged with rage and sorrow—he's practically crying at the end. "Asleep at the Light" became a Christian radio hit, as did the comical "Dear John Letter (to the Devil)" and the country-rocking "Soften Your Heart." At this juncture, Green moved his Last Days Ministries headquarters from California to Lindale, Texas, and started his own label, Pretty Good Records. He announced in 1980 that his next album, *So You Wanna Go Back to Egypt,* would be sold for a variable price and given away to those who couldn't afford to pay for it. This was considered a radical move, though it did cause some Christian artists to reconsider their album and concert ticket pricing policies. An estimated 200,000 copies of *Egypt* were eventually distributed at little or no cost.

So You Wanna Go Back to Egypt was another effort toward uplifting and invigorating the faithful. The title track drew a humorous parallel between the road-weary followers of Moses and the lackluster Christians of today. Green looked into his own heart and asked for strength in "I Want to Be More Like Jesus" and "Romans VII." The most memorable track here is "O Lord You're Beautiful," a stirring hymn that went on to become a worship music standard. *Songs for the Shepherd* (1982) was devoted entirely to songs of praise, ranging musically from genial pop ("You Are the One") to country waltzes ("Draw Me") and slinky blues/rock ("O God Our Lord").

On July 28, 1982, Green was killed along with two of his children and nine other passengers when his small aircraft crashed near his Lindale home. Pretty Good Records gathered together previously unreleased Green recordings and released *The Prodigal Son* in 1983 and *Jesus Commands Us to Go* the following year. While these albums lack the thematic unity of the albums Green released during his lifetime, they do contain some worthwhile moments, such as *Prodigal Son*'s well-crafted and dramatically performed title track.

Other Christian artists have followed in Green's path to combine music and ministry—singer/songwriters as different as **Carman, Rebecca St. James,** and the late **Rich Mullins**. Musically, Green's recordings sound almost naïve by today's standards. He was definitely not "cool"—in fact, his in-your-face preaching and lack of personal reserve were among his most admired qualities.

Repackagings of Green's music continued to appear from Sparrow in the 1980s and

'90s. *No Compromise: Remembering the Music of Keith Green,* a multi-artist tribute album, was released by Sparrow in 1992. Last Days Ministries remains active under the guidance of Melody Green.

For Him Who Has Ears to Hear
    (Sparrow, 1977)
 No Compromise (Sparrow, 1978)
So You Wanna Go Back to Egypt
    (Pretty Good, 1980)
The Keith Green Collection (Sparrow, 1981)
Songs for the Shepherd (Pretty Good, 1982)
The Prodigal Son (Pretty Good, 1983)
Jesus Commands Us to Go (Pretty Good, 1984)
The Ministry Years, Volume I
    (Sparrow, 1988)
The Ministry Years, Volume II
    (Sparrow, 1989)
Because of You: Songs of Testimony
    (Sparrow, 1998)
Here Am I, Send Me: Songs of Evangelism
    (Sparrow, 1998)
Oh Lord, You're Beautiful: Songs of Worship
    (Sparrow, 1998)
Make My Life a Prayer to You: Songs of
    Worship (Sparrow, 1998)

GUARDIAN
Formed 1982 in Santa Ana, California

Originally a heavy metal act, Guardian underwent an intriguing transmutation during the 1990s. Over the years, the group became unpredictably eclectic in its sound, capable of everything from head-banging metal to acoustic excursions and Nirvana-esque alternative rock. Guardian's approach to Christian themes in its lyrics changed as well, gaining more subtlety and humor as its career progressed.

The band was first launched by bassist David Bach and singer Paul Cawley in 1982 as Fusion. Over the next four years, Fusion changed its name to Guardian, added drummer Rikk Hart and guitarist David Caro, then replaced Caro with Tony Palacios. The band gradually worked its way to prominence in the Southern California rock club scene, trading in the sort of anthemic Christian metal that had made **Stryper** popular. Signing with the secular Enigma label, it recorded its debut album, *First Watch,* with Stryper guitarist Oz Fox producing. The result was a solid melodic metal effort, featuring such heroic declarations of faith as "Livin' for a Promise," "Saints Battalion," and "Rock in Victory."

Though response to *First Watch* was positive, complications began to plague the band. The pressures of touring prompted Hart and Cawley to leave the group in 1990; they were eventually replaced by singer Jamie Rowe and drummer Karl Ney. Around this time, the band's management and record label urged it to play down its Christian faith in its songs. Refusing to compromise, Guardian left Enigma and signed with Pakaderm Records, a custom label founded by producers John and Dino Elefante and distributed by Word. *Fire and*

Love, released in 1990, proved the wisdom of the group's decision—one of the best Christian metal albums of its time, it spawned a major secular crossover hit with "Power of Love." *Fire and Love* became the first of two Guardian albums to be distributed by Epic Records to the secular market, further expanding the band's reach.

Guardian began to tinker with its sound on *Miracle Mile* (1993), adding a funkier feel to its rhythms. Rowe's raw-throated vocals and Palacios's searing guitar solos remained the focal points, powering tunes like "Shoeshine Johnny" and "Sweet Mystery." Rather than play it safe, the group shifted to a more acoustic-oriented sound on

Guardian, with lead singer Jamie Rowe (far right)
Photo by Michael Wilson

1994's *Swing, Swang, Swung.* Matching rock swagger with street-preacher fervor, Guardian delivered a swampy set of tunes more intimate and personal than its previous work. There's a loose, playful quality to *Swing, Swang, Swung* that makes the Christian testimony in its lyrics all the more credible. Each member contributed songs to this album; Bach's "Endless Summer" and Palacios's "See You in Heaven" are among the standouts.

More changes were to come. *Buzz* (1995) found the group plunging into grunge rock, alienating some of its *Fire and Love*– era fans with an angst-tinged tone. Singer/songwriter **Steve Taylor** produced the album and cowrote a number of its songs, contributing his razor-sharp lyric wit to "This Old Man" and other tracks. Guardian collaborated with Taylor on a second album, 1997's *Bottlerocket.* An extension of *Buzz*'s sonic direction, *Bottlerocket* boasted such memorable cuts as the quirky "Are We Feeling Comfortable Yet?" and a rousing treatment of the old hymn "This Little Light of Mine." In addition to these discs, the band also released a pair of Spanish-language albums in the mid-'90s.

In 1998, Bach left the group to accept an executive position at ForeFront Records. A number of self-released discs—most notably 1999's *Live*—helped keep the group's fan base happy for the next few years. Though officially inactive as of 2002, Guardian held out the possibility of future tours and recording projects.

First Watch (Enigma, 1989)
Fire and Love (Pakaderm/Word, 1990)
Miracle Mile (Pakadern/Word, 1993)
Swing, Swang, Swung (Pakaderm/Myrrh, 1994)
Nunca Te Dire Adios (Myrrh, 1995)
Buzz (Myrrh, 1995)
Promesa (Myrrh, 1997)
Bottlerocket (Myrrh, 1997)
Smashes (compilation)(Myrrh, 1999)
Live! (G-Man, 1999)

MARK HEARD
**Born December 16, 1951,
in Macon, Georgia; died August 16,
1992, near Los Angeles, California**

Widely respected among his peers, singer/
songwriter Mark Heard has remained a
cult favorite since his untimely death in
1992. His songs were distinguished by
their uncommonly well-crafted lyrics, filled
with startling images and brilliant turns
of phrase. After years of moderate success,
he distanced himself from the Christian
music industry and released his best work
on his own Fingerprint label.

Born in Macon, Georgia, Heard was
musically active by the time he reached
high school. In 1972, he independently
released the LP *Setting Yesterday Free* with
the group Infinity Plus Three. He attended

the University of Georgia and scraped
by with a number of jobs, including one
for a company manufacturing automatic
chicken feeders and orthopedic mattresses.
After meeting **Larry Norman** in Atlanta
in the mid-'70s, Heard signed with
Norman's Solid Rock Productions and
released *On Turning to Dust* in 1978. This
folk/rock song collection was followed by
a similar effort, 1979's *Appalachian Melody*.
The latter album contained the sweetly
melodic "Castaway," one of Heard's better
early efforts.

Something of a Christian intellectual,
Heard spent time studying at L'Abri, a
retreat founded by American philosopher
Francis Schaeffer in Switzerland. Out of
this experience came *Fingerprint*, issued
by the Swiss label Palmfrond in 1980.
This album (released only in Europe)
contained such folksy fare as "Well-Worn
Pages" and "Gimme Mine." Back in the
States, he began recording for Home Sweet
Home Records, releasing seven albums
(including two "best of" packages) for the
label between 1981 and 1985. Except for
the mostly acoustic *Eye of the Storm*, these
LPs presented Heard's songs in Byrds/Tom
Petty–like rock settings. Heard grew considerably as an artist during this period,
avoiding Christian lyric cliches in his
dissection of moral maladies. His feel for
a strong pop hook was evident on infectious tracks like "Stranded at the Station"
and "One Night Stand." The sense of
outrage that would inform his later work

came through on "The Pain that Plagues Creation," one of his few Christian radio hit singles.

Heard's releases on Home Sweet Home were decidedly better than average, but they only hinted at how good his work would become in later years. Frustrated with creative restrictions within the Christian music industry, he signed with A&M-distributed What? Records in hopes of reaching a larger listenership. Recording under the band name Ideola, he released *Tribal Opera* (1987), a techno-pop-slanted effort that failed commercially. He kept busy for the remainder of the '80s as a session musician, producer, and engineer, working with **Randy Stonehill** and **the Choir,** among others.

In 1990, Heard founded Fingerprint Records with partners Chuck Long and Dan Russell. *Dry Bones Dance,* his first release for the label, was a quantum leap forward creatively. Freed from constraint, he delivered a set of highly literate, emotionally honest tunes, remarkable for their ability to restate familiar Christian verities in new ways. Much of the album has a Cajun/Tex-Mex feel, guitar-driven and spiced by Heard's accordion. But it's the beautifully bittersweet lyrics that truly shine here—"House of Broken Dreams," "Strong Hand of Love," and "Rise from the Ruins" are panoramic depictions of man's suffering and God's grace. *Dry Bones Dance* sold well enough to enable Heard to release a follow-up, 1991's *Second*

Hand. Tough-minded, exquisitely rendered sketches of human frailty make this another outstanding effort. Among its finest moments is "What Kind of a Friend," a hymn-like tune probing moral subtleties (e.g., "What kind of friend would stoop so low/as to shield your eyes from the mirror's gaze?")

Heard's revulsion at the state of the Western world came to a head on *Satellite Sky* (1992), his last album to appear in his lifetime. From the bitter satire of "Freight Train to Nowhere" to the apocalyptic regret of "We Know Too Much," there's a palpable sense of anger here. Heard's singing matches the intensity of his material—his voice bellows, cracks with emotion, yet never quite loses control. Most of the tracks are scorching rockers, many set to a martial tempo. There are gentler songs as well, particularly "Love Is So Blind," a portrait of a saintly innocent. "Orphans of God" is a sweeping vision of benighted humanity, a prayer for the flawed believer. But the album's most powerful song—possibly the best he ever wrote—is the final one, "Treasure of the Broken Land." Set to an anthemic melody, the lyric is both a lament for a lost loved one and a vision of a merciful Savior alive on Earth. At once pain-wracked and triumphant, "Treasure of the Broken Land" is thrilling to hear.

On July 4, 1992, Heard suffered a heart attack while performing at the Cornerstone Festival near Chicago. After finishing his set, he was rushed to the hospital, treated, and released. He returned to his home near Los Angeles, where he suffered a second, more serious attack that left him in a coma. He never recovered; on August 16, he was taken off life support. At the time of his death, Heard was assembling a sampler of his Fingerprint recordings for distribution by a larger label. This collection, *High Noon*, was issued through Myrrh Records in 1993. A year later, Fingerprint (via Word/Epic) released *Strong Hand of Love*, a tribute album with covers of Heard songs by **dc Talk's** Kevin Smith, **Bruce Cockburn, Randy Stonehill, Ashley Cleveland, Rich Mullins, Phil Keaggy,** and others. An expanded two-CD version of this tribute, *Orphans of God*, appeared in 1996. Most of Heard's catalog is currently available on CD via Fingerprint.

Setting Yesterday Free
    (independent release, 1972)
On Turning to Dust (AB, 1978)
Appalachian Melody (Solid Rock, 1979)
Fingerprint (Palmfrond, 1980)
Stop the Dominoes (Home Sweet
    Home/Benson, 1981)
Victims of the Age (Home Sweet Home, 1982)
Eye of the Storm
    (Home Sweet Home/Myrrh, 1983)
Ashes and Light
    (Home Sweet Home/Myrrh, 1984)
Best of Mark Heard: Acoustic
    (Home Sweet Home/Myrrh, 1985)

Best of Mark Heard: Electric
    (Home Sweet Home/Myrrh, 1985)
Mosaics (Home Sweet Home/Myrrh, 1985)
Tribal Opera (as Ideola) (What?/A&M, 1987)
Dry Bones Dance (Fingerprint, 1990)
Second Hand (Fingerprint, 1991)
Satellite Sky (Fingerprint, 1992)
High Noon (Fingerprint/Myrrh, 1993)

KIM HILL
Born 1963 in Starville, Mississippi

Gifted with a powerful alto voice, Kim Hill broke into the upper ranks of Contemporary Christian artists in 1988 after the release of her self-titled debut album. At the time, there were few outstanding female singer/songwriter/guitarists in the genre, and she soon won acclaim both in the Christian and secular press. After a brief stint as a secular country artist, she returned to the Christian market with an emphasis on praise and worship music.

Hill was born in Starville, Mississippi. After attending Mississippi State University, she moved to Nashville and ultimately signed with Reunion Records. Her 1988 debut LP yielded such Christian radio hits as "Faithful" and "Change Your Heart." *Talk About Life*, her 1989 follow-up album, was a particularly strong effort, showcasing Hill's muscular vocals (reminiscent at times of Annie Lennox) and producer Brown Bannister's sleekly modern production. The moody "Snake in the Grass" and surging

"Inside of You" were among its noteworthy tracks. "Testimony," a midtempo statement of faith, became her first number one Christian radio single.

In 1991, *Brave Heart* found Hill delving further into her trademark folk/rock style, and was her most successful album to date. "Satisfied" earned her a chart-topping Christian radio hit the following year. Then, in 1994, Hill made the leap into the mainstream market by signing with BNA and releasing a country album, *So Far So Good*. While the album contained such worthy tracks as "Janie's Gone Fishing," it only sold moderately and Hill was dropped by BNA.

Returning to the Christian market, she released *The Fire Again* in 1997. That same year, she began her association with Renewing the Heart, a national ministry for women similar to the Promise Keepers. Her work as a worship leader was captured on *Renewing the Heart Live* (Star Song, 1998), which went on to win a GMA Dove Award for praise and worship album of the year. This album and its follow-up, 1999's *Renewing the Heart: For Such a Time as This*, featured Hill leading a choir of several hundred women in performance at Nashville's Belmont Church.

Hill also renewed her solo career as a Contemporary Christian artist during this time, releasing *Arms of Mercy* in 1998. This album found Hill updating her potent mixture of roots-rock and folk-influenced melodies with impressive results.

Kim Hill (Reunion, 1988)
Talk About Life (Reunion, 1989)
Brave Heart (Reunion, 1991)
So Far So Good (BNA, 1994)
The Fire Again (Star Song, 1997)
Renewing the Heart Live (Star Song, 1998)
Arms of Mercy (Star Song, 1998)

DALLAS HOLM
Born November 5, 1948,
in St. Paul Park, Minnesota

An early Jesus Music artist, Dallas Holm was a link between traditional gospel and Christian rock. Less loud and radical than contemporaries like **Larry Norman,** this Texas-based singer/songwriter/guitarist avoided harder-edged sounds in favor of a gently inspirational approach. He enjoyed his greatest success with the backup group Praise in the late 1970s and '80s.

A native Minnesotan, Holm was inspired by Elvis Presley as a youngster and, by his high school days, was playing in a rock combo. After accepting Christ at age 16, he tried to find a way to combine his love for rock with his faith. He began by performing his own Christian songs in jails, on street corners, and at church gatherings. By the late 1960s, he was using music as part of his work as a youth pastor in the Dallas/Ft. Worth area. This attracted the attention of evangelist David Wilkerson, who made Holm part of his traveling crusades. (The author of the popular book *The Cross and the Switchblade,*

Wilkerson was initially a bitter critic of rock music. He later changed his views.)

Holm's early albums for the Zondervan and Impact labels presented straightforward worship songs in tasteful rock settings. His career took a major step forward when he formed Praise with bassist Randy Adams, drummer Ric Norris, keyboardist Tim Johnson, and LaDonna Gatlin Johnson (sister of the hit-making Gatlin Brothers country group). *Dallas Holm & Praise…Live* (Greentree, 1977) captured the group's in-concert energy, becoming one of the few Christian albums of the era to achieve gold status. The album's centerpiece song was the fervent "Rise Again," which became one of the biggest Christian radio hits in history. "Rise Again" went on to win a GMA Dove Award in 1978, with Holm winning songwriter and male vocalist of the year awards and Praise selected as mixed group of the year.

In 1980, Dallas Holm and Praise left the Wilkerson ministry and embarked on their own career, with Rick Crawford replacing Adams on bass. Further popular singles followed, including "Tell 'Em Again," "A Broken Heart," "Losing Game," and "Hitting the Road." Holm kept up with the times musically, adding synthesizer and cranking up his guitar a notch. On *Change the World* (Dayspring, 1985), he led Praise through such numbers as "Prayer Warriors," "It's War," and the title track, punching up his tried-and-true gospel message with modern rock dynamics.

Holm continued to record in the following decade, releasing his most recent album, *Before Your Throne,* in 1999. He also remains active as the director of Praise Ministries and participates in the Christian Motorcyclists Association. (Note: Discography is selective.)

For Teens Only (Zondervan, 1971)
Peace, Joy & Love (Impact, 1974)
Dallas Holm & Praise…Live
  (Greentree, 1977)
Tell 'Em Again (Greentree, 1979)
This Is My Song (Greentree, 1980)
Signal (Greentree, 1983)
Change the World (Dayspring, 1985)
Behind the Curtain (Dayspring, 1988)
The Early Works (Benson, 1991)
Face of Mercy (Benson, 1995)
Before Your Throne (Diamante, 1999)

THE INNOCENCE MISSION
Formed 1982 in Lancaster, Pennsylvania

Shimmering in sound and wistful in sentiment, the Innocence Mission has been creating its own version of Christian folk/rock for some 20 years. The group was founded by Karen Peris (vocals, keyboards, acoustic guitar), her future husband Don Peris (guitar), Mike Bitts (bass), and Steve Brown (drums) while all four attended a Catholic high school in Lancaster, Pennsylvania. Venturing into nearby Philadelphia, they became a club favorite and earned praise in the local press. In 1986, they independently released a five-song EP, *Tending the Rose Garden*. Three years later, they made their major label debut with a self-titled album on A&M Records.

At the time, *The Innocence Mission* seemed somewhat derivative of 10,000 Maniacs, with Karen Peris's singing style inviting comparisons to Natalie Merchant. A closer listening to the album's songs reveals some unique elements, however—Karen's lyrics are steeped in mystical Catholicism, while Don's electric guitar work has its own distinctive subtleties. An antique sweetness pervades the songs, hinting at a divine presence even in melancholy moments. Among the highlights is "Medjugorje," inspired by visions of the Virgin Mary seen near a small Bosnian town. An otherworldly spirit is even more evident on *Umbrella* (1991), an album rich with atmospheric sounds and nostalgic imagery. "Every Hour Here," "Evensong," and "Now in This Hush" are haunting meditations on God from a childlike perspective.

The Innocence Mission continued in this vein on 1995's critically praised *Glow*; unfortunately, the demise of A&M halted the band's career upswing. Steve Brown left the group shortly before the 1999

release of *Birds of My Neighborhood*, prompting the remaining members to adopt a stripped-down sound. As a threesome, the group independently released *Christ Is My Hope* (2000), featuring creative reworkings of such timeless hymns as "It Is Well with My Soul" and "O Sacred Head Surrounds." *Small Planes*, a compilation of previously unreleased recordings from the band's archives, appeared in 2001.

The Innocence Mission (A&M, 1989)
Umbrella (A&M, 1991)
Glow (A&M, 1995)
Birds of My Neighborhood (RCA, 1999)
Christ Is My Hope (independent release, 2000)
Small Planes (What Are Records?, 2001)

JARS OF CLAY
Formed 1994 in Greenville, Illinois

Jars of Clay achieved the unlikely feat of scoring a secular hit at the start of its Christian music recording career. The quartet's moodily intelligent brand of folk/rock found a wide audience with its self-titled debut album. Later albums have found the group refining its sound, adding more electric rock to its acoustic base.

Founding members Dan Haseltine (lead vocals), Matt Bronleewe (guitar),

Stephen Mason (bass), and Charlie Lowell (keyboards) assembled Jars of Clay while music students at Greenville College in rural Illinois. Dormitory jam sessions turned serious when a demo of the newly formed group helped them win the Gospel Music Association's Spotlight Competition in 1994. After Bronleewe turned over the guitarist's slot to Matt Odmark, the band relocated to Nashville and secured a record deal with Essential Records. *Jars of Clay,* the group's debut album, was released in 1995. An understated but still compelling work, the album included two tracks produced by King Crimson guitarist Adrian Belew. One of these was "Flood," a plea for God's protection that matched insistent guitar strumming with a chamber music interlude. Released as Jars of Clay's first single, the tune became a Top 40 secular hit as well as a Christian radio favorite. The impact of "Flood" helped boost their first album past the double-platinum sales mark. Further singles from *Jars of Clay*—including "Lovesong for a Savior," "Liquid," and "Blind"—similarly combined acoustic rock with classical shadings.

The group earned a GMA Dove Award for new artist of the year in 1996. Expectations were high for its follow-up album, 1997's *Much Afraid.* Recorded in London, this release featured auxiliary band member Greg Wells on drums and bass. Electric guitars and keyboards are increasingly prominent this time, accenting the more upbeat

Jars of Clay. Left to right: Dan Haseltine, Matt Odmark, Stephen Mason, and Charlie Lowell
Photo by Michael Wilson

lyric mood on many of the songs. The brightly melodic "Overjoyed" and wistfully hopeful "Five Candles" were among the album's Christian radio hits. While *Much Afraid* was not the secular market success that the first one had been, it demonstrated that Jars of Clay was a band of substance with potential to grow further. *Much Afraid* went on to win platinum certification and a Grammy for pop/contemporary gospel album of the year.

Enlisting the aid of producer Dennis Herring (known for his work with Counting Crows and **the Innocence Mission,** among others), Jars of Clay decided to aim their third album at a more secular audience. *If I Left the Zoo* (1999) attempted to present Christian themes in less direct language, reaching out to the spiritually timid in songs like "Famous Last Words" and "Goodbye, Goodnight." Still, there was plenty of explicit praise for the Savior in such tracks as "Unforgettable You," "No One Loves Me Like You," and "River Constantine." Sonically, the band stretched out further, adding touches of British pop and old-fashioned acoustic country. Lowell's piano was given more exposure and Odmark's electric guitar had freer reign. *If I Left the Zoo* was an artistic breakthrough for Jars of Clay, looser in feel and displaying a greater maturity.

After a nearly three-year absence, Jars of Clay returned to record-making with *The Eleventh Hour* in 2002. This self-produced album avoided the eclectic arrangements of their previous CD in favor of straight-ahead folk/rock tunes. "I Need You," its first single, combined a propulsive rhythm with a simple, plaintive message. "Revolution," another strong track, was an aggressive rocker that had the potential to become another secular hit.

In addition to their albums, Jars of Clay released a four-song Christmas EP in 1995, and contributed original songs to the film soundtracks for *Moses: Prince of Egypt* and *Long Kiss Goodnight.* (For more on Matt Odmark, see pages 74–79.)

Jars of Clay (Essential/Silvertone, 1995)
Much Afraid (Essential/Silvertone, 1997)
If I Left the Zoo(Esssential/Silvertone, 1999)
The Eleventh Hour
   (Essential/Silvertone, 2002)

JOY ELECTRIC
Formed 1994
in Orange County, California

Committed Christians and confirmed electronic-pop devotees, Joy Electric is practically a subgenre unto itself. This two-member group composes and performs its music on analog synthesizers, disdaining computer-driven samplers and drum machines. Joy Electric traces its origins back to 1992, when Orange County, California, natives Ronnie and Jason Martin began recording under the name Dance House Children. Jeff Cloud, another local techno-music enthusiast, joined the group a year later. *Rainbow Rider,* Dance House Children's 1993 release, helped secure them a contract with Tooth & Nail Records. After Jason Martin decided to leave the group, the two remaining members carried on as Joy Electric, releasing their debut album, *Melody,* in 1994.

Joy Electric took its inspiration from such secular techno-rock groups as Kraftwerk, Tangerine Dream, and Human League. Martin and Cloud were particularly drawn to the use of Moogs and other early synthesizers. They applied this technology to melodic songs with varying amounts of Christian content. At first, they found little acceptance, and their 1995 EP *Five Stars for Failure* reflected their downbeat mood at the time. Still, they persevered, with Martin building his own synthesizers in hopes of creating a unique sound. "Monosynth," a tribute to their favorite instrument, gained them some notice. The 1997 EP *Old Wives Tales* captured the quirkiness of the group—such tracks as "The Cobbler" and "Marigoldeness" were chirping, chiming ditties built around fantasy lyric motifs. Martin's fey, slightly dreamy vocals had a British tinge to them as he sang over percolating low-tech keyboard beats.

Christiansongs (1999) found Joy Electric singing more assertively about its faith. Such songs as "Children of the Lord" and "Voice of the Young" had a rousing anthem-like quality to them. "I Sing Electric" added a darker mood, while "Lift Up Your Hearts" took a jab at self-absorbed rock artists. The group toured in support of the album, slowly expanding its cult following.

As a side project, Martin established his own independent label, Plastiq Musiqu, in 1998. Its first release was *You Are Obsolete* by synth-pop group House of Wire.

Melody (Tooth & Nail, 1994)
Five Stars for Failure (EP)
　(Tooth & Nail, 1995)
We Are the Music Makers
　(Tooth & Nail, 1996)
Old Wives Tales (EP)
　(Tooth & Nail, 1997)
Robot Rock (BEC, 1997)
The Land of Misfits (EP) (BEC, 1998)
Christiansongs (BEC, 1999)

PHIL KEAGGY
Born March 23, 1951,
in Youngstown, Ohio

One of Christian rock's earliest innovators, Phil Keaggy has continued to make vital, intriguing music into his third decade as a recording artist. Known for his guitar virtuosity and Beatles-influenced melodies, he has earned the respect of peers in both the Christian and secular music realms. Keaggy's music has retained a sweetly innocent quality over the span of his career, remaining true to the spirit of the early Jesus Music period.

Ohio-born Keaggy learned to play guitar as a child despite the loss of his right-hand middle finger in an accident at age four. By his midteens, he was playing and recording with such local groups as the Squires and the New Hudson Exit. In 1968, he formed Glass Harp with bassist Daniel Pecchio and drummer John Sferra, a psychedelic power trio that went on to record three albums for Decca Records. It was during his years with this group that Keaggy experienced a life-changing tragedy. On Valentine's Day, 1970, he emerged from a harrowing LSD trip to learn that his mother had been killed in an automobile accident hundreds of miles away. Her loss devastated him and led him to accept Christianity. This decision changed the course of both his life and his music.

Keaggy began writing Christian songs while still a member of Glass Harp. In August 1972, he quit the band and moved to a Christian fellowship in upstate New York. He made his solo debut two years later with *What a Day* on the independent New Song label. This modest but winning effort showcased Keaggy's high tenor vocals, fluent guitar prowess, and blissful lyric outlook. After a 1973 stint with **Love Song,** he released 1976's *Love Broke Through,* another gracefully tuneful, Beatles-influenced work. Further albums followed on a yearly basis, each displaying Keaggy's increasingly subtle melodic gifts and amazingly versatile instrumental abilities. Folk, blues, jazz, and baroque classical were all present in his unique sonic stew.

Phil Keaggy
Photo by Michael Wilson

The 1980s found Keaggy recording for a series of labels, releasing particularly strong albums on the Myrrh label at the end of the decade. *The Wind and the Wheat* (1987) brought him his first GMA Dove Award for best instrumental album of the year. Shifting gears, he recorded the rock-slanted *Phil Keaggy and Sunday's Child* album (1988) with such Christian music luminaries as **Randy Stonehill, Mark Heard,** and **Rick Cua.** His electric guitar work took on added heft and bite on 1990's *Find Me in These Fields,* with especially ferocious playing heard on "Carry On" and "Strong Tower." Another track from this album, "This Side of Heaven," brought Keaggy one of his biggest Christian radio singles. Besides recording, he toured frequently with Stonehill and other artists during this period.

Many of Keaggy's releases in the '90s were instrumental works, among them the GMA Dove Award–winning *Beyond Nature* (Myrrh, 1991). His 1998 CD *Phil Keaggy* marked his return to the role of singer/songwriter after a three-year absence. Such tracks as "Tender Love" and "A Sign Came Through a Window" showed that his way with a classically tinged pop melody hadn't diminished with time. His ever-eclectic output has continued into the new century. *Inseparable,* a two-disc album featuring Keaggy on all instruments, and *Lights of Madrid,* a largely acoustic jazz/classical instrumental collection, both appeared in 2000. (Note: Discography is selective.)

What a Day (New Song, 1974)

Love Broke Through (New Song, 1976)

Emerging (New Song, 1977)

The Master and the Musician (New Song, 1978)

Ph'lip Side (Sparrow, 1980)

Town to Town (Sparrow, 1981)

Play Through Me (Sparrow, 1982)

Underground (Nissi, 1984)

Way Back Home (Nissi, 1986)

The Wind & the Wheat
(Maranatha/Myrrh, 1987)

Phil Keaggy and Sunday's Child
(Myrrh, 1988)

Find Me in These Fields (Myrrh/Epic, 1990)

Beyond Nature (Myrrh/Epic, 1991)

Crimson & Blue (Myrrh, 1993)

Time: 1970–1995 (Myrrh, 1994)

True Believer (Sparrow, 1996)

Acoustic Sketches (Sparrow, 1997)

Invention (with Keaggy, King, Dante)
(Sparrow, 1997)

Phil Keaggy (Myrrh, 1998)

Inseparable (Canis Major, 2000)

Lights of Madrid (Word Artisan, 2000)

KING'S X
Formed 1980 in Springfield, Missouri

Hailed as "the thinking man's heavy metal band" by *Entertainment Weekly*, King's X has served up melodic hard rock from a Christian perspective for more than two decades. The trio's musical reach has been broad, encompassing 1960s-vintage psyche-delia, classic R&B stylings, and grandiose art-rock touches. Tempering its evangelical message with more conventional romantic themes, the band has managed to appeal to both fellow believers and a substantial number of secular fans.

Lead singer/bassist Doug Pinnick was the driving force behind the group's formation. Born in Joliet, Illinois, in the early 1950s, he was raised by his great-grandmother in a strict Pentecostal environment. He remained close to his religious heritage even as he absorbed musical influences as diverse as Motown and Led Zeppelin. After attending college, he joined a Christian community in Florida and became involved in the local music scene. Moving back to Joliet, he put together his own Christian music combo and helped organize a communal church group called the Shiloh Fellowship. Still restless, Pinnick moved to Springfield, Missouri, where he teamed up with key-boardist Matt Spransy in the progressive rock unit Servant.

When this project had run its course, Pinnick began playing with drummer Jerry Gaskill, a former student at Springfield's Evangel College. The two of them backed up **Phil Keaggy** on a brief tour before forming their own group in 1980. Adding guitarist Ty Tabor, they became the Edge, a New Wave/rock–slanted cover group that spent five years touring the rock-club cir-cuit. In 1985, the band moved to Houston, where it came under the wing of manager Sam Taylor, known for his work with ZZ Top. Recognizing the Edge's potential,

King's X, with lead singer Doug Pinnick (far left)
Photo by Allen Clark

Taylor urged Pinnick to emphasize his R&B leanings as a vocalist. Taylor also suggested that the trio change its name to King's X (a reference to the mark that God puts on His faithful).

The group began to attract notice with its ambitious yet well-honed sound, built around three-part vocal harmonies and unusual rhythm shifts. While forthright in expressing its beliefs, King's X aimed beyond the confines of Christian music from the very beginning. Signing with the secular Megaforce/Atlantic label, it earned a degree of critical praise with its debut album, 1988's *Out of the Silent Planet.* Mixing riff-driven tracks like "Power of Love" with romantic fare such as "Goldilox," the group's sound was very much its own. Lyrically, the songs kept the accent on the positive, though "In a New Age" came down hard on neo-pagan religions.

A year later the group released *Gretchen Goes to Nebraska,* a concept album that combined elements of *Alice in Wonderland, The Wizard of Oz,* and C. S. Lewis's *Chronicles of Narnia.* The songs followed the title character on a spiritual journey with strongly Christian overtones. "Mission" dealt with the relevance of the church in today's world, while "Over My Head" celebrated music as a vehicle for the divine. *Gretchen* may be the band's best effort overall, a compelling interweaving of harsh and delicate sonic textures that took the group far from the limitations of typical hard rock.

In 1990, *Faith Hope Love* brought King's X to a large mainstream audience. The group scored its first hit with the swirling "It's Love"; other worthy songs here include the funk/rock number "We Are Finding Who We Are" and the folk-tinged "I'll Never Get Tired of You." Several cuts offered an unmistakably Christian message—"Legal Kill" and "Mr. Wilson," for instance, were pointed attacks on abortion. While Pinnick remained the band's most recognizable voice, both Gaskill and Tabor sang lead on some *Faith Hope Love* tracks. *King's X* (1992) and *Dogman* (1994) brought further refinements of the band's trademark sound.

After leaving Atlantic Records, King's X resurfaced with *Tape Head* on Metal Blade in 1998. Gradually, the band began to move away from its R&B/rock underpinnings toward a fresher approach. *Manic Moonlight*

(2002) found it experimenting with electronic beats and samples. Despite this somewhat jarring departure, Pinnick's vocal style and the band's strong sense of melodiousness provided a link to earlier efforts.

In addition to recording with King's X, both Pinnick and Tabor have released solo albums.

Out of the Silent Planet
  (Megaforce/Atlantic, 1988)
Gretchen Goes to Nebraska
  (Megaforce/Atlantic, 1989)
Faith Hope Love (Megaforce/Atlantic, 1990)
King's X (Atlantic, 1992)
Dogman (Atlantic, 1994)
Ear Candy (Atlantic, 1996)
Best of King's X (Atlantic, 1997)
Tape Head (Metal Blade, 1998)
Please Come Home...Mr. Bulbous
  (Metal Blade, 2000)
Manic Moonlight (Metal Blade, 2002)

JENNIFER KNAPP
Born April 12, 1974, in Chanute, Kansas

A folk/rock singer/songwriter of unusual ability, Jennifer Knapp ranks among the most promising Christian artists to appear in the mid-1990s. Her first three albums displayed an aggressive yet nuanced vocal style, reminiscent at times of Tracy Chapman or the Indigo Girls' Amy Ray. As a lyricist, Knapp has concentrated on personal confession rather than storytelling, mixing

vivid references to the life of Christ with emotion-charged pleas for grace. Her talents have been recognized by the Christian music community (she won a GMA Dove Award for new artist of the year in 1999) and mainstream pop critics alike. Still in her twenties, Knapp seems likely to gain wider recognition in years to come.

Born in a small Kansas town, Knapp was raised by a divorced father and experienced a difficult childhood. After a somewhat wild adolescence, she became a Christian while studying music education at Pittsburg State University in Pittsburg, Kansas. Her new-found faith spurred her on to become a Christian artist/writer, and she soon won a following by performing at local venues. She received her crucial break when **dc Talk** member Toby McKeehan heard one of her self-released CDs, *Wishing Well*. Recognizing her talents, he signed Knapp to his own independent label, Gotee Records.

Audio Adrenaline front man Mark Stuart produced Knapp's 1997 debut CD, *Kansas*. On the whole, its songs had a funky melodiousness that lent a bit of grit to her diary-like lyric ruminations. Declarations of weakness and humility before God comprise the overriding theme of the album—at times, Knapp's unremitting self-reproach gets excessive. While she may express doubts about her worthiness, though, her vocals are definitely self-assured. *Kansas*'s best tracks include "Undo Me" (a 1999 GMA Dove Award winner for rock song of the year), the reggae-tinged "Romans," and the gently prayerful "Faithful to Me." Knapp helped her career gain momentum by winning a spot on Sarah McLachlan's Lillith Fair concert tour.

Kansas earned gold record status, raising expectations for Knapp's 2000 follow-up, Lay It Down. While not a radical departure from her first album, this effort added more rock and hip-hop influences to her sound. "You Answer Me" and "All Consuming Fire" are particularly intriguing, marrying potent grooves with expressions of Christian devotion and awe of the divine. "Peace," Lay It Down's closing number, displayed her fluent touch on acoustic guitar.

For her third album, 2001's The Way I Am, Knapp worked with producer Tony McAnany (Madonna, Sinead O'Connor) and such noted New York session men as bassist Tony Levin and drummer Vinnie Cauliuta. The result was a distinct creative advance—the songs here are more mature, the production full-bodied and compelling. While as intense in her declarations as ever, Knapp's lyric thrust is more poetic this time, touching on themes like the Crucifixion with a subtler pen. Tunes such as "By and By" and "Say Won't You Say" have the feel of mainstream hits without their messages having been diluted. "Around Me" shows a new jazzy side to her music, while "Light of the World" is tinged with a silky electronica feel. The

Way I Am is a strong bid for mainstream success from an artist only beginning to reach her peak.

Kansas (Gotee, 1997)
Lay It Down (Gotee, 2000)
The Way I Am (Gotee, 2001)

MICHAEL KNOTT
Date and place of birth undisclosed

Southern California–based singer/songwriter Michael Knott has operated on the outskirts of Contemporary Christian music for more than two decades. His torment-filled lyrics and abrasive music have treated Christian themes from the viewpoint of modern society's misfits and losers (although his latest album retells the story of King David). Sonically, Knott's music recalls the manic highs and lows of X and Nirvana; lyrically, his intricate wordplay brings to mind Patti Smith, Jim Carroll, and similar poet/songwriters. Though unknown to most music fans (including Christian ones), Knott has built up a formidable body of work, both as a solo artist and as the leader/instigator of several band projects.

Knott's recording history is convoluted—he has released more than two dozen albums under a variety of names for numerous major and small-time labels. He first gained notice in the early 1980s with the band Lifesavers (initially spelled

"Lifesavors"), a pioneering Christian punk band active mostly on the West Coast. This group mutated into LSU (an acronym for Life Savers Underground), which stirred considerable interest with its 1987 release *Shaded Pain*. Serious in intent and uncompromising in sound, the album depicted the struggle for faith in a brutal world. Knott's ominous vocals and feedback-drenched guitar were harsh by Christian music standards of the day. Though the album was more a critical than a commercial success, Knott persevered, releasing albums with LSU and under his own name at a steady pace into the early 1990s. Some were astringently punk in approach, others more melodic. All of them challenged notions of what a Christian musician could (or should) say. The title track of his 1994 album, *Rocket and a Bomb*, for instance, was a cry of rage and despair addressed to "Mrs. God" (referring to the church as the bride of Christ, apparently).

In 1996, Knott took a stab at reaching a mainstream audience with yet another group, the Aunt Bettys. Signing with the secular EastWest label (an imprint of Elektra Records), the four-member group released a blistering album's worth of tunes that rank among Knott's best work. Addiction, violence, poverty, and predatory love are among the topics here—at times the presence of God seems far away from the ugly scenarios Knott unfolds. Yet there are also tracks such as "Jesus" and "Double" that introduce Christ as a last, desperate hope amidst the failure and madness. Sadly, *Aunt Bettys* didn't win Knott his place in the secular market and he resumed recording for Christian-oriented labels.

Ever the maverick, Knott surprised even his fans with 2001's *Life of David*, a song cycle dealing with the Old Testament figure in a surf-rock setting. The album, an unflinching portrait of the biblical king/poet/warrior's glories and sins, was a worthy addition to Knott's impressive catalog.

SOLO:
Screaming Brittle Siren (Blonde Vinyl, 1992)
Rocket and a Bomb (Brainstorm, 1994)
Strip Cycle (Tooth & Nail, 1995)
Fluid (Alarma, 1995)
The Definitive Collection (KMG, 1998)
Life of David (Metro One, 2001)
WITH LIFESAVERS:
Us Kids (Swing, 1981)
Dream Life (Refuge, 1983)
A Kiss of Life (Frontline, 1986)
Poplife (Blonde Vinyl, 1991)
Huntington Beach (Brainstorm, 1995)
WITH LSU / LIFE SAVERS UNDERGROUND:
Shaded Pain (Frontline, 1987)
This Is the Healing (Blonde Vinyl, 1991)
The Grape Prophet (Blonde Vinyl, 1992)
Cash in Chaos/World Tour (Siren, 1993)
Grace Shaker (Alarma, 1994)
Bring It Down Now (Gray Dot, 1995)
Dogfish Jones (Light/Platinum Christian, 1998)
WITH THE AUNT BETTYS:
Aunt Bettys (EastWest/Elektra, 1996)

THE LOST DOGS
Formed 1992 in Southern California

Launched as a one-time-only affair, the Lost Dogs have continued to record and tour for more than a decade. At the start, the band comprised singer/songwriters Derri Daugherty (**the Choir**), Gene Eugene (**Adam Again**), Mike Roe (**the 77s**), and Terry Taylor (**Daniel Amos**), all of whom had worked together on previous recording or touring projects over the years. In contrast to its members' primary bands, the Lost Dogs have tended to be more casual and acoustic-oriented in approach. While much of their output has had an upbeat country flavor, some songs have had a moodier alternative-rock feel.

Scenic Routes (1992), the Lost Dogs' first album, featured "Breathe Deep (the Breath of God)," a panoramic vision of human unity. The group scored a surprise Christian radio hit in 1993 with "Pray Where You Are"—the tune's rollicking Bob Dylanesque wordplay served to highlight its reverent spirit. The Lost Dogs have continued to intersperse serious spiritual musings with bursts of pure silliness (such as "Bad Indigestion," a graphic ode to the effects of road food) on subsequent albums. Surviving the unexpected passing of Eugene in 2000,the remaining members released *Real Men Cry* as a trio the following year.

Scenic Routes (BAI, 1992)
Little Red Riding Hood (BAI, 1993)
The Green Room Serenade Vol. One (BAI, 1996)
The Best of the Lost Dogs (KMG, 1999)
Gift Horse (BEC, 1999)
Real Men Cry (BEC, 2001)

LOVE SONG
Formed 1970 in Costa Mesa, California

The harmonizing folk/rock quartet Love Song has taken on legendary status since its 1970–74 heyday. Carrying on the tradition of such Southern California icons as the Beach Boys and the Mamas & the Papas, this pioneering group lent its fervently Christian songs a mellow glow, clearing a path for other artists to follow. Cofounder Chuck Girard has continued into the present day as a solo artist.

Of the four, Girard had achieved the most notoriety as a secular musician before joining the group. A native of Santa Rosa, he began his career as a member of the Castells, a singing group best known for its hits "Sacred" (number 20, 1961) and "So This Is Love" (number 21, 1962). From there, he joined the Hondells, which scored a number 9 hit in 1964 with "Little Honda." He began performing Christian music after meeting Jay Truax, then a member of the secular hard-rock group

Spirit of Creation. The two formed a duo in 1967, attempting to sing the praises of the Lord in nightclubs with marginal success. Girard's life changed in earnest when he began attending Calvary Chapel in Costa Mesa, California, a youth-oriented church that became a major outpost of the emerging Jesus Music phenomenon. Truax began coming to the Chapel as well, as did musician friends Tom Coomes and Fred Field. Out of this shared experience came Love Song, featuring Girard on keyboards, Coomes and Field on guitars, and Truax on bass. All four members contributed to the group's soaring vocal harmonies. The band made its recording debut by contributing to the *Everlastin' Living Jesus Music Concert* compilation album released by Maranatha! Music (Calvary Chapel's record label) in 1971.

After a lineup shift replacing Field with Bob Wall on lead guitar, Love Song released its self-titled first album on Good News Records in 1972. This LP captures the joyfully expectant mood of young Jesus movement adherents during the early 1970s. Its soft-rock sound recalls both the carefree spirit of classic surf-pop music and the down-home amiability of Crosby, Stills & Nash. "Little Country Church" celebrates the inclusive spirit of Calvary Chapel, while "Two Hands" extends an invitation for non-believers to take part. Girard's high, light vocals shine throughout, executing some smooth falsetto moves on "Welcome Back." Coombs adds his own jazzy influence

on such tracks as "Let Us Be One." *Love Song* went on to sell 250,000 copies and became popular in such far-flung locales as Wichita, Kansas, and the Philippines— oddly enough, its title track topped the local charts in Manila, leading the band to perform there.

Love Song toured constantly, singing and spreading the gospel at churches, schools, and elsewhere. In 1973, guitarist Wall was replaced by **Phil Keaggy,** who took a detour from his solo career to perform with the group. After more touring on the West Coast, the band released its second Good News album, *Final Touch,* in 1974. After a farewell national tour, the group disbanded. Two years later, they came back together for a one-off reunion tour, documented on the two-disc *Feel the Love* album (1977). In 1995, Girard and Coombs revived Love Song once more, recording updated versions of their classic material for the album *Welcome Back.*

Girard has been the most visible ex-band member, with a debut solo album appearing on Good News in 1975. An extension of the Love Song sound, *Chuck Girard* mixes feisty surf-pop ("Rock'n'Roll Preacher") with moodily reverent ballads ("Everybody Knows for Sure") and solemn traditional-style hymns ("Sometimes Alleluia"). His 1979 single "Take a Hand" was a Christian radio hit. While his songs didn't receive much Christian radio exposure in the 1980s, he continued recording and touring. His 1996 independent album *Voice of the Wind* sought to capture the sound and feel of a live worship service. As the founder of the nonprofit Chuck Girard Ministries, he has sung and evangelized in Europe, Australia, Asia, and South Africa. His daughter, Alisa Girard, is a member of the Christian pop trio **ZOEgirl.**

Love Song (Good News, 1972)
Final Touch (Good News, 1974)
Feel the Love (Good News, 1977)
Welcome Back (Maranatha, 1995)
CHUCK GIRARD SOLO:
Chuck Girard (Good News, 1975)
Glow in the Dark (Good News, 1976)
Written on the Wind (Good News, 1977)
Take It Easy (Good News, 1979)
The Stand (Good News, 1980)
Voice of the Wind (NewPort, 1996)

BARRY MCGUIRE
Born October 15, 1937,
in Oklahoma City, Oklahoma

First and foremost, Barry McGuire is identified with "Eve of Destruction," a folk/rock protest number that topped the Top 40 charts in September 1965. In a strange way, this bitter condemnation of war, racism, and a host of other sins served as a prelude to his later career as a Christian artist. After accepting Christ, McGuire sought to provide a positive alternative to the all-consuming rage expressed in his most famous recording.

McGuire first gained notice as colead singer with the New Christy Minstrels, lending his jovial growl to "Green, Green" (1963) and other hits. Signing with Dunhill Records as a solo artist, he was given "Eve of Destruction" to record along with a batch of other tunes by songwriters P. F. Sloan and Steve Barri. McGuire snarled his way through the song's Bob Dylanesque lyrics, turning a doomsday tirade into an unlikely smash. Unfortunately, further hits were not forthcoming, and by 1970 he was at a low both personally and professionally. A chance encounter with a "Jesus freak" on the streets of Hollywood led to his exploration of the Bible and subsequent conversion. After joining Agape Force, a Christian community in Sanger, California, he rededicated his music to his faith. His first Christian album, *Seeds,* was released by Myrrh Records in 1973. Three years later, he took part in the musical *Firewind,* cowritten by **John Michael Talbot** and also featuring **Keith Green,** and **2nd Chapter of Acts'** Matthew Ward.

McGuire's sound now had a mellower feel than during his secular days. Much of his recording output for Myrrh reflected the contentment he'd found since accepting Christ—the rough edges of his voice were avoided in favor of a smoother delivery. Tunes like "Anyone but Jesus" and "Happy Road" had a country/rock sing-along quality, while "Love Is" and "Callin' Me Home" were meditative ballads. In 1978, he released "Cosmic Cowboy," his most popular song as a Christian artist and one of the biggest Christian singles of the 1970s. A good-humored country/pop tune with string orchestration and disco elements, the song portrayed the Savior as a sky-riding wrangler leading McGuire to a Western-style heaven. (This vision of Christ as a hero on a flying steed is a reoccurring one in Christian music, extending back to **Judee Sill** and, most recently, turning up in **Earthsuit**'s 2001 recording "Whitehorse.")

During the next decade, McGuire delved increasingly into children's music. "Bullfrogs and Butterflies"—a catchy kids' song about personal transformation—became a Christian radio hit in 1980. He continued to record albums aimed at both adults and youngsters and toured in the United States and overseas. He relocated to New Zealand in the mid-1980s.

Eve of Destruction (Dunhill, 1965)
Seeds (Myrrh, 1973)
Lighten Up (Myrrh, 1975)
To the Bride (Myrrh, 1975)
C'mon Along (Sparrow, 1976)
Have You Heard (Sparrow, 1977)
Cosmic Cowboy (Sparrow, 1978)
Inside Out (Sparrow, 1979)
Best of Barry McGuire (Sparrow, 1979)
Barry McGuire as the Polka Dot Bear:
    The Story of Creation (Birdwing, 1980)

Finer than Gold (Sparrow, 1981)
Pilgrim (Live Oak, 1991)

SARAH MASEN
Born December 1, 1975, in Royal Oak, Michigan

Soft voiced and quietly serious, Sarah Masen is among Christian music's harder-to-classify singer/songwriters. Her treatment of Christian themes has avoided blatant evangelism in favor of more subtle treatment of spiritual themes.

Masen was raised in a conservative evangelical home in the Detroit suburbs. She listened almost exclusively to Christian music growing up and began writing songs by her teenage years. She continued to develop as a singer and guitarist while majoring in English at Detroit's William Tyndale College. After performing locally at coffeehouses and other venues, she released an independent album, *The Holding*, in 1995. Coproduced by **the Choir**'s Derri Daugherty, its songs were bittersweet in mood and sparse in sound. Masen's voice conveyed fragility and yearning as she mused about her faith in songs like "Peacefully" and "Dear Friends." Her lyrics seemed like sung diary entries, with doubts and hesitations intact. *The Holding* was at times a tentative work, but one that held promise. (In 1999, the album was reissued by the Tooth & Nail–affiliated BEC label.)

Sarah Masen
Photo by Michael Wilson

"Shine" followed the song up the charts as well. Hoping to reach beyond the Christian market, Masen went on a Borders bookstore tour of Europe in the summer of 1997. Though "All Fall Down" received some secular airplay, Masen remained largely unknown to mainstream fans.

Carry Us Through (1998) reflected her desire for more creative freedom. Produced once again by Peacock, this release was stylistically diverse and lyrically provocative. As with *Sarah Masen*, much of the album dealt with the idea of community from a Christian perspective. Masen told interviewers that she wanted her music to initiate a dialogue about faith, rather than be considered a form of ministry. Some *Carry Us Through* tracks, such as "75 Grains of Sands," received Christian radio airplay, though Masen didn't feel entirely at ease with the criteria set by the Gospel Music Association and other industry gatekeepers as to what constituted a Christian song.

While sorting these matters out, Masen took a sabbatical from recording. In 1997, she gave birth to her first child, Dorothy Day (named for the revered American Catholic social worker and activist). She and her husband, David Dark, studied Christian history and philosophy during this time, which added a broader perspective to her songwriting. In 2000, she began recording with producer John Jennings (known for his work with Mary Chapin Carpenter) on her first album for Word, *The Dreamlife of Angels*. Atmospheric and

This sense of exploration—both artistic and religious—was continued on 1996's *Sarah Masen,* her first nationally distributed release. This album was produced by **Charlie Peacock** for his newly launched re:think label and was intended to reach secular as well as Christian audiences. *Sarah Masen*'s songs were a bit more upbeat than those on *The Holding,* dressed up in folk/ rock textures. "All Fall Down" gave Masen a hit single on the first try—built around a catchy guitar hook, it was one of the quirkier entries on the Christian airwaves in mid-1996. "Downtown" and intentionally ragged in places, this album marked a definite sonic departure. The mood of the songs is often playful and quaint, enhanced by acoustic guitar, organ, and understated drums. "Love Is Breathing," "Midnight," and "She Stumbles through the Door" are among the better tracks on this evocative (if lyrically oblique) song collection.

Unfortunately, *The Dreamlife of Angels* fell victim to a corporate shake-up at Word after its early 2001 release. Christian radio largely passed it by, though the track "Girl on Fire" received some exposure on secular stations. Plans call for Masen to release an acoustic album on her own sometime in 2002.

The Holding (independent release, 1995; BEC, 1999)
Sarah Masen (re:think, 1996)
Carry Us Through (re:think/Sparrow, 1998)
The Dreamlife of Angels (Word, 2001)

RANDY MATTHEWS
Born c. 1950, location unknown

Long-haired singer/songwriter Randy Matthews was among the first wave of Jesus Music troubadours in the early 1970s. His scruffy looks and raggedy country/rock sound were considered daring for the era. Matthews was especially noted for his free-wheeling live act, filled with road stories and personal testimonials to Christ's glory.

The son of a founding member of the Jordanaires (Elvis Presley's backup vocal group), Matthews sang and played in a psychedelic rock group as a teenager. After high school, he joined a gospel quartet called the Revelations, adding a rock influence to its traditional sound. In between tours, he attended Ozark Bible College. After a two-year stint with the Revelations, Matthews enrolled in Cincinnati Bible Seminary, where he began to apply his music toward street ministry. Among his projects was the Jesus House, a weekly gathering place for young Christians. Matthews also played in a group called the Sons of Dust during this time. He began to perform across the country, touring on a shoestring and performing wherever he could find listeners.

In 1970, Matthews signed with Word Records and began recording a solo album. Released the following year, *Wish We'd All Been Ready* was a slickly produced song collection that muted the singer's rock instincts. Matthews let his hair down on his next recording, which was initially rejected by Word as too extreme. He convinced them to launch a subsidiary label to market Christian rock, and so became the first artist signed to Myrrh Records. *All I Am Is What You See* (Myrrh, 1972) turned out to be a grittier-sounding album, toning down the production and allowing the electric guitars more prominence. Matthews's best moments include a pair of acoustic ballads: "Johnny" (a nonpreachy account of accepting Christ) and "Time to Pray" (a caressing ballad that recalls Bread and other soft-rock groups of the time). He celebrated his southern gospel roots in "Country Faith," cutting loose with a deep southern twang.

Son of Dust, released in 1973, was probably his most interesting work, full of energy and bite. Taking arrangement cues from Neil Young's Harvest album, Matthews dressed up his tunes with acoustic piano, banjo, and pedal steel. He took risks on songs like "Brown-Eyed Woman," a swampy track with somewhat elusive lyrics. The key song was "Didn't He," an intense narrative of the Crucifixion sung by Matthews with subdued drama. Son of Dust was an archetypal Jesus Music album, capturing the unkempt zeal of a hippie street revival. Two years later came Now Do You Understand?, a double-disc live album capturing Matthews performing solo. His storytelling abilities and folksy humor are in evidence here, as is his ability to command a crowd with just his voice and acoustic guitar.

Matthews released another album on his own in 1976 (Eyes to the Sky), then formed a short-lived trio with Christian rockers Danny Taylor and Mike Johnson. Taking a break from recording in the late '70s, he resumed with his Randy Matthews album, released by Spirit Records in 1980. Such tracks as "Small Circle of Friends" found him belting out gospel-rooted rock with a passionate Joe Cocker–like rasp. "Ball and Chain" gave him a Christian radio hit in 1982.

Out of step with Contemporary Christian music's increasing sophistication, Matthews remains true to his Jesus Music beginnings, performing for church gatherings in the Southeastern United States. He is said to have a new album in the works.

Wish We'd All Been Ready (Word, 1971)
All I Am Is What You See (Myrrh, 1972)
Son of Dust (Myrrh, 1973)
Now Do You Understand? (Myrrh, 1975)
Eyes to the Sky (Myrrh, 1976)
The Best of Randy Matthews (Myrrh, 1977)
Randy Matthews (Spirit, 1980)
Plugged In (Spirit, 1981)
Streets of Mercy (Spirit, 1987)
The Edge of Flight (Wave, 1990)

JULIE MILLER
Born July 12, 1956, in Waxahachi, Texas

Alternative-country artist Julie Miller writes and sings Christian music with a distinctively dark tinge. Much of her work deals with loneliness, degradation, and suffering, with the healing presence of God seen amid life's torments. After aiming her albums toward the Christian market, Miller began recording for the secular Hightone label and has won increasing mainstream recognition.

Miller (whose maiden name is Julie Griffin) was raised in a troubled Christian home in a small town south of Dallas, Texas. Escaping from her abusive upbringing, she moved to Austin in the early 1970s and began singing with various local country, blues, and rock bands. Still unhappy, she attempted suicide and ended up in a mental institution for several months. A rediscovery of her faith began to turn her life around, as did a romantic relationship with singer/guitarist Buddy Miller. The couple eventually moved to New York together, where their group began to attract record company interest. At the start of the 1980s, Miller walked away from her band and music in general to embrace a more Christ-centered life. Buddy Miller's decision to accept Christianity led to the couple's marriage in 1981. The Millers eventually relocated to Southern California and became part of the country/rock music scene there, with Julie Miller attracting notice for her emotive, childlike voice and confessional songwriting. Signing with Myrrh, she released *Meet Julie Miller* in 1990.

From the start, Miller stood apart from most Contemporary Christian artists. Her tremulous singing conveyed vulnerability rather than spiritual strength and her songs could be disturbingly personal. Still, her lyrics were undeniably faith-based and her folk/pop music was often catchy (if a little left of center). *Meet Julie Miller* achieved exposure through such singles as "How Could You Say No," "What Would Jesus Do?," and "Mystery Love." Her second Myrrh album, *He Walks through Walls* (1991), kept her on the airwaves with the single "Never Gonna Give Up on You."

But Miller was not grooming herself to be a Christian radio hit-maker—if anything, her work grew more introspective and moody as her career progressed. *Orphans and Angels*, released in 1993, had a sparse, almost ghostly sound—such tracks as "All My Tears," "Nobody But You," and "Praise to the Lord, Amen" had the feel of ancient backwoods hymns. There were lighter moments as well, particularly the singles "Angels Dance" and "Put a Little Love in Your Heart" (a cover of the 1969 Jackie DeShannon hit).

Breaking away from the Christian music mainstream, Miller released *Invisible Girl* on Street Level/R.E.X. in 1994. Much of this album deals with sorrow, loss, and redemption in unflinching terms. While it yielded another popular single ("Nobody's Child"), *Invisible Girl* was her last release for a Christian record label. Miller began to gain wider exposure in 1995—Emmylou Harris covered "All My Tears" on her *Wrecking Ball* CD and Miller sang and cowrote songs on husband Buddy's debut album for Hightone, *Your Love and Other Lies*. Hightone signed her as well, releasing her album *Blue Pony* in 1997. Beautiful in its melancholy, the album gives Miller room to sketch out stories of the abused and the unbalanced. "By Way of Sorrow" and "I Call on You" are bittersweet prayers for grace; "Letters to Emily" finds God's presence in the details of life. "The Devil Is an Angel" is a theologically interesting tale of a seductive stranger, sung by Miller with a sense of hard-won knowledge.

Broken Things (1999) was a companion piece to *Blue Pony,* similar in its themes of human frailty and divine mercy. The Millers released their first official album together, *Buddy and Julie Miller,* in 2001; highpoints included "Rachel," Julie's elegy for one of the victims of the Columbine High School massacre.

Meet Julie Miller (Myrrh, 1990)
He Walks through Walls (Myrrh, 1991)
Orphans and Angels (Myrrh, 1993)
Invisible Girl (Street Level/R.E.X., 1994)
Blue Pony (Hightone, 1997)
Broken Things (Hightone, 1999)
WITH BUDDY MILLER:
Buddy and Julie Miller (Hightone, 2001)

MORTIFICATION
Formed 1990 in Australia

Hard music and zealous faith are fused together in Mortification, which rose to the top of the Christian metal heap in the mid-1990s. Since then, the band has continued to record and tour despite leader Steve Rowe's recurring battles with cancer.

Mortification grew out of a late 1980s-era Australian metal combo, Lifeforce. Two of the group's members—bassist Rowe and guitarist Cameron Hall—broke away and joined with drummer Jayson Sherlock to form a heavier-sounding unit in 1990. As lead singer and general mastermind, Rowe infused Mortification with an uncompromising ferocity lyrically and musically. Those with a taste for harsh, hard rock found the band's gory imagery and lacerating sound pleasingly brutal. The trio's songs consistently drove home the message of Christ's power and Satan's eventual defeat. *Break the Curse,* the group's 1990 debut album, threw down the gauntlet to the devil with tracks like "New Beginnings" and "Blood Sacrifice."

Replacing Hall with Michael Carlisle on guitar, Mortification adopted a punk-meets-metal grind-core sound on its 1991 self-titled album (the first to be released in the United States). Rowe's raw-throated vocals delivered fire-and-brimstone sermons as his group churned and seethed behind him. Sounding like a feverish Old Testament prophet, he railed against sin in "The Destroyer Beholds," "Satan's Doom," and similar cuts. *Scrolls of the Megilloth* (1992) plunged the listener into a nightmarish landscape of tormented humanity, drawing upon Scripture for the jagged imagery of its title track. For all his fondness for horrific word-pictures, songwriter Rowe rarely lost sight of his mission to glorify the Savior. The concept of Christ's unbreakable blood covenant with mankind became his particular focus.

By the time *Primitive Rhythm Machine* was released in 1995, Mortification's lineup consisted of Rowe, guitarist Lincoln Bowen, and drummer Keith Bannister. Among the most extreme releases in the band's catalog (which is saying a great deal), *Primitive Rhythm Machine* decried drug abuse ("Toxic Shock"), condemned the world's violence ("Seen It All"), and offered hope in Christ's resurrection ("Providence"). Following the release of a "best of" compilation, the group began releasing its works on Rowe's own label. A hectic international touring schedule took the group to such far-flung spots as Brazil, Norway, and South Africa, performing to Christian and secular fans alike. Signing a licensing deal with Metal Blade Records in the United States, the band gained access to the mainstream rock market for its 1999 release *Hammer of God*. During the late '90s, Rowe also released projects by other bands from Australia and elsewhere via Rowe Records.

Casting a shadow over such breakthroughs was Rowe's struggle to beat cancer. Diagnosed with leukemia in 1996, he survived against long odds and continued to tour and record. He kept up a grueling pace even after his disease returned, heroically performing across America in 2001 while gravely ill. The band's future seemed in doubt at the start of 2002.

Break the Curse (Nuclear Blast, 1990)
Mortification (Intense, 1991)
Scrolls of the Megilloth (Intense, 1992)
Post Momentary Affliction (Intense, 1993)
Live Planetarium (Intense, 1993)
Bloodworld (Intense, 1994)
Primitive Rhythm Machine (Intense, 1995)
The Best of… Five Years (Intense, 1995)
Envision Evangeline (Rowe, 1996)
Triumph of Mercy (Rowe, 1998)
Hammer of God (Rowe/Metal Blade, 1999)

NICOLE C. MULLEN
Born 1967 in Cincinnati, Ohio

One of 2000's most impressive comebacks was that of singer/songwriter Nicole C. Mullen, largely absent from the Christian radio airwaves since the early 1990s. Her self-titled album for Word combined hip-hop grooves with early 1970s-style funk and acoustic guitar accents. Mullen's streetwise yet spiritual lyrics and elegantly nuanced vocals placed her in a class with Lauryn Hill, Des'ree, and other modern R&B divas.

A native of Cininnati, Mullen (born Nicole Coleman) began singing in church choirs at a young age. Moving to Dallas in 1984, she signed her first recording contract with Frontline Records while still a Bible-college student. During this same period she met (and later married) singer/songwriter David Mullen and began working as a backup singer/choreographer for **Amy Grant** and **the Newsboys,** among others. She was also active as a studio singer, recording with such artists as **Kim Boyce** and Tim Minor.

In the early 1990s, Mullen released a number of Top Ten Christian radio singles on Frontline, including "Don't Let Me Go," "Wish Me Love," "Show Me," and "Miracles." Together with her husband, she cowrote a number of Christian hits, including **Jaci Velasquez**'s "On My Knees," which won a GMA Dove Award for song of the year in 1998. She branched out into animation work by contributing the voice of Serena the Cat to the Dove Award–winning children's video *Yo! Kids* and singing the "Larry Boy Theme Song" for the popular *VeggieTales* series.

Mullen's reemergence as a Christian pop/R&B artist showed that her talents had only deepened with time. Her *Nicole C. Mullen* album (2000) featured well-crafted, engagingly personal songs that dealt with themes of gang violence ("Granny's Angel"), interracial unity ("Black, White, Tan"), and urban poverty ("Blowin' Kisses"). Such tunes as "Butterfly" and "Homemade" were bittersweet depictions of her childhood. Her mix of southern roots music and a positive Christian message recalled the Staple Singers and other classic gospel groups. One track, "Redeemer," was a soaring ode to the Creator that had the makings of a worship music standard. It topped the Christian singles charts and went on to win a GMA Dove Award for 2000 song of the year; Mullens won a Dove for songwriter of the year as well.

After the album's release, Mullen participated in the 2000 Billy Graham Crusade and other Christian events. She has also taken part in the Kids Across America summer camp, an outreach mentoring program for inner-city youth. In 2001, she released her much-anticipated second album for Word, *Talk About It.*

Nicole C. Mullen (Word, 2000)
Talk About It (Word, 2001)

RICH MULLINS
Born October 21, 1955, in Richmond, Indiana; died September 19, 1997, in LaSalle County, Illinois

Singer/songwriter Rich Mullins was a revered figure in Contemporary Christian music even prior to his untimely death in 1997. His work combined a wide-eyed fervor with considerable technical skills as a composer and lyricist. Mullins won the admiration of his peers for his humility and selflessness as much as for his talents. He remains an exemplary model of a Christian artist living the principles of his faith.

Born and raised in rural Indiana, Mullins attended Cincinnati Bible College before joining Zion Ministries. In 1981, Zion released an album of Mullins's songs, *Behold This Man*. One of its tunes, "Sing Your Praise to the Lord," was discovered by **Amy Grant,** who turned it into a chart-topping Christian radio hit in 1982. This led Mullins to sign a song publishing deal and, after a stint as a music minister in Grand Rapids,

Rich Mullins
Photo by Michael Wilson

Michigan, to become a Reunion Records recording artist. His self-titled first album established him as a rising Christian artist, yielding such singles as "A Few Good Men" and "Verge of a Miracle." His 1988 single "Awesome God" became a worship music classic—powerful in its simple message, it rode a haunting, timeless melody.

By the release of his 1989 album *Never Picture Perfect*, Mullins had fully established himself as an insightful interpreter of Scripture. Less scholarly in approach than an artist like **Michael Card,** his songs often restated biblical verities in fresh, highly personal ways. *Never Picture Perfect*'s "My One Thing" and "While the Nations Rage" had a compelling vulnerability to them, underscored by the rough edges in Mullins's voice.

Mullins combined his music career with a commitment to charitable works. In 1989, he founded the Kid Brothers of St. Frank, a religious order inspired by St. Francis of Assisi. After earning a degree in music education from Friends University in Wichita, Kansas, in 1995, he moved to the Navajo reservation in northeastern Arizona and served as a music teacher. His acts of service and humble lifestyle stood in contrast to the rarified glamour increasingly associated with the Christian music industry.

Fans grew to value Mullins's authenticity as a songwriter. He became a master at unreeling long, vivid lyric lines, at times reminiscent of 1970s-era Bruce Springsteen or Jackson Browne. This Walt Whitmanesque invocation of the holy amidst the ordinary was displayed on 1993's *A Liturgy, a Legacy & a Ragamuffin Band.* (The last phrase in the title was inspired by Christian author Brennan Manning's *Ragamuffin Gospel*, an inspirational work aimed at hard-pressed, less-than-perfect believers.) This album features both beautifully rendered praise songs ("The Color Green") and character sketches of Christian common folk ("Hard," "I'll Carry On"). Perhaps Mullins's most satisfying work, *A Liturgy* expresses a fundamentalist Christian's vision of American tradition with poetic eloquence and an open heart.

By the mid-'90s, Mullins was touring with the Ragamuffin Band, a rock-oriented combo that added muscle to his stage sound. Signing with Myrrh Records, he spent much of 1997 writing songs and rehearsing with his group for his next album. Before recording could begin, however, Mullins was killed in a traffic accident near Peoria, Illinois. The Ragamuffin Band decided to complete the projected album, ultimately released by Myrrh as *The Jesus Record*. This two-CD release featured a host of artists—including Amy Grant, **Michael W. Smith,** and **Ashley Cleveland**—interpreting Mullins's final songs, as well as rough recordings the singer/songwriter had made of his tunes shortly before his death. While only partially a true Mullins album, *The Jesus Record* stands as a moving closing state-ment from one of Contemporary Christian music's most-loved artists. "My Deliverer" (sung by Ragamuffin Band member Rick Elias) went on to win a GMA Dove Award for song of the year in 1999.

Rich Mullins (Reunion, 1986)

Pictures in the Sky (Reunion, 1987)

Winds of Heaven, Stuff of Earth (Reunion, 1988)

Never Picture Perfect (Reunion, 1989)

The World as I Best Remember It, Vol. 1 (Reunion, 1991)

The World As I Best Remember It, Vol. 2 (Reunion, 1992)

A Liturgy, a Legacy & a Ragamuffin Band (Reunion, 1993)

Collection of Songs (Reunion, 1996)

The Jesus Record (Myrrh, 1998)

MxPx
Formed 1992 in Bremerton, Washington

Punk/pop trio MxPx has managed to break into the upper ranks of the secular music world without forsaking its Christian beginnings. Its joyful brand of melodic thrash recalls the Descendents, Black Flag, and other legends of the 1980s Southern California punk scene. The band's faith shows in its positive lyric outlook, shorn of the nihilism associated with hard-core punk. Recent albums have found its sound maturing and drawing upon more diverse influences.

Founding members Mike Herrera (vocals, bass) and Yuri Ruley (drums) first came together as 15-year-olds while attending Central Kitsap High School in Bremerton, Washington. The band's original name was Magnified Plaid, which was shortened to MxPx after guitarist Tom Wisniewski joined the band. Admittedly crude at first, the band won fans through its brash energy and optimistic attitude. Independent Christian label Tooth & Nail signed the three and released their debut album, *Pokinatcha,* in 1994. Touring to promote the release, MxPx mostly played for fellow young Christians at church-sponsored events. From the start, though, the group avoided evangelizing in favor of writing songs from its own teenaged point of view—which happened to be Christian.

The band's cheerful ferocity quickly found an audience, particularly in

Southern California. Further releases, including *Teenage Politics* and *On the Cover* (both 1995, the latter featuring covers of classic and obscure rock tunes), found its skill levels increasing. In 1996, MxPx had the honor of sharing the stage with the Sex Pistols at Seattle's Bumbershoot festival. That same year saw the release of *Life in General*, which expanded the group's fan base still further. *Life in General* is a double-time travelogue through the life of a Christian punk rocker—Herrera sings about the trials of decent, God-fearing teens in tunes like "Do Your Feet Hurt" and "The Wonder Years." Even funny stuff like the mock-rockabilly "Chick Magnet" (an MTV video hit) has a wholesome ring to it. The band's family-friendly values seem to reinforce rather than undermine the hyperactive earnestness of its pop/punk sound.

MxPx remained connected with fellow believers, performing at Cornerstone, TomFest, and similar events and racking up much of its record sales at Christian bookstores. At the same time, the band reached out to secular fans by playing nightclubs and appearing on the 1998 Warped tour with bands like Rancid and the Deftones. A&M Records saw the group's potential and signed it for the secular market. *Slowly Going the Way of the Buffalo*, the band's 1998 A&M debut, won it a mainstream hit single with "I'm OK, You're OK" and went on to reach gold certification. Two years later

came *The Ever Passing Moment*, a pop/rock effort that recalled Elvis Costello's early work in its use of keyboards, waltz-time melodies, and other touches. The album's single "Responsibility" found the band's brash-but-thoughtful attitude still intact.

Pokinatcha (Tooth & Nail, 1994)
Teenage Politics (Tooth & Nail, 1995)
On the Cover (EP) (Tooth & Nail, 1995)
Life in General (Tooth & Nail, 1996)
Move to Bremerton (Tooth & Nail, 1996)
Slowly Going the Way of the Buffalo
    (A&M/Tooth & Nail, 1998)
Let It Happen (Tooth & Nail, 1998)
At the Show (Rock City/Tooth & Nail, 1999)
The Ever Passing Moment (A&M-
    Interscope/Tooth & Nail, 2000)
The Renaissance (EP) (Fat Wreck
    Chords/Caroline, 2001)

THE NEWSBOYS
Formed 1986
in Mooloolaba, Australia

Playful and prayerful, the Newsboys have ranked among the top Christian rock bands since the mid-1990s. This Australian combo serves up tasty pastiches of pop music styles from the past three decades, laced generously with gospel content. Weathering the loss of their lead singer in 1997, they've continued with consistent success as both a recording and touring entity.

The Newsboys came together in Mooloolaba (on Australia's North Coast) in 1986. Members Peter Furler (drums/vocals), John James (vocals), Sean Taylor (bass), and Phil Yates (guitar) were an eager but struggling group when they hooked up with manager Wes Campbell, who helped shape them and build up a base of support among local Christian churches and youth groups. At the same time, the band began playing Australian secular venues, touring the rowdy club and pub circuit. In 1987, they came to the United States and barely scraped by on a shoestring budget. Their break came when they talked their way into an unscheduled spot at Atlantafest, an important Christian music festival. Their well-received set helped lead to a contract with Refuge Records.

Read All About It, the Newsboys' debut album, was released by Refuge in 1988. The band replaced Yates with Jonathan Genge on guitar, signed with Star Song, and released 1990's *Hell Is for Wimps.* Two singles on the album—"All I Can See" and "Simple Men"—earned Christian airplay. More changes followed: Genge left, guitarist Vernon Bishop joined, and keyboardist Cory Pryor was added. This lineup recorded *Boyz Will Be Boyz* (1991), which yielded two more Christian hits,

"One Heart" and "Stay with Me." It was Bishop's turn to exit next—Furler and James took over guitar duties for 1992's *Not Ashamed,* which proved a major turning point. The album's title track—cowritten with **Steve Taylor,** the album's producer—was an upbeat expression of Christian self-esteem that became a major hit. "Where You Belong/Turn Your Eyes on Jesus" and "Upon This Rock" also did well as singles. Sonically, *Not Ashamed* melded 1960s and '70s-era pop styles together with humor and a hint of irony. The band's zany-but-wholesome image fully emerged here, satirizing American kitsch-culture while simultaneously testifying about Jesus.

After *Not Ashamed,* the roster shifted once again—Jeff Frankenstein replaced Pryor, Jody Davis became the new guitarist, and Duncan Phillips signed up as percussionist. This lineup went into the studio with Steve Taylor to make 1994's *Going Public.* The key track on the album was "Shine," a rollicking tune that advocated embodying Christian faith rather than merely preaching it. A sunny summation of what the Newsboys stood for, "Shine" went on to become a huge radio single and win a GMA Dove Award for rock recorded song of the year. "Spirit Thing," similar to "Shine" in message, and "Truth and Consequences," a sassy sermon about dating ethics, extended their hit streak. *Going Public* earned them their first gold record and won a Dove as 1995's rock album of the Year. Phillip Joel took over the bassist's slot at this point.

Take Me to Your Leader (1996) was a third Newsboys/Taylor collaboration, packed with more cheeky, good-natured tunes. The title number laid deft wordplay on top of a catchy track, while "Reality" rode on a shimmering pop groove. Pushing at the boundaries of goofiness was "Breakfast," a jivey farewell to a deceased friend that name-checked Captain Crunch as well as God. All of these tracks (as well as three others) rose to the upper reaches of the Christian singles charts, helping *Take Me to Your Leader* reach the gold-level sales mark.

In 1997, the band broke Christian concert attendance records when it played to a crowd of 30,000 in Houston. It also saw the departure of lead singer James; he was replaced by Furler, who turned over drumming duties to Phillips. The Newsboys' next release, 1998's *Step Up to the Microphone,* evidenced some retooling in their sound. Produced by Furler, the album reflected more of a hip-hop and '90s alternative-rock influence. The lyrics— mostly written by band members—were more straightforward than Taylor's had been. Furler's vocals lent an Aussie-accented edge to tracks like "WooHoo" and the title song, two "Shine"-like anthems that became hit singles. "Entertaining Angels," a semi-spacey praise message awash in electric guitar, seemed to have secular hit potential, though its success was confined to Christian radio.

The R&B quotient was increased on *Love Liberty Disco* (1999), again produced by Furler. There's less satire and more serenity in the lyrics here, complemented by percolating beats and sweet string backdrops. "Say You Need Love" and "Beautiful Sound" are as cheerful as their titles indicate. "Good Stuff" stirs up some funk/rock energy, while "Fall on You" has a slightly eerie electronica mood. Overall, the album is easy to like, even if certain tracks are overly frothy. The Newsboys toured in support of *Love Liberty Disco* in the spring of 2000, performing inside an inflatable "air dome" they carried with them from city to city.

Shine: The Hits, a "best of" compilation, appeared in 2000. The Newsboys were back in 2002 with *Thrive,* scoring a hit with the album's first single, "It Is You." (For more about the Newsboys, see pages 80–83.)

Read All About It (Refuge, 1988)
Hell is for Wimps (Star Song, 1990)
Boyz Will Be Boyz (Star Song, 1991)
Not Ashamed (Star Song, 1992)
Going Public (Star Song, 1994)
Take Me to Your Leader
    (Star Song/Virgin, 1996)
Step Up to the Microphone
    (Star Song/Virgin, 1998)
Love Liberty Disco (Sparrow, 1999)
Shine: The Hits (Sparrow, 2000)
Thrive (Sparrow, 2002)

NICHOLE NORDEMAN
Born January 3, 1972,
in Victorville, California

Introspective singer/songwriter Nichole Nordeman scored a noteworthy debut with her 1998 album *Wide Eyed.* Its piano-based tracks and questioning spirit invited comparisons with the work of secular songstress Sarah McLachlan. Vocally, the two artists share a keening upper range and dusky lower tones. But whatever the similarities, Nordeman's lyric perspective is definitely her own, rooted deeply in her Christian faith.

Born in the desert town of Victorville, California, Nordeman spent her later childhood years in Colorado. Moving to Los Angeles, she supported herself as a waitress while honing her singing and composing talents. Her fortunes changed after she entered a songwriting contest sponsored by the Gospel Music Association. She placed first with her composition "Why," a well-crafted account of the Crucifixion from the viewpoint of a child. Not long after, she secured a recording deal with Sparrow and, in 1998, released her first album, *Wide Eyed.* Christian radio embraced her music, with its Adult Contemporary–formatted stations giving "To Know You," "Who You Are," and "I Wish the Same" considerable airplay.

This Mystery, her 2000 follow-up release, found Nordeman expanding her sonic palette. Its tracks had more of an R&B influence, underscored by her cover of the Stevie Wonder tune "As." Such original songs as "Tremble," "Help Me Believe," and the title track emphasized the awesome, humbling presence of God. In "Every Season," she reaffirmed her faith as she comes to terms with a friend's passing. *This Mystery* received warm reviews in both the Christian and secular press and helped Nordeman win a GMA Dove Award for female vocalist of the year in 2001.

Wide Eyed (Sparrow, 1998)
This Mystery (Sparrow, 2000)

LARRY NORMAN
Born April 8, 1947,
in Corpus Christi, Texas

It's hardly an exaggeration to say that Larry Norman is Contemporary Christian music's founding father. His stature compares with that of Bob Dylan and John Lennon in the secular rock realm. In the late 1960s, he demonstrated that rock'n'roll and evangelism could mix and produce something artistically valid—a highly debatable proposition at the time. Besides writing and recording some of the genre's seminal songs, he has been important in launching the careers of other Christian artists. Despite suffering health problems in recent years, Norman has remained a stubbornly independent voice outside of Christian music's corporate confines.

Norman was born in Corpus Christi, Texas, and moved to San Francisco with his family three years later. As a fourth grader in 1956, he fell in love with Elvis Presley's music and was inspired to write and perform his own songs. He preached the gospel with his music, following in the footsteps of his father, who witnessed for Jesus in prisons and on street corners. Norman's musical talents earned him an appearance on the *Ted Mack Original Amateur Hour* in 1959. Rather than become an entertainer, though, he dreamed of reaching young people outside the church with culturally relevant Christian songs.

Moving to San Jose, he formed the rock sextet People with guitarist Geoff Levin. The group signed with Capitol Records and scored a number 14 pop hit with "I Love You" in 1968. Norman ran into problems with the label, however, when he pushed to have a picture of Christ on the cover of his band's album *We Need a Whole Lot More of Jesus and a Lot Less Rock and Roll*. When Capitol refused, Norman quit People and went solo. In 1969, Capitol released his *Upon This Rock* LP, considered by many to be the first Contemporary Christian music album.

More than 30 years later, *Upon This Rock* still conveys the blend of reverence and rebellion that uniquely pervades Norman's work. In some ways, the album is a snapshot of a time when more than a few Christians believed that Judgment Day was imminent. Norman expressed this view in

Larry Norman (on left), with brother Charles
Photo courtesy of Larry Norman

his classic "I Wish We'd All Been Ready," an exquisitely written, intentionally scary glimpse of the coming apocalypse. But he could also have fun with the idea of a mortal faced with God's presence—"Moses in the Wilderness" retold a Bible story in comical hipster lingo, while "Ha Ha World" was a wry song-skit set to a churning folk/rock groove. Norman dressed up some tunes in orchestral arrangements and presented others as bare-bones acoustic numbers. There are dark piano ballads and sunny gospel/pop numbers. *Upon This Rock* is both an aggressively evangelical document and a collection of funny, dramatic, highly entertaining pop/rock songs. Norman's idiosyncratic personality—at times kooky, at others commanding—binds it all together.

As a live performer, Norman was confrontational, a gadfly stinging the lazily pious. His stage presence—long blonde hair framing an unsmiling face, black shirt and jeans, brown saddle shoes—didn't conform to the image of the happy guitar-strumming singer for Jesus. In between songs, he would criticize the church for its moral slackness and lack of commitment to the poor and needy. All of this made it difficult to get bookings at Christian coffeehouses and other venues at times. But Norman began to find an audience among young believers, the vanguard of the "Jesus movement" that would gather force in the early 1970s.

Leaving Capitol, Norman started his own record company, One Way, with financial help from Pat Boone. A pair of live albums, *Street Level* and *Bootleg*, appeared by the end of 1969. He continued to tour, often in tandem with protege **Randy Stonehill.** Norman's growing notoriety attracted the interest of MGM, who signed him to its Verve subsidiary. In 1972, he released what became his best-known work, *Only Visiting This Planet.* Recorded at London's Air Studios with arrangement help from the legendary George Martin, this album is more sonically polished and thematically diverse than *Upon This Rock.* There are some gentle folk pieces here, including "The Outlaw," an account of Christ's life, and "Pardon Me," one of the album's two love songs. Much of the album, though, is given over to rocked-up Christian commentaries and protest songs. Songs like "I Am the Six O'Clock News" and "The Great American Novel" tear into racism and hypocrisy, while "Why Don't You Look into Jesus" warns against self-destructive behavior in blunt language ("you got gonorrhea on Valentine's Day/and you're still looking for the perfect lay...")." On the upbeat side is "Why Should the Devil Have All the Good Music," Norman's rockabilly-style personal anthem. A rerecorded "I Wish We'd All Been Ready" is included as well. *Only Visiting This Planet* ranks among the most enduring Christian rock albums ever released by virtue of its technical excellence, articulate moral fervor, and sly sense of the absurd.

Whatever shot Norman had at secular success was bungled when MGM interfered with his song choices for his next album, 1973's *So Long Ago the Garden.* The label apparently vetoed several Christian songs in favor of poppy love tunes like "Fly, Fly, Fly," the LP's opening track. Though the album lacks the cohesiveness of his earlier releases, there are some memorable tracks here, especially the ominous "Be Careful What You Sign" (a retelling of *Faust*) and "Nightmare #71," a bluesy Bob Dylanesque epoch of world destruction complete with the sinking of California and the resurrection of Harpo Marx. Whatever its merits, *So Long Ago the Garden* soured Norman on MGM, and he left to launch another label, Solid Rock. He was back in 1976 with *In Another*

Land, a return to the tightly focused Jesus Music of *Upon This Rock.* Some of his best songs are found here, including "Six Sixty Six," a glimpse of the Antichrist; "I Am a Servant," a testimonial of faith set to a gorgeous melody; and "Hymn to the Last Generation," a grand pop/rock aria. Norman tackles everything from southern rock ("Shot Down") to 1920s-style theater music ("The Sun Began to Rain") and acquits himself nicely—all the while paying homage to the Savior. Norman capped off the '70s by performing for President Jimmy Carter at the White House.

Solid Rock developed into a haven for other noteworthy Christian artists, releasing albums by Randy Stonehill, **Mark Heard,** and **Daniel Amos,** among others. Norman steered an increasingly independent course as Christian music became more corporate in the late '70s. His music—and his personality—didn't seem to fit in with the formulas that began to dominate the genre. In 1980, he formed yet another record label, Phydeaux (named for his dog), through which he released such albums as *Something New Under the Son,* a collection of raw blues/rock tracks of less explicit Christian content. A series of live albums, including *The Israel Tapes, Come as a Child* and *Stop This Flight,* appeared in the early and mid-1980s. Touring took him to Europe, Australia, and beyond. He even scored a rare Christian radio hit in 1989 with "Somewhere Out There."

In 1990, Norman suffered a serious heart attack. Though health limitations forced him to cut back on touring, he continued to release new studio and live recordings independently throughout the '90s. *Copper Wires* (1998) was an enjoyably retro-folk/rock album that included a remake of People's "I Love You" and a twangy version of the hymn "I Am a Pilgrim." *The Vineyard,* a two-CD 1999 release, caught the intimacy of his solo acoustic shows particularly well. Despite continued heart problems, he released another studio album, *Tourniquet,* in 2001. Among its tracks was a new version of "Feed the Poor," a call to social action that reaffirms his Christian idealism.

Norman's songs have been recorded by an amazingly disparate list of artists, from Sammy Davis, Jr. to post-punk rocker Frank Black. In 1995, ForeFront Records released the tribute album *One Way: The Songs of Larry Norman.* Until recently, though, Norman's early recordings had been out of print for years. Solid Rock began to remedy this in the late '90s by reissuing *Upon This Rock, Only Visiting This Planet, In Another Land,* and other essential albums on CD. (Note: Discography is selective.)

Upon This Rock (Capitol, 1969)
Street Level (One Way, 1969)
Bootleg (One Way, 1969)
Only Visiting This Planet (MGM/Verve, 1972)
So Long Ago the Garden (MGM/Verve, 1973)

In Another Land (Solid Rock, 1976)

Streams of White Light into Darkened Corners
(AB, 1977)

Roll Away the Stone (Phydeaux, 1980)

The Israel Tapes (Phydeaux, 1980)

Something New Under the Son
(Phydeaux, 1980)

Come as a Child (Phydeaux, 1983)

Quiet Night (Stress, 1983)

Stop This Flight (Six Blue Lions, 1984)

Archaeology (Phydeaux, 1986)

Rehearsal for Reality (Royal, 1986)

Down Under (Royal, 1986)

Home at Last (Solid Rock/Benson, 1989)

The Best of Larry Norman (Royal/Word, 1990)

Stranded in Babylon (Solid Rock/Sonrise, 1994)

Omega Europe (Street Level, 1994)

Totally Unplugged (Street Level, 1994)

Children of Sorrow (Street Level, 1994)

A Moment in Time (Street Level, 1994)

Copper Wires (Solid Rock, 1998)

The Vineyard (Solid Rock, 1999)

Blarney Stone (Solid Rock, 2000)

Tourniquet (Solid Rock, 2001)

OUT OF EDEN
Formed 1992 in Nashville, Tennessee

R&B/urban trio Out of Eden's silken sound has earned it popularity in both the Christian and secular music realms. Often compared with mainstream all-female groups like EnVogue and TLC, members Lisa Kimmey Bragg, Andrea Kimmey Baca, and Danielle Kimmey match smooth-flowing grooves with uplifting spiritual content.

Hailing originally from Richmond, Virginia, the Kimmey sisters began performing early in childhood. Their mother, singer/musician DeLice Hall, used to feature them as the opening act in her concerts. (Hall now serves as a music instructor at Nashville's Fisk University.) Ministry was also part of their heritage—several of their ancestors were ministers and bishops in the African Methodist Episcopal Church. Lisa, Andrea, and Danielle were known to practice sermons in shopping malls. Combining preaching and singing came easily, and the sisters became serious about a Christian music career in their teens. After moving to Nashville with their mother in 1992, they adopted the name Out of Eden and began recording demos, one of which found its way to Toby McKeehan of **dc Talk.** McKeehan signed the trio to his newly created Gotee Records label, which released their debut album *Lovin' the Day* in 1994.

Lovin' the Day was released at a time when few African-American artists recorded for the Contemporary Christian market. Typically, music with a spiritual content by black performers was considered "black gospel," a distinct and separate category. Out of Eden sought to break through these barriers with a hip, high-gloss sound very much in keeping with 1990s mainstream pop trends. The sisters succeeded in gaining Christian radio airplay with such *Lovin' the Day* singles as "Lovely Day" and "Good Thing." At the start, the trio combined beguiling vocal harmonies and soul-searching lyrics with enticing hip-hop rhythms. This combination began to win fans outside of Christian music after the release of their second CD, 1996's *More than You Know.* The tune "Greater Love" received exposure on Black Entertainment Television, while the album's title track was included on the soundtrack to the film *Dr. Doolittle.* A 1996 appearance on the UPN show *Moesha* brought them to an even wider audience.

Tours with dc Talk and secular artist Monica, as well as appearances with the Billy Graham Crusade, won Out of Eden further fans. The group headed in a more pop direction with 1999's *No Turning Back,* an appealing mixture of programmed and acoustic sounds. The album's songs— all cowritten and/or coproduced by Lisa Kimmey—offer encouragement to the down-hearted and misguided. Tracks like "Here's My Heart" and "Open Up Your Heart" express the Savior's love for humankind in romantic language. "Sarah Jane," the album's closing number, asks for compassion for children gone wrong. Beyond the lyric content, the caressing vocal textures of the Kimmeys convey a healing quality. Their sincerity and unforced sweetness make *No Turning Back* easy to like.

Out of Eden's fourth album, *This Is Your Life,* was released in early 2002.

Lovin' the Day (Gotee, 1994)
More than You Know (Gotee, 1996)
No Turning Back (Gotee, 1999)
This Is Your Life (Gotee, 2002)

OUT OF THE GREY
Formed 1990 in Nashville, Tennessee

One of the most consistent Christian hit-makers of the 1990s, Out of the Grey built its sound around Christine Dente's honeyed vocals and husband Scott Dente's crisp, clean guitar work. This Nashville-based duo presented itself as a modern Christian married couple, dealing with life's stresses and disappointments from a faith-centered standpoint. The group kept a low profile following a long string of popular singles, then returned with a new album in late 2001.

The Dentes met in 1985 while both were attending Boston's Berklee School of Music. They married two years later and relocated to Nashville by the end of the decade. Adopting the name Out of the Grey, they signed with Sparrow Records and began working with producer **Charlie Peacock.** From the start, the duo's song-writing showed a feel for combining con-trasting parts into a pleasing whole. "Wishes," from their 1991 self-titled debut album, is a case in point—the angular, nervous rhythms in the verses flow into a melodic chorus, with Christine Dente's supple voice making the shift easily. Peacock contributed significantly to the band's sound, cowriting many of its tunes and bringing a sophistication to its band arrangements.

Out of the Grey toured with **Steven Curtis Chapman** in 1991 and enjoyed a high profile on Christian radio the following year. *The Shape of Grace*, released in 1992, contained two of the duo's biggest hits, the catchy R&B/pop number "Nothing's Gonna Keep Me from You" and the percolating pop tune "Steady Me." The band's hits became smoother over time, losing some of the edginess of the first album. "All We Need" (from 1994's *Diamond Days*) was a serene celebration of God sung with blissful assurance by Christine. The pair's technical fluency veered into excessive perfection at times. Their most distinctive songs touched upon family relationships. "So We Never Got to Paris" (found on their 1995 album *Gravity*) dealt with the joys and regrets of married life with clear-eyed maturity. Parting company with Peacock, they recorded *See Inside* with longtime **Amy Grant** producer Brown Bannister. This 1997 release had a leaner, funkier sound than earlier albums, giving the Dantes a chance to groove on tracks like "Not a Chance."

After the release of a "best of" compilation in 1998, Out of the Grey left the Sparrow fold and went without a label for several years. The group ultimately signed with Rocketown Records and, in December 2001, released a comeback album, *6.1*. (This release was its sixth all-new album and its first for Rocketown, hence its title.) This time, the duo worked with producer Monroe Jones (**Third Day, Caedmon's Call**), who helped retool and update their familiar sound. The festive single "Shine Like Crazy" rekindled some of the spark from the band's earliest days.

In addition to her work with Out of the Grey, Christine Dente joined forces with **Susan Ashton** and **Margaret Becker** to record the 1994 album *Along the Road*.

Out of the Grey (Sparrow, 1991)
The Shape of Grace (Sparrow, 1992)
Diamond Days (Sparrow, 1994)
Gravity (Sparrow, 1995)
See Inside (Sparrow, 1997)
Remember This: The Out of the Grey
  Collection (Sparrow, 1998)
6.1 (Rocketown, 2001)

OVER THE RHINE
Formed 1989 in Cincinnati, Ohio

The (mostly) melancholy songs of Over the Rhine are indirectly rather than overly Christian. Though a favorite with Christian alternative rock fans, the group has used its faith primarily as background instead of subject matter. Now downsized to its two founding members, Over the Rhine continues to make compelling music of elusive, intuitive meaning.

The band's history began at Marion College, a small Quaker institution in Canton, Ohio, where keyboardist/bassist/songwriter Linford Detweiler and singer/

acoustic guitarist Karin Bergquist met as music students in the mid-1980s. Several years after graduation, the two started a band together in Cincinnati, Ohio, taking its name from the city's historic Over-the-Rhine neighborhood. Rounding out the lineup were lead guitarist Ric Hordinski and drummer Brian Kelly. The group became popular locally and released an independent album, *'Til We Have Faces,* in 1991.

Signing with I.R.S. Records, Over the Rhine released *Patience* in 1992. The album showcased Bergquist's moody vocal stylings and Detweiler's cerebral lyrics, along with the atmospheric sound of the band as a whole. Some songs have a wry, paradoxical humor—one track asks, "How Does It Feel (to Be on My Mind)?" Most of *Patience,* though, luxuriates in a thoughtfully bittersweet space, pondering loss in "Jacksie" and separation in "I Painted My Name." Two years later came *Eve,* a more rock-slanted work that showed off Bergquist's jazzier side. Glimmers of an elusive presence flit through the lyrics here—the subject of "Confessions of a Guilty Bystander" could be Christ as well as a mortal loved one.

Parting company with I.R.S., the band released the CD *Good Dog Bad Dog* on its own Imaginary Records label in 1996. Even more downbeat than previous efforts, it proved to be the band's strongest work. Detweiler's ability to match his somberly poetic lyrics to a wide range of musical

Over the Rhine, with Karin Bergquist and Linford Detweiler (center)
Photo by Michael Wilson

forms is impressive, and Bergquist's skill at performing them is even more so. "Latter Days" and "Poughkeepsie" are positively beautiful in their bleakness. This album also contains "A Gospel Number," a quirky request for salvation addressed explicitly to Jesus. The sparse, ghostly sound of this self-produced and -recorded effort fits the material perfectly. Later that same year, Over the Rhine released an album of Christmas music, *The Darkest Night of the Year.* Taking liberties with familiar melodies, the band put its own folk/jazz spin on "Silent Night" and lent a dark cast to "It Came Upon a Midnight Clear." Some classically tinged originals were included as well. Chilly but lovely in spots, *The Darkest Night of the Year* ranks with **Bruce Cockburn**'s *Christmas* as a holiday collection of real imagination and charm.

By the end of the '90s, Hordinski and Kelly had left the group. Detweiler and Bergquist (now a married couple) toured several times as members of the Cowboy Junkies. Keeping Over the Rhine active with a rotating cast of support players, they signed with Backporch (a Virgin Records subsidiary) and released *Films for Radio* in 2001. Coproducing with Christian music veteran **Dave Perkins,** the band experimented with programmed drums and other ambient electronic touches. "The World Can Wait" and "When I Go" are among the noteworthy tracks on this thoughtfully unsettling album.

'Til We Have Faces (Scampering Songs, 1991; I.R.S., 1995)
Patience (I.R.S., 1992)
Eve (I.R.S., 1994)
Good Dog Bad Dog (Imaginary, 1996)
The Darkest Night of the Year (Imaginary, 1996)
Films for Radio (Backporch/Virgin, 2001)

TWILA PARIS
Born December 28, 1958, in Ft. Worth, Texas

Honey-voiced Twila Paris has devoted herself to inspirational music for more than two decades. Her gossamer-textured singing and well-crafted songwriting have kept her following faithful since the early 1980s. Over the years, Paris has updated her Adult Contemporary sound to incorporate rock and New Age music elements. A number of her best-known songs—including "Lamb of God," "How Beautiful," and "We Will Glorify"—have been included in church hymnals.

Paris's family has deep roots in both ministry and music—her great-grandparents were revivalist preachers in the Arkansas/ Oklahoma area and her grandmother composed religious songs. Her father, a minister and songwriter, encouraged her to begin singing in church at a young age. She began piano studies at age six and sang in choirs in high school. After studying for a year at a Christian discipleship school, she decided to concentrate on faith-based singing and songwriting. Her first recordings were self-released and distributed on cassette. After years of hard work, she signed with the Milk & Honey label and released her debut album, *Knowing You're Around*, in 1981.

Following in the wake of **Amy Grant,** Paris didn't aim for similar crossover popularity. She concentrated instead on distinguishing herself as a praise and worship music artist. This she did handily—her success began with the 1982 Christian radio hit "Humility," a breezy pop number extolling the Lord. Further singles on Milk & Honey also did well, particularly

1984's "The Warrior Is a Child," a confession of vulnerability with a military motif that remains her biggest hit. Paris sang these songs with exact phrasing and great vocal command, and with a hint of Broadway in her voice. Her composing abilities showed equal polish, displaying in songs like "Keeping My Eyes on You" and "We Bow Down" an ability to rework timeless Christian themes in 1980s-style pop modes.

Switching to the Star Song label, Paris released her well-regarded *Cry for the Desert* album in 1990. Next came her 1991 CD *Sanctuary*, which paired her with producer/arranger/keyboardist Richard Souther. This album placed her silken vocals in ethereal New Age–like musical surroundings to striking effect. Her lyrics began to change as well—1993's *Beyond a Dream* dealt with her family's roots in songs like "Seventy Years Ago." *Where I Stand* (1996), her first album for Sparrow, brought her pop/rock sound further up-to-date. The 1990s saw Paris winning GMA Dove Awards for her work, including ones for praise and worship album of the year (for *Sanctuary*), song of the year (for "God Is in Control," 1995), and female vocalist of the year (for 1993, 1994, and 1995). In 1993, she coauthored (with Wheaton College professor Robert Webber) her first book, *In This Sanctuary*, published by Star Song Communications.

In 2000, Paris recorded *Bedtime Prayers: Lullabies and Peaceful Worship*, an album for children that had a similar feel to *Sanctuary*. Appropriately, the album's release coincided with the birth of her first child.

Knowing You're Around
(Milk & Honey, 1981)
Keepin' My Eyes on You
(Milk & Honey, 1982)
The Warrior Is a Child
(Milk & Honey, 1984)
The Best of Twila Paris
(Milk & Honey, 1985)
Kingdom Seekers (Star Song, 1985)
Same Girl (Star Song, 1987)
For Every Heart (Star Song, 1988)
Cry for the Desert (Star Song, 1990)
Sanctuary (Star Song, 1991)
A Heart that Knows You (Star Song, 1992)
Beyond a Dream (Star Song, 1993)
Where I Stand (Sparrow, 1996)
Perennial: Worship Songs for the Seasons
of Life (Sparrow, 1998)
True North (Sparrow, 1999)
Bedtime Prayers: Lullabies and
Peaceful Worship (Sparrow, 2000)
Greatest Hits (Sparrow, 2001)

SANDI PATTY
Born July 14, 1957,
in Oklahoma City, Oklahoma

A diva of enduring appeal, Sandi Patty has won millions of admirers through her heartfelt interpretations of classic hymns, modern inspirational songs, and pop ballads. Often called "the Voice," she ranks among the most honored artists in Contemporary Christian music, with 33 GMA Dove Awards and three Grammys. Scandal surrounding her 1992 divorce had a negative impact on her career, though she has continued to record and perform for large audiences.

Patty's debut singing performance was as a two year-old in church. She spent time during her childhood touring with her minister father's singing group, the Ron Patty Family. Music continued to be her passion as she grew older, studying

Sandi Patty
Photo by Thunder Image Group

voice at San Diego State University before pursuing a music degree at Indiana's Anderson College. Work as a background singer on commercials for Juicy Fruit gum and Steak-n-Shake Restaurants helped pay the bills while she attended school. At Anderson, she performed with the group New Nature and met musician John Helvering, who went on to become her husband, arranger, and business partner. With his encouragement, she recorded and self-released her first album, *For My Friends.* As the result of a printer's error on the album's cover, she adopted "Sandi Patti" as her professional name at the start of her recording career (she went back to "Patty" in the mid-1980s).

Undeniably gifted as a song interpreter, Patty soon attracted national attention as a featured soloist with legendary gospel composer Bill Gaither's group. She entered the front ranks of Christian artists after signing with Impact Records and releasing *Lift Up the Lord* in 1982. This album helped her win GMA Dove Awards for artist and female vocalist of the year, the first of many Doves she would win in years to come. *More than Wonderful*, a 1983 live album, became her first release to earn gold certification. This LP provided a good showcase of her impressive vocals skills and on-stage humor. Patty could thrill audiences with her near-operatic vocal skills, yet still shine on intimate, restrained numbers. "We Shall Behold Him," *More than Wonderful's* closing tune, was indicative of the expertly controlled emotion she brings to inspirational songs.

A steady series of albums continued to appear throughout the '80s. The Grammy-winning *Mornings Like This* (Word, 1986) was a particular favorite with fans, yielding the Christian radio hits "Love in Any Language" and "They Say," a duet with R&B/pop singer Deniece Williams. Modern rock influences began appearing in her albums, particularly on 1988's *Make His Praise Glorious.* Though firmly in the Contemporary Christian music camp, Patty has received some attention in the secular entertainment world. In 1986, A&M Records (then partnering with Word on a number of projects) released a version of the "Star Spangled Banner" sung by Patty as part of an album supporting the Statue of Liberty–Ellis Island Foundation. The recording was eventually broadcast as part of ABC-TV's Fourth of July programming, stirring tremendous favorable reaction. This led to increased appearances on secular award shows, TV specials, and international concert dates. Appearances at the 1988 Republican national convention and 1989 presidential inauguration further secured her stature.

As her star rose, Patty was depicted in the Christian press as a model Christian wife, raising her children with husband John back home in Anderson, Indiana. The 1992 announcement of her divorce shocked her fans. This was followed in 1995 with the confession of two affairs during her marriage, creating a controversy that prompted Christian stations to drop her songs for a time. Riding out the controversy as best she could, Patty continued to record and tour. *Le Voyage* (Word/Epic, 1993) was an interesting creative departure, a pop/rock song cycle based on the theme of spiritual pilgrimage. Subsequent releases found her back in a more familiar inspirational mode. She won yet another GMA Dove Award, this time for Spanish language album of the year, for *Libertad Me Das* (1998). In the secular realm, her renditions of the Gershwin standards "Someone to Watch Over Me" and "Summertime" received wide radio exposure via the Music of Your Life syndicated network. By the end of the 1990s, she had sold more than 11 million recordings.

Patty continues to keep a high profile through performances with symphony orchestras, often mixing Broadway tunes and patriotic songs with gospel material. In 2000 she released her latest Word CD, *These Days.*

Sandi's Song (Milk & Honey, 1979)
Love Overflowing (Impact, 1981)
Lift Up the Lord (Impact, 1982)
More than Wonderful (Impact, 1983)
The Gift Goes On (Impact, 1984)
Songs from the Heart (Impact, 1984)
Hymns Just for You (Word, 1985)
Mornings Like This (Word/A&M, 1986)

Make His Praise Glorious
   (Word/A&M, 1988)
Sandi Patti and the Friendship Company
   (Word/A&M, 1989)
The Finest Moments (Word/A&M, 1989)
Another Time, Another Place (Word, 1990)
Le Voyage (Word/Epic, 1993)
Find It on the Wings (Word, 1994)
Artist of My Soul (Word, 1998)
Libertad Me Das (Word, 1998)
Together (Kathy Troccoli and Sandi Patty)
   (Word, 1999)
These Days (Word, 2000)

CHARLIE PEACOCK
Born August 10, 1956,
in Yuba City, California

A highly influential figure, Charlie Peacock (born Charles William Ashworth) is Christian music's leading Renaissance man. His interlocking involvements as an artist, songwriter, and producer—as well as the quality of his work—invite comparisons with Todd Rundgren. Peacock has also been active as a record label founder, arts seminar leader, and author. An outspoken critic of the Christian music industry, he has sought to market his music in the secular realm as well.

Growing up in the Sacramento area, Peacock first began performing in clubs as a secular musician in the 1970s. In 1980, he launched the trio Vector with Jimmy Abegg (later a member of the Ragamuffin Band) and Steve Griffith. After becoming a Christian, Peacock embarked on a solo career and released his first album, *Lie Down in the Grass*, on Sacramento-based Exit Records in 1984. Featuring members of **the 77s** on some tracks, this first effort displayed Peacock's interest in Third World rhythms. The percussion-driven title track suggests an African influence, while "One, Two, Three (That's OK)" and "Turned on an Attitude" add ska and reggae accents. Peacock's light, jazz-tinged vocals glide through the lyrics, Christian in content but understated in their pronouncements. Not long after *Lie Down in the Grass*'s initial release, A&M signed a distribution pact with Exit and rereleased the album with two new (and slightly more secularly oriented) tracks.

After parting ways with A&M, Peacock recorded his self-titled second album with producer Nigel Grey, best known for his work with the Police. Released by Island Records in 1986, *Charlie Peacock* continued to experiment with grooves and textures, edging away from rock and toward R&B/pop. This album also marked his last project for some years as a secular artist. In 1989, he moved to Nashville and quickly established himself as an in-demand producer and songwriter. Over the next 10 years, he would work with such Christian artists as **Avalon, Margaret Becker, Lisa Bevill, Bob Carlisle, Kim Hill, Phil Keaggy, Out of the Grey,** and Brent Bourgeois, to name only a few. Signing with Sparrow as an artist, he released

The Secret of Time in 1990. This song collection contained the uplifting "Almost Threw It All Away," which became a chart-topping single on Christian radio. Increasingly, Peacock was now writing and singing tunes in a classic soul/gospel mode, inviting comparisons with Smokey Robinson and similar greats. Such *Secret of Time* tracks as "Dear Friend" and "Big Man's Hat" (both radio hits) combined elegant songwriting with thoughtful, cliché-free lyrics.

Peacock was back in 1991 with *Love Life,* a groundbreaking album that touched upon human sexuality within a Christian context. Though the lyrics dealt with married love, the sensual nature of tracks like "Kiss Me Like a Woman, Love Me Like a Man" made Sparrow uneasy. Christian radio wasn't quite ready for this sort of song; the biggest hit from this album was "In the Light," a celebration of the Holy Spirit with a propulsive African feel. Later in 1991, Sparrow released *West Coast Diaries Vols. 1–3,* a trio of albums featuring demos and live recordings. First appearing as independent releases in the late '80s, this series was a mixed bag of tunes of varying roughness and polish. More for the serious Peacock fan than the average listener, they nevertheless contain some high points, such as the in-concert performances on *Vol. 2* and a sleek treatment of Paul Simon's "Mrs. Robinson" (with the sarcasm of the "Jesus loves you" lines downplayed) on *Vol. 3*. Peacock was

back in 1994 with an all-new album, *Everything that's on My Mind*; its best-known tune was the infectious "One Man Gets Around," yet another Christian radio favorite.

By the mid-1990s, Peacock had become a leading figure within the Christian music mainstream, credited with helping to raise standards of songwriting and production within the genre. Beyond his own recordings, his songs were turned into massive hits by **Amy Grant** ("Every Heartbeat") and **dc Talk** ("In the Light") in 1991 and 1996, respectively. He won GMA Dove Awards for producer of the year in 1995, 1996, and 1997, and received a Dove for modern/ alternative rock recorded song in 1996. Still, his success was tempered by a sense that the Christian genre was artistically restricted and spiritually shallow. These concerns prompted him to launch the Art House, an ongoing educational forum held at his home from 1991 to '96. Musicians, writers, and theologians participated in the forum's freewheeling discussions, designed to broaden the parameters of Christian-inspired art. This search for answers reflected Peacock's own desire to take control of his music. Toward that end, he founded and self-financed his own label, re:think Records, in 1996.

Strangelanguage, his next album, appeared on re:think that same year. This project moved away from the R&B stylings of his Sparrow albums and toward a contemporary weave of ambient electronica sounds and

'60s psychedelic rock. Peacock's lyrics explored questions of human vanity and divine mercy in poetic ways; songs like "The Harvest at the End of the World" and "Liquid Days" evoked biblical imagery with a subtle touch. Besides *Strangelanguage,* re:think also released albums by singer/ songwriter **Sarah Masen** and the band Switchfoot. The goal of re:think was to present Christian artists directly to the mainstream market. Before the label fully had a chance to take root, however, Peacock decided to abandon the role of record executive and sold his interest in re:think to Sparrow Records. In 1999, he released *Kingdom Come,* a return to a more organic pop/rock sound. This album captured some of the loose exploratory feel heard on *West Coast Diaries,* with guest appearances by singer **Ashley Cleveland** and banjo virtuoso Bela Fleck, among others.

The close of the 1990s saw Peacock producing albums by **Audio Adrenaline, Twila Paris,** and **Michelle Tumes.** In 2001, he collaborated with African vocal group Ladysmith Black Mambazo on a track for the multi-artist compilation album *Roaring Lambs.* Perhaps his most significant work during this time was the book *Crossroads* (Broadman & Holman, 1999), a provocative study of Contemporary Christian music. In its pages, he questioned the very premise of the genre, calling for greater engagement in mainstream culture along with a deeper understanding of

Scripture. Peacock sought to further his own biblical knowledge by working on a master's degree at Convent Theological Seminary in St. Louis in 2000–01. He returned to Nashville in late 2001 and founded a new publishing company, Printshop Music Group. Plans called for him to release several new projects in 2002. (For more about Charlie Peacock, see pages 84–88.)

Lie Down in the Grass (Exit, 1984; A&M/Exit, 1985)
Charlie Peacock (Island/Exit, 1986)
The Secret of Time (Sparrow, 1990)
Love Life (Sparrow, 1991)
West Coast Diaries, Vols. 1–3 (Sparrow, 1991)
Everything that's on My Mind (Sparrow, 1994)
Strangelanguage (re:think, 1996)
The Very Best of Charlie Peacock: In the Light (re:think, 1996)
Kingdom Come (re:think/Sparrow, 1999)

DAVE PERKINS
Born October 4, 1948, in Camden, New Jersey

Though best known in the Christian music world as a producer, songwriter and guitarist, Dave Perkins has released memorable albums as an artist as well. Born to a keyboardist father and vocalist mother, he performed with his family at churches and on radio broadcasts in the Northeast as a child. In early adulthood, he embarked on a legal career, then switched back to music. Stints as a sideman with Carole King, Jerry Jeff Walker, and other artists kept him busy into the mid-1970s. A rediscovery of his belief in God led to his emergence as a Christian singer/songwriter and band-leader later in the decade. In the early to mid-1980s, he produced albums by such Christian music notables as **Steve Taylor, Phil Keaggy, Randy Stonehill,** and **Rick Cua.** He released his debut as an artist on the Word-distributed What? label in 1986. *The Innocence* was a bracing collection of rock anthems, reminiscent of U2 and **the Call** in its martial tempos and ringing idealism. Such tracks as "Harvest Home," "Make Me Feel," and "Catacombs" grappled with spiritual warfare, fueled by Perkins's incendiary guitar work.

The Innocence failed to make much of a commercial dent, in part due to What? Records' demise. Perkins went on to join forces with Steve Taylor in Chagall Guevara, a secularly slanted rock combo that recorded a well-regarded album for MCA before sputtering out in the early '90s. From there, Perkins and fellow Chagall guitarist Lynn Nichols became the duo Passafist, releasing a self-titled CD in 1994. This intriguing slice of industrial rock betrays a Christian influence amidst thickly layered guitars, pounding drum lines, and distorted vocals. Tracks like "Christ of the Nuclear Age" display a social consciousness as well as an underlying faith. Since then, Perkins has kept a low profile as an artist but has

continued as a producer, working with **Over the Rhine** on its 2001 album *Films for Radio.*

The Innocence (What?, 1986)
Passafist (with Lynn Nichols) (R.E.X., 1994)
WITH CHAGALL GUEVARA:
Chagall Guevara (MCA, 1991)

PETRA
Formed 1972 in Ft. Wayne, Indiana

Now entering its fourth decade, Petra is remarkable for its durability alone. For many years, the group was considered the world's most popular Christian rock band. While its commercial stature has slipped somewhat, it continues to record and tour with the same missionary zeal it has always displayed. Tried and true if not trendy, Petra remains one of the most recognized Christian groups among secular music fans.

The Petra story starts with singer/songwriter/guitarist Bob Hartman (born December 26, 1949, in Byron, Ohio), who began playing with rock bands at age 15. By his early twenties, he was part of the Christian group Rapture, a short-lived combo that also included future Petra bassist John DeGroff. After that group's demise, DeGroff moved to Ft. Wayne, Indiana, and enrolled in the Christian Training Center, a non-accredited church institution. Hartman soon followed and began studying for the ministry. Rather than become a preacher, he decided to form a new group with DeGroff and guitarist Greg Hough. Adding drummer Bill Glover, the four performed regularly at the Adam's Apple, a local Christian coffeehouse. After some false starts, they named themselves Petra, the Greek word for "rock." Gradually, they overcame opposition to their hard rock sound among more conservative believers and earned a following. In 1973, they relocated to Nashville.

Signing with Myrrh Records, Petra released its self-titled debut album in 1974. The band's ranks expanded to include lead singer Greg X. Volz in 1976; a veteran Jesus Music performer, Volz turned down an offer to join secular rockers REO Speedwagon in favor of signing up with Petra. After another modest-selling LP for Myrrh, the group moved to Star Song and released 1979's *Washes Whiter Than*, which contained its first Christian radio hits, "Why Does the Father Bother" and "Yahweh Love." The following year, a band shakeup resulted in the departure of DeGroff, Hough, and Glover. Hartman and Volz reassembled Petra with bassist Mark Kelly, drummer Louie Weaver, and keyboarist John Slick. This lineup released *Never Say Die* (1981), best known for "The Coloring Song," a simple statement of faith that became a Christian Adult Contemporary radio favorite, and "For Annie," a ballad dealing with teen suicide.

More Power to Ya (1982) typifies the strengths and limitations of Petra during the early '80s. Hartman, the band's leader and chief songwriter, shows his ability to craft catchy hooks on tunes like the title track, "Rose Colored Stained Glass Windows," and "Judas's Kiss." His lyrics are straightforward exhortations to the faithful, forsaking poetic ambiguity for clarity of message. As a singer, Volz is akin to such secular rock front men as Boston's Barry Goudreau and Styx's Dennis DeYoung, sweet-voiced if a little shrill at times. The band's approach remained consistent even as new refinements were added. Synthesizers were prominent on 1984's *Beat the System*, courtesy of added keyboardist John Lawry. While some fans missed the harder sounds of earlier efforts, the album did yield such popular Christian singles as "Hollow Eyes," "Witch Hunt," and the title track.

Petra survived the loss of Volz in 1985. (As a solo artist, Volz went on to score such Christian radio hits as "The River Is Rising," "Walk Towards the Light," and "Waiting on Someday" in the late '80s and early '90s.) Taking his place was John Schlitt, former lead singer with the secular band Head East. A somewhat grittier sounding vocalist than Volz, Schlitt made his Petra recording debut with 1986's *Back on the Street*. This album veered away from the high-gloss production of *Beat the System* and back toward the guitar-powered basic rock of earlier releases. Hartman began writing songs with a spiritual warfare theme, filling albums like *This Means War!* (1987) and *On Fire!* (1988) with Christian calls to righteous combat. The group's 1988 single "Get on Your Knees and Fight Like a Man" defined its ideal of a prayer warrior. Driving the point home further, Petra released its own version of the hymn "Onward Christian Soldiers" the following year.

In 1991, Petra won GMA Dove Awards for both the album *Beyond Belief* (1990) and its title track. The group's next album, 1991's *Unseen Power*, earned another Dove as well as a Grammy. By that point, the band had become a Christian music institution, a reliable hit-making entity if not the flashiest act around. A 1996 Petra tribute album was titled *Never Say Dinosaur*, ironically referring to the group's less-than-hip image. Hartman and Schlitt took it all in stride, continuing to enjoy Christian radio hits like "Just Reach Out" and "Mark of the Cross" throughout the '90s and holding on to their faithful following. As the band entered the twenty-first century, it could look back on some six million units in total sales. Its stature was further acknowledged when it became the first Christian band to be enshrined at the Hard Rock Cafe.

Recent Petra releases have shown some renewed vigor and new ideas. *No Doubt* (winner of a 1996 GMA Dove for rock album of the year) ran the gamut from growling Aerosmith-like numbers ("Heart of a Hero") to ballads of humility and repentance ("We Hold Out Our Hearts to You"). Hartman's decision to retire from touring and concentrate on songwriting

put the spotlight increasingly on Schlitt. The late '90s Petra lineup—Schlitt, drummer Louie Weaver, guitarist Pete Orta, bassist Lonnie Chapin, and keyboardist Trent Thompson—offered an intriguing revision of the band's history on 1999's *Double Take*. The album featured stripped-down (and in some cases rewritten) acoustic versions of such signature tunes as "Creed," "Praying Man," and "This Means War." *Double Take* gave evidence that life still remained in this so-called "dinosaur band."

Petra (Myrrh, 1974)
Come and Join Us (Myrrh, 1977)
Washes Whiter Than (Star Song/A&M, 1979)
Never Say Die (Star Song/A&M, 1981)
More Power to Ya (Star Song/A&M, 1982)
Not of This World (Star Song/A&M, 1983)
Beat the System (Star Song/A&M, 1984)
Captured in Time and Space
  (Star Song/A&M, 1986)
Back on the Street (Star Song, 1986)
This Means War! (Star Song, 1987)
On Fire! (Star Song, 1988)
Petra Praise: The Rock Cries Out
  (Dayspring, 1989)
Beyond Belief (Dayspring, 1990)
War and Remembrance: 15 Years of Rock (Star
  Song, 1990)
Unseen Power (Dayspring, 1991)
Wake-up Call (Dayspring, 1993)
No Doubt (Word/Epic, 1995)
Petra Praise 2: We Need Jesus (Word, 1997)
God Fixation (Word, 1998)
Double Take (Word, 1999)

LESLIE PHILLIPS/ SAM PHILLIPS
Born June 28, 1962, in East Hollywood, California

The story of how Leslie Phillips (Christian market artist) morphed into Sam Phillips (secular market artist) is a fascinating one. Hailed as the "queen of Christian rock" at the start of her recording career, she increasingly pushed against the boundaries of Contemporary Christian music until she left the genre behind altogether. Resuming recording under a new name, both her sound and her persona evolved far from those displayed in her early work. Judging by her songs, Phillips's journey into the secular entertainment world has marked an evolution of her religious views as well.

In interviews, Phillips has traced the longing heard in her music back to her parents' divorce during her teenage years. Growing up in the Los Angeles area, she began writing songs and performing them in church at age 14. Four years later, she was signed to Myrrh Records, which released her debut album, *Beyond Saturday Night*, in 1983. Compared to later efforts, Phillips's vocals here sound unsure and overwrought. The songs allude to hurt and confusion, but find hope in Christ. "Bring Me Through" strikes a particularly desperate note, balanced by the certainty of "I'm Finding" (a Christian radio hit). *Beyond Saturday Night*, while something of an awkward

start, served to launch her as a star-to-be in the Christian music world.

Phillips kept releasing albums on Myrrh at a steady pace and toured Christian venues. She received a good deal of Christian radio airplay, scoring a chart-topping single with "Your Kindness" in 1986. As her singing and songwriting gained maturity and focus, she began edging away from explicitly God-centered material. Her transitional phase is best captured on *The Turning* (1987), her final LP for Myrrh. The contrast between this album and her first is striking—singing more in her lower range, she fills her songs with a restless, moody spirit. The lyrics here convey frustration, a sense of entrapment, alluding both to romantic relationships and her niche in the Christian music industry. There are still clear-cut expressions of faith, such as "Libera Me" and "God Is Watching You." Overall, though, *The Turning* suggested that Phillips was exploring new creative and personal options. This was underscored by **T-Bone Burnett**'s adventuresome production, spiced with oddly syncopated rhythms, backwards guitars, and other unexpected touches.

Meeting Burnett turned out to be a key event in Phillips's life—the two became a couple and eventually married. He helped her secure a deal with Virgin Records and re-create herself as a secular artist. Changing her name to Sam Phillips (partially in homage to Elvis Presley's first producer), she returned to the studio to record *The Indescribable Wow* (1988). Her decision to "go secular" provoked much criticism from her old fans— some felt betrayed, as if she'd renounced Jesus along with her involvement in the Christian music industry. Phillips made it clear in interviews that, while she remained a Christian, she had grown tired of the restrictions and conservatism she had labored under for years. *The Indescribable Wow* reflects her sense of freedom; most of the songs are depictions of romance, etched with rue and venom. Her spiritual side is mostly shown in disdain for greed and materialism, as in "Holding on to the Earth." Burnett's production this time brings to mind the tuneful eclecticism of the Beatles' *Rubber Soul/Revolver* period, with dabs of harpsichord and quirky strings.

From there, Phillips's albums grew increasingly idiosyncratic. *Cruel Inventions* (1991) had a tart, irritated tone, expressing feelings of alienation and betrayal. Increasingly, her songs cast her as an aggrieved party, a put-upon skeptic in a world of deceit; her cover of John Lennon's "Gimme Some Truth" on 1994's *Martinis and Bikinis* was an apt choice. Phillips's laser-precise dissections of human weakness (including her own) gave an edge of cruelty to her mid-'90s albums. As ever, her gift for writing pop/rock melodies remained outstanding, no matter how dark her lyrics became.

Sam Phillips
Photo by Michael Wilson, courtesy of Nonesuch Records

It's interesting to speculate how Phillips would have fared in the Christian music industry had she begun recording 10 years later, when its creative restrictions were growing less severe. Would Leslie have led the way for other upstart Christian recording artists? Would Sam never have been born?

AS LESLIE PHILLIPS:
Beyond Saturday Night (Myrrh, 1983)
Dancing with Danger (Myrrh, 1984)
Black and White in a Grey World
     (Myrrh, 1985)
The Turning (Myrrh/A&M, 1987)

AS SAM PHILLIPS:

The Indescribable Wow (Virgin, 1988)

Cruel Inventions (Virgin, 1991)

Martinis and Bikinis (Virgin, 1994)

Omnipop (It's Only a Flesh Wound Lambchop)
   (Virgin, 1996)

Zero, Zero, Zero: The Best of Sam Phillips
   (Virgin, 1999)

Fan Dance (Nonesuch, 2001)

PLUS ONE
Formed 1999

Christian "boy band" Plus One was launched to be the evangelical answer to 'NSYNC, the Backstreet Boys, and similar pop vocal groups. The youthful quintet enjoyed considerable media attention after releasing its 2000 debut, going on to successfully tour and earn a gold album.

Members Gabe Combs, Nate Cole, Jerry Mhire, Jason Perry, and Nathan Walters were all in their late teens or early twenties when selected for the group. The catalyst for Plus One's creation was manager Mitchell Solarek, who sent out an open audition call through Christian youth ministry channels. Three of the singers chosen were sons of preachers; most had experience performing at churches. After initially considering the name Blue, the fivesome was dubbed Plus One and sent into the studio under the guidance of multi-Grammy-winning producer David Foster. Coproducing and contributing songs to the project were such proven secular hit-makers as Eric Foster White (Britney Spears, Backstreet Boys), Rodney Jerkins (Whitney Houston, Brian McKnight), and Robbie Nevil (Jessica Simpson, Brandy). During the album-making process, the band members shared living quarters in San Francisco and, later, Los Angeles.

Plus One's debut CD, *The Promise,* was released in early 2000 on Foster's 143 Records label (distributed by Atlantic). Its tracks were dance/pop numbers reflecting the skills of the writer/producers involved. The quintet's harmonies were intricately arranged, as slick as those of its secular counterparts. The album's lyrics, though, were different from typical boy-band fare—overt sexiness was replaced by family-oriented messages about friendship and faith. Tunes like "Written in My Heart" (the group's initial hit), "God Is in This Place," and the title track demonstrated that the formula was an appealing one. Plus One proved it was more than a studio creation by touring with **Jaci Velasquez** in the fall of 2000; the group's shows mixed singing and choreography with moments of worship. *The Promise* went on to receive gold certification. A second album, *Obvious,* appeared on 143 in early 2002.

The Promise (143/Atlantic, 2000)

Obvious (143/Atlantic, 2002)

P

P.O.D.
Formed 1992 in San Diego, California

Loud, aggressive, and loaded with street credibility, P.O.D. broke big into the secular rock market in 2000. The four-member band had already become a solid favorite with Christian alternative rock audiences thanks to frequent touring and a series of independent releases. Combining rap, hip-hop, reggae, and rock, the group presented its testimonials of faith with a hard-hitting sonic attack.

P.O.D.—which takes its name from the banking term "payable on death"—was founded by guitarist Marcos Curiel and drummer Wuv (born Noah Bernardo, Jr.) in the gritty South Bay (or Southtown) section of San Diego. By 1993, singer Sonny Sandoval and bassist Traa (Mark Daniels) had joined its ranks. The band gained a local following by performing anywhere it could, including skate-parks, church basements, and farms. With the help of Wuv's father, the group formed its own Rescue label and released *Snuff the Punk* (1993), *Brown* ('96), and *Live at TomFest* ('97). These CDs revealed both the band's raw power and its soul-bearing honesty. Such tracks as *Brown*'s "Full Color" dealt with mortality and the healing power of Christ in compellingly authentic terms. P.O.D.'s unpreachy Christian testimony helped win the group a devoted legion of fans, which the band dubbed "the warriors." This core following provided a base to reach out to secular audiences, which in turn led to a deal with Atlantic Records in 1997.

P.O.D.'s Atlantic debut, *The Fundamental Elements of Southtown*, proved one of the best rock albums released in 1999, secular or Christian. Comparable to the rap/rock sound of Rage Against the Machine, the album's uncompromising moral stance set it apart and helped win the group wide media attention. "Southtown," a hard-slamming ode to P.O.D.'s neighborhood, became a radio and MTV hit and helped *Southtown* reach gold certification. The raucous "Rock the Party (Off the Hook)" was a successful follow-up single. Some questioned if all the secular success represented a diluting of the band members' faith; touring as part of Ozzy Osbourne's Ozzfest concert package drew even more concern. In interviews, the four reaffirmed both their Christianity and their desire to reach nonbelievers.

Satellite, released in 2001, added more melody and vocal harmony to P.O.D.'s mix of scorching guitar riffs and rapped vocals. One of the album's singles, "Youth of the Nation," which was inspired by a shooting incident at a San Diego–area high school, became a secular hit in early 2002.

Snuff the Punk (Rescue, 1993)
Brown (Rescue, 1996)
Live at TomFest (Rescue, 1997)
The Warriors (EP) (Tooth & Nail, 1999)
The Fundamental Elements of Southtown
    (Atlantic, 1999)
Satellite (Atlantic, 2001)

POINT OF GRACE
Formed 1990 in Arkadelphia, Arkansas

Blending R&B, gospel, and girl-group–style pop, Point of Grace has been a consistent favorite with Christian radio programmers and music buyers. The slickness of the quartet's recordings is balanced by the wholesome, woman-next-door qualities of its members, with its most popular tunes featuring inspirational lyrics sung in close harmony over smoothly produced tracks.

The origins of the group go back to Norman, Oklahoma, where Denise Jones and Heather Floyd had been friends since

Point of Grace. Clockwise from top left: Denise Jones, Terry Jones, Heather Floyd, and Shelley Phillips
Photo by Thunder Image Group

elementary school. During their high school years, they formed a vocal trio with Terry Jones (no relation to Denise). All three went on to attend Ouachita Baptist University in Arkadelphia, Arkansas, where they formed the Ouachitones and performed at local churches. After expanding to a quartet with the addition of Shelley Phillips, they redubbed themselves Say So and embarked on a summer 1991 performing tour of churches and youth camps. The group had a knack for arranging gospel material into sparkling Andrews Sisters–like harmonies. The women's talents gained them entry into the 1992 Christian Artists Vocal Competition, held at Estes Park, Colorado, where their grand-prize finish led to a contract with Word Records. Before recording their debut, they settled on the name Point of Grace, taken from the writings of Christian author C. S. Lewis.

Point of Grace's self-titled first album was phenomenally popular, yielding six high-charting Christian singles, among them "I'll Be Believing," "One More Broken Heart," and "Faith, Hope & Love." From the start, the group's sound had a strong R&B undercurrent, with a black gospel influence evident in its vocal moves. While the songs came from a variety of outside writers, the group's material was unified by its themes of hope and healing. It was a winning combination from the start—the *Point of Grace* album went gold and earned the band a GMA Dove Award for new artist of the year.

The group's second album, *The Whole Truth* (1995), likewise went gold and was the source of more major Christian hits, including the rock-tinged "Gather at the River" and the sleekly grooving "God Is with Us." *Life, Love & Other Mysteries* (1996) was even more successful, breaking the platinum sales barrier and launching such singles as the buoyant "Circle of Friends." Point of Grace went on to win both artist and group of the year Dove Awards in 1996. The group's next two CD releases, *Steady On* and *A Christmas Story*, both reached gold certification. *Rarities & Remixes* (2000) contained a sampling of its best-known work in remixed form, along with some lesser-known tracks.

Point of Grace managed to sell more than two million albums during its first decade without expanding beyond the Christian market. *Free to Fly*, its 2001 album, showed signs that the band might be developing crossover potential. Its lead track, "By Heart," closely resembled a secular pop love song, with references to the Deity confined to a capitalized "You." Time will tell if Point of Grace seriously pursues a secular hit.

Point of Grace (Word, 1993)
The Whole Truth (Word, 1995)
Life, Love & Other Mysteries (Word, 1996)
Steady On (Word, 1998)
A Christmas Story (Word, 1999)
Rarities & Remixes (Word, 2000)
Free to Fly (Word, 2001)

ANDY PRATT
Born c. 1947

Singer/songwriter Andy Pratt is one of the more obscure artists in these listings, though undeservedly so. A critic's favorite during the earlier, secular phase of his career, he went on to record several worthy Christian projects during the 1980s before slipping out of sight almost completely. Pratt's highly expressive (if quirky) voice and sensitive songs remain to be rediscovered by a larger audience.

Pratt came from a patrician background—his great-great grandfather was the cofounder of Standard Oil and Brooklyn's Pratt Institute bears his family's name. He learned to play guitar while attending prep school and continued to play music while attending Harvard University. His first musical involvement of note was the band Butter, which secured a deal with MGM Records in the late 1960s before breaking up. From there, Pratt signed as a solo artist with Polydor, releasing the whimsical if unfocused LP *Records Are Like Life* in 1970. Two years later he stirred interest on Boston rock stations with "Avenging Annie," an operatic story-song based on Woody Guthrie's "Ballad of Pretty Boy Floyd." Pratt originally wrote the song for a woman's voice, and he sang his version of it almost entirely in falsetto. The Who's Roger Daltrey covered "Avenging Annie" in 1977.

After an unsuccessful self-titled album on Columbia, Pratt moved to Nemperor Records, which released his LP *Resolution* in 1976. His songs were better realized here, touching upon highly personal themes of love and loss in richly melodic pop/rock settings. Increasingly, his lyrics traced his spiritual searching, which ultimately led him to Christianity. His 1977 album *Shiver in the Night* was the first to explicitly mention Jesus in a song. He devoted much of his next album, 1979's *Motives*, to honoring Christ. Pratt brings passion and vulnerability to his readings of "Savior" and "Cross on the Hill"—he truly sounds "slain in the spirit" here, overcome by rapture and awe. Musically, *Motives* often has a jazz/pop feel, built upon Pratt's acoustic piano work. Sadly, this album proved no more commercial than its predecessors.

Leaving Nemperor, Pratt released his *Fun in the First World* EP on the independent Enzone label in 1982. On this five-song disc, he scolds mankind for its materialism ("Paper Money") and warns of the coming divine judgment ("Fun in the First World," "Burn Up in the Fire"). The music here is New Wave-ish techno-pop, adding an edge to Pratt's end-times message. Except for some Boston airplay, *Fun in the First World* hardly made a ripple. Since then, Pratt's recording history has been sporadic. He resurfaced in 1989 with *Perfect Therapy*, recorded in the Netherlands and released in the United States by the small Fortress

label. A sleek, keyboard-heavy album, it lacks some of the sonic nuances of his previous work. Still, Pratt's dramatic sense of melodic dynamics and beguiling high-register vocals are evident on tracks like "Pass Away" and "More than the Sky." And, as ever, he expresses his faith with the joy of a wide-eyed innocent.

Currently living in Europe, Pratt is said to be working on a new album.

Shiver in the Night (Nemperor, 1977)
Motives (Nemperor/CBS, 1979)
Fun in the First World (EP) (Enzone, 1982)
Not Just for Dancing (Aztec, 1985)
Perfect Therapy (GMI/Fortress, 1989)
Resolution: The Andy Pratt Collection
    (Razor & Tie, 1996)

RESURRECTION BAND/ REZ BAND
Formed 1973 in Milwaukee, Wisconsin

The raw blues/rock of Resurrection Band set it apart from other Jesus Music artists in the early 1970s. The band combined social activism with musical evangelism, ministering to the poor as well as recording and touring.

Singer/guitarist Glenn Kaiser (born January 21, 1953) formed the group in

Milwaukee. Both of his parents had been involved in pop and jazz music in their younger days. Growing up poor in rural Wisconsin, he turned his energies toward music and began performing with a series of bands in his early teens. After a period of drug use and reckless living, he accepted Christ and started Resurrection Band at age 19. Not long after its formation, the group became part of Jesus People U.S.A. (JPUSA), a Christian community working with the poor and homeless on Chicago's south side. Kaiser and his bandmates—singer Wendi Kaiser (Glenn's wife, born April 8, 1953), lead guitarist Stu Heiss, bassist Jim Denton, and drummer John Herrin—served as part of JPUSA's street outreach program, performing in parks, shopping centers, and anywhere else they could attract a crowd.

The band's first release was a limited-edition promotional cassette, *Music to Raise the Dead* (1974). Resurrection Band didn't begin to reach a national audience, though, until it signed with Star Song and recorded 1978's *Awaiting Your Reply.* The album's music was hard-hitting (if sometimes heavy-handed), featuring Glenn's bluesy growl and Wendi's Grace Slick–like wail. "Wave" preached the Good News to a Led Zeppelin–like trudging tempo, with the Kaisers trading lead vocals. "The Return" was a slow-simmering ballad celebrating the Second Coming. Beyond spiritual themes, the band increasingly tackled social and political issues in its songwriting. Moving to Light Records, the group released 1980's *Colours,* an unsparing portrait of a downtrodden and anxiety-filled America, with tracks like "City Streets" and "American Dream" addressing the chaos and confusion of modern life. Helping drive the lyrics home was Heiss's lead guitar work, riffing frantically on the opening track "Autograph."

Rez Band (as it came to be known in the 1980s) raised the intensity level further on *Mommy Don't Love Daddy Anymore* (1981), an album that mixed ferocious hard rock with frantic New Wave tempos. Among the targets this time were moral slackness ("First Degree Apathy") and the blandness of typical Christian pop music ("Elevator Muzik)." "Lovin' You" introduced a techno-pop element, surrounding a worshipful lyric with driving synthesizers as well as guitars. *D.M.Z.* (1982) alternated between angry broadsides ("Babylon," "White Noise") and paeans to the Savior ("So in Love with You," "I Need Your Love"). A number of the album's tracks, including "Military Man" and "No Alibi," received a good deal of Christian radio airplay.

Further albums continued to appear throughout the 1980s and '90s. The band formed Grrr Records, based out of its offices at JPUSA. One of the group's most ambitious releases on Grrr was *Lament,* a concept album based on the Book of Lamentations. Rez Band's most recent album, *Ampendectomy,* appeared in 1997. Glenn Kaiser has released a number of solo albums on Grrr as well, including 1993's *All My Days: Songs of Worship* and 1999's *Time Will Tell.*

JPUSA has been the focus of controversy in recent years. In 1994, Christian author Ron Enroth accused the community of practicing corporal punishment on adult members, separating children from "unfit" parents, and performing ritual exorcisms. In 2001, a series of articles in the *Chicago Tribune* questioned JPUSA's financial practices, including its demand that members turn down payment for work on its various projects. As an elder of the community, Glenn Kaiser vigorously came to its defense, launching a series of letter-writing campaigns to help refute the charges.
(Note: Discography is selective.)

Awaiting Your Reply (Star Song, 1978)
Rainbow's End (Star Song, 1979)
Colours (Light, 1980)
Mommy Don't Love Daddy Anymore
   (Light, 1981)
D.M.Z. (Light, 1982)
Hostage (Sparrow, 1984)
Between Heaven 'n Hell (Sparrow, 1985)
Silence Screams (Grrr/Word, 1988)
Innocent Blood (Grrr/Word, 1989)
Civil Rites (Grrr/Ocean, 1991)
Lament (Grrr/R.E.X., 1995)
The Light Years (Light, 1995)
Ampendectomy (Grrr, 1997)

CHRIS RICE
Born 1962 in Clinton, Maryland

A youth minister–turned–recording artist, Chris Rice has become popular thanks to his down-to-earth depictions of Christian living. He was born and raised in the Washington, D.C., suburbs, where his parents owned a Christian bookstore. Rice became active in church programs at an early age. His work with children and teens grew to include music as part of worship services. Developing his singing and song-writing over time, he edged into a music career after moving to Nashville in 1987. In 1993, **Kim Boyce** scored a Christian radio hit with his song "By Faith." **Kathy Troccoli, Amy Grant,** and **Michael W. Smith** went on to record his compositions as well.

Rice continued to serve as a traveling minister, visiting Christian youth camps and retreats across the country even as his songs won greater attention. When Michael W. Smith launched his Rocketown label, he signed Rice as its first artist. *Deep Enough to Dream,* Rice's 1997 debut album, proved that his thoughtfully tuneful style had broad appeal. Such tunes as "Clumsy" and "Sometimes Love" rose high on the Christian singles charts. Rice's sweet-toned, guileless vocal style drew comparisons with James Taylor, and his insightful lyrics won him a solid following, especially among younger audiences. *Past the Edges* (1998) added more elaborate production touches, earning him airplay with such tunes as "Smellin' Coffee" and "And Your Praise Goes On." The success of *Past the Edges* helped Rice win a GMA Dove Award for male vocalist of the year in 1999.

Despite strong sales, critical praise, and the recognition of his peers, Rice considered dropping out of recording in favor of returning to youth ministry full time. He released his third CD, *Smell the Color 9*, in 2000, with the understanding that his involvement in its promotion would be limited. Tunes like the album's title track and "Questions for Heaven" found him wrestling with nagging spiritual quandaries— as ever, his songs seemed an extension of his role as a Christian teacher and worship-leader. In 2001, he released *The Living Room Sessions*, an instrumental album featuring classic hymns played by Rice on his piano at home.

Deep Enough to Dream (Rocketown, 1997)
Past the Edges (Rocketown, 1998)
Smell the Color 9 (Rocketown, 2000)
The Living Room Sessions (Rocketown, 2001)

REBECCA ST. JAMES
Born July 26, 1977, in Sydney, Australia

A self-described "radical" Christian, singer/songwriter Rebecca St. James combines an unwavering commitment to the gospel with a high-energy rock/techno-pop sound. Beginning her recording career at age 16, she has risen to become one of America's outstanding young evangelists and a role model for Christian teens. Her albums are groove-driven celebrations of a Bible-centered lifestyle, at once morally rigorous and ultra-catchy.

Rebecca St. James Smallbone, the eldest of seven siblings, spent her earliest years in Australia. Her father, Thomas Smallbone, encouraged her singing talents while he worked as a Christian concert promoter. In 1991, she performed with **Carman** on a tour of her homeland. Not long after, a failed concert promotion venture left the Smallbone family destitute. Moving to the United States, they settled near Nashville, Tennessee, and cleaned houses to make ends meet. The local Christian music community became aware of St. James's talents, and she was signed to ForeFront Records in 1994.

St. James's self-titled debut album was an immediate success, spawning such Christian radio hits as "Here I Am" and "Everything I Do." Remarkably focused and confident for a 16-year-old, she earned a GMA Dove Award nomination for new artist of the year in 1995. She returned in 1996 with *God,* an even more impressive album. Producer Tedd T. achieved a potent synthesis of modern music styles on this record, deftly layering distorted electric guitars, clattering drums, and massed harmonies. St. James's vocals are as bold as the music, accented with slurs, growls, and whispers that sound positively sensual. Yet none of this studio sophistication clashes with her message—on such songs as the title track, "Go and Sin No More," and "Me without You" (all chart-topping Christian radio singles), she conveys a simple and undiluted devotion to the Heavenly Father. *God* went on to sell more than 350,000 copies and received a Grammy nomination for best rock/gospel album.

Pray (1998) added more of a hip-hop feel to *God's* sonic approach, with tape loops and drum programs lending a hypnotic quality to her expressions of devotion. St. James's cover of **Rich Mullins**'s "Hold Me Jesus" rides a simmering groove, while "Peace" glides on a dance club–style rhythm track. At times, St. James's singing takes on a breathy desperation—clearly, she is no passive seeker after religious truth. Genuine evangelical fire lights up "Mirror" (yet another Christian radio hit) and "Lord You're Beautiful" (a passionate reworking of a **Keith Green** tune). In "Omega," the album's closing track, St. James speaks her testimony with a quiet but compelling fervor. *Pray* manages to convey old-time religion and still sound cutting-edge cool— no small achievement. It went on to earn a 1999 Grammy for best rock/gospel album.

The Smallbone family has been actively involved in St. James's career throughout, with her father serving as manager and her siblings helping out on tour. Live, St. James is an evangelist as much as an entertainer,

filling her elaborately staged concerts with preaching and question-and-answer sessions. She is an advocate of premarital abstinence, encouraging couples to refrain from intimacy (including kissing) before tying the knot. Her theological stance is aggressive and uncompromising, calling on Christians to turn away from carnality, vanity, and materialism. She has helped spread her message through the youth-oriented devotional books *40 Days with God* and *You're the Voice: 40 More Days with God* (issued by Thomas Nelson Publishing in 1996 and 1997, respectively).

In 2001, St. James released *Transform*. Working with a new producer, Matt Bronleewe (a former member of **Jars of Clay**), she ventured deeper into Euro-dance territory and added string orchestrations. *Transform* brought her still more Christian radio hits, including "Reborn" and "In Me." (For more about Rebecca St. James, see also pages 89–94.)

Rebecca St. James (ForeFront, 1994)
God (ForeFront, 1996)
Christmas (ForeFront, 1997)
Pray (ForeFront, 1998)
Transform (ForeFront, 2001)

2ND CHAPTER OF ACTS
Formed 1971 in Los Angeles, California

Known for its stellar vocal harmonies, 2nd Chapter of Acts was a unique combination of talents. The group was very much a family affair—members Annie Herring, Matthew Ward, and Nelly Ward Griesen were siblings; Herring's husband Buck produced their albums and served as sound engineer on tour. The trio's songs were an unlikely hybrid of old-fashioned hymnody, 1970s-era hard rock, and American theater music. Over the course of the group's 17-year career, it remained committed to musical ministry and avoided trendy updates of its style.

Herring was the first of the Ward children to concentrate on music. Raised in the Catholic faith in rural North Dakota along with her eight siblings, she began singing in the church choir and found inspiration in the Latin mass. Annie moved with her family to the Sacramento area in 1963. Five years later, the death of her mother prompted her to embrace the evangelical Christianity of her boyfriend, Buck Herring. After the passing of her father in 1970, she and Buck (now married and living in Los Angeles) took in her younger sister Nelly and brother Matthew. The three siblings began working up harmonized versions of the inspirational Christian songs that Annie Herring was composing on piano. Encouraged by friends, they started performing in public as 2nd Chapter of Acts in early 1971.

Among those impressed by the trio was Pat Boone, who arranged for the three to record for MGM Records. Their debut 1972 single, "Jesus Is," featured 13-year-old Matthew Ward's vocals. After the release of the follow-up, "I'm So Happy," MGM decided not to release an album by the group. 2nd Chapter moved on, touring extensively with **Barry McGuire** before signing with Myrrh Records and releasing its first album, 1974's *With Footnotes*. This LP featured "Easter Song," a brief but compelling hymn written by Annie that received secular as well as Christian radio airplay.

2nd Chapter continued to perform at coffeehouses and church-sponsored events, winning over audiences with its youthful enthusiasm and stirring vocals. The group collaborated with McGuire on the two-disc concept album *To the Bride* (1975) and joined forces with **Phil Keaggy** on a similar project, *How the West Was One* (1977). Such singles as "Mansion Builder" and "Rod & Staff" found favor on the Christian airwaves during the late '70s. Switching to Sparrow, 2nd Chapter released the ambitious *The Roar of Love* (1980), a song cycle based on C. S. Lewis's allegorical novel *The Lion, the Witch, and the Wardrobe*. A Christian rock operetta of sorts, the album's music was built upon complex melodies, stop-start tempo shifts, and blazing guitar interludes (featuring guest star Phil Keaggy). As vocal soloists, Matthew displayed a measure of R&B swagger, while Annie's pure tones recalled her church choir background.

Untouched by New Wave rock and other hip influences, 2nd Chapter continued to release albums with distinctive sounds.

The group's music defied easy secular comparisons—at times, its early '80s work suggests ABBA in an off-Broadway musical, or Queen following up "Bohemian Rhapsody" with a praise song. Really, the group remained very much itself. *Rejoice* (1981) added some rock pyrotechnics courtesy of guitarist/synthesizer player Kerry Livgren (from the band Kansas). The album's effusive title track became one of the group's biggest Christian hits in early 1982. Further albums and singles followed, including *Hymns* (1986), the first of three albums devoted to (mostly) traditional sacred songs.

Far Away Places (1987) contained another major Christian radio hit, the rousing "Humble Yourself." Remaining true to its essence, 2nd Chapter filled this album with sweet arias ("You Are All in All"), shimmering sing-alongs ("I Reach Out"), and melo-dramatic rockers ("It's No Masquerade"). Even more than the music, the message remained constant—extolling Christ was always the group's reason for being, from beginning to end.

Tiring of the road and looking to spend more time with their families, the members of 2nd Chapter embarked on a final tour in 1988. Both Matthew and Annie had been releasing solo projects since the 1970s, and they continued to do so after the band's breakup. *20*, a com-prehensive anthology of 2nd Chapters's recordings, appeared in 1992. (Note: Discography is selective.)

With Footnotes (Myrrh, 1974)
In the Volume of the Book (Myrrh, 1975)
How the West Was One (with Phil Keaggy)
   (Myrrh, 1977)
Mansion Builder (Sparrow, 1978)
The Roar of Love (Sparrow, 1980)
Rejoice (Sparrow, 1981)
Singer Sower (Sparrow, 1983)
Night Light (Live Oak, 1985)
Hymns (Live Oak, 1986)
Far Away Places (Live Oak, 1987)
Hymns II (Live Oak, 1988)
Hymns Instrumental (Live Oak, 1989)
20 (Sparrow, 1992)
ANNIE HERRING SOLO:
Through a Child's Eyes (Sparrow, 1976)
Search Deep Inside (Sparrow, 1981)
Waiting for My Ride to Come (Live Oak, 1990)
There's a Stirring (Sparrow, 1992)
Glimpses (Spring Hill, 1997)
Wonder (Spring Hill, 1998)
MATTHEW WARD SOLO:
Toward Eternity (Sparrow, 1979)
Armed and Dangerous (Live Oak, 1987)
The Matthew Ward Collection (Benson, 1992)
Point of View (Benson, 1992)
My Redeemer (Newport, 1997)
Even Now (Discovery House Music, 2000)

THE 77s
Formed 1979 in Sacramento, California

The 77s have released one of the most eclectic bodies of work in Christian music. Centered around singer/guitarist Michael

Roe, the group evolved from an uneven New Wave–styled combo in the early 1980s into a far more confident blues/folk/rock unit later in the decade. More recent albums have shown further growth and artistic diversity. Roe's sly, eloquent songs and unfettered guitar flights have come to define the band's essence. Though under-exposed in both the Christian and secular markets, the 77s have continued to record and tour in various configurations, sup-ported by a loyal coterie of fans.

Sacramento's Warehouse Ministries served as the launching pad for the band in the late 1970s. Founding members Roe, Mark Tootle (keyboards/guitar/vocals), Jan Eric Volz (bass/guitar), and Mark Proctor (drums/vocals) came together as part of the church's artistic outreach program. The group—originally called the Scratch Band—performed every weekend at the Warehouse and earned an enthusi-astic local fan base. At the start of 1982, they recorded their debut album, *Ping Pong Over the Abyss*, at the Warehouse's own recording facility, Sangre Studios. The Scratch Band changed its name to he 77s just prior to the album's release on the Word-distributed Exit label. (Note: The band's name has appeared on various releases and in print as "the Seventy Sevens," "the 77s," and "77's.")

Ping Pong Over the Abyss was an earnest but derivative album, the work of a band still finding its own voice. Self-consciously ominous vocals and herky-jerky, overly busy arrangements make the release sound dated today. In contrast to later efforts, the lyrics have a strident edge in their condemnation of secular humanism and New Age religion. "Someone New" and a stripped-down cover of Ry Cooder's "Denomination Blues" are the album's best tracks. The 77s displayed a clearer sense of identity on 1984's *All Fall Down*, released to the secular market by Exit in tandem with A&M. Roe's guitar work shows a more pronounced blues influence on tracks like "Mercy, Mercy" and "You Don't Scare Me." The lyrics were more subtle and revealing as well. *All Fall Down* received some exposure on mainstream radio and via MTV.

Replacing drummer Proctor with Aaron Smith (former sideman with Ray Charles and the Temptations), the 77s returned with a self-titled album released by Exit/Island in 1987. Roe emerges here as a commanding rock guitarist and a singer/ songwriter of nuance and honesty, able to rip through ferocious leads one moment and dissect moral issues in a subdued setting the next. Every track on this album is strong— particular standouts include "What Was in That Letter" (a meditation of the power of the Word with screaming guitar volleys), "The Lust, the Flesh, the Eyes and the Pride of Life" (a chiming folk/rock track about wrestling with temptation), and "Bottom Line" (an understated, sweetly melodic ode to God). The album's final track, "I Could Laugh," is a brooding acoustic number with a Lou Reed–like dark edge. In the latter, Roe traces the descent of an alienated hipster into sin and self-loathing, leaving him in the shadow of God's final judgment. Such fine performances, though, went largely unheard. Underpromoted by Island, *The 77's* quickly sank in the marketplace.

Tootle and Volz had left the group by the late 1980s, leaving Roe as the sole original member. Under the moniker 7&7 Is, Roe released a collection of new recordings, demos, and outtakes as *More Miserable than You'll Ever Be* on the Alternative label in 1990. That same year, Broken Records released *Sticks and Stones*, a further assortment of demos and previously unheard material, including such impressive tracks as "Perfect Blues" and "MT." A live album, *88*, appeared on Broken in 1991 and included several new tunes along with a manic version of the Yardbirds' "Under, Over, Sideways, Down."

The 77s gained new blood when guitarist David Leonhardt and bassist Mark Harmon joined forces with Roe and Smith. This lineup recorded *The Seventy Sevens*, released by BAI/Word in 1992. Impressive in its creative reach, the album counterpoints serene melodies and vocal harmonies (reminiscent of Brian Wilson's work at times) with hard, even downright nasty guitar and drum work. The lyrics have a similarly broad scope, addressing man's need for God with humor, irony,

and unforced tenderness. A Christian sense of divine love fills "Kites without Strings" and "The Rain Kept Falling in Love." The band is equally adept at sleek, chiming folk/rock ("Phoney Eyes") and grease-spattered blues/boogie ("Nuts for You"), managing to sound intelligently reverent either way. Also notable is the tune "Pray Naked" (the album's original title until Word objected), an elaborately arranged song-suite with a playful but spiritual lyric message.

Still on a creative upswing, the 77s sounded a bit tougher and spookier on 1994's *Drowning with Land in Sight*. A '70s-style hard rock influence is more prominent here, showing itself in tracks like "Snake" (wherein Roe takes on the voice of Satan) and "Snowblind" (a confession of weakness and confusion). The band went so far as to cover Led Zeppelin's "Nobody's Fault but Mine"; the new version, surprisingly enough, received a measure of Christian radio airplay. Free expression had its limits, however—the track "Dave's Blues" contained the phrase "kicked my ass," which was censored by Word. As with *The Seventy Sevens* album, Roe's lyrics zero in on the sufferings and absurdities of Christians, combining irony with empathy in about equal measure.

The second edition of the 77s passed into history when Leonhardt and Smith left the band after *Drowning with Land in Sight*. Roe moved on and released *Safe as Milk* (1995), a solo outing on the VIA label with contributions from his former bandmates. This album contains some of Roe's most interesting and provocative work, freed from the constraints of his previous recording situations. The intentions of some songs are hard to read—tunes like "Go with God but Go" and "Till Jesu Comes" are so goofily earnest as to border on the tongue in cheek. Another track, "The Stellazine Prophesy," is a demonic sales pitch for a mind-numbing drug set to a funk/rock groove. Still another highpoint is "It's for You," a catchy acoustic folk tune that lambastes an arrogant nonbeliever in fairly racy terms ("You shot your wad when you named yourself God..."). The music here varies from simple guitar/vocal numbers to delicately layered atmospheric pieces and piano-based ballads.

Meanwhile, Roe and Harmon linked up with drummer Bruce Spencer to reactivate the 77s, releasing 1995's *Tom Tom Blues* on Brainstorm. This album is full of attitude, delivering hard-rocking put-downs like "Rocks in Your Heads" and wallowing in alienation in "You Still Love Me." The band has effortless command of classic blues/rock riffs and rhythms, with Roe growling his way through the gleefully downbeat lyrics. "Earache" indulges in drum solos and note-gargling guitar work, all in good fun. For contrast, there's the simmering "Flowers in the Sand," a gentler number spiced with a "wah-wah" solo. The following year, Roe returned with *The Boat Ashore*, another "solo" outing, with Harmon and Spencer

providing backup. More sonically unified than *Safe as Milk* and softer than *Tom Tom Blues,* this release (on the Innocent Media label) showcases the jazzier side of Roe's guitar playing. God returns as a focal point in the title track and "Thanks a Million."

The band inaugurated its own Fools of the World label with the 1996 live acoustic album *Echoes o' Faith.* In 1999, they released *EP,* a collection of five pop/rock tunes mostly dealing with damaged relationships. A full album, *A Golden Field of Radioactive Crows,* appeared in 2001. The rockabillyish "Mean Green Season" and the deceptively sunny "Related" (inspired in part by the death of Roe's longtime collaborator Gene Eugene) were among the best moments here. Released near the twentieth anniversary of the 77s first album, *A Golden Field* shows the remarkable level of vigor and imagination they continue to possess.

In addition to the above, Roe has toured and recorded with **the Lost Dogs** since 1992. (For more about the 77s, see pages 95–101.)

Ping Pong Over the Abyss (Exit, 1982)
All Fall Down (Exit/A&M, 1984)
The 77s (Exit/Island, 1987)
Sticks and Stones (Broken, 1990)
88 (BAI, 1991)
The Seventy Sevens (BAI/Word, 1992)
Drowning with Land in Sight (Myrrh, 1994)
Tom Tom Blues (Brainstorm, 1995)
Echoes o' Faith (Fools of the World, 1996)

EP *(Fools of the World, 1999)*
A Golden Field of Radioactive Crows
    (Fools of the World, 2001)
MICHAEL ROE SOLO:
More Miserable than You'll Ever Be
    (as 7&7 Is) (Alternative, 1990)
Safe as Milk (VIA, 1995)
The Boat Ashore (Innocent Media, 1996)

JUDEE SILL
Born 1944; died 1979

It is debatable whether the late Judee Sill was ever really a Christian. Scattered information indicates that she held an assortment of spiritual beliefs, influenced at times by Theosophy and Rosicrucianism. What *can* be said is that her work as a singer/songwriter drew upon Christian symbolism in fascinating ways. Moreover, her songs had a prayer-like quality to them, as if she were asking God to rescue her from her troubled life. If Sill was a seeker rather than a believer, her music nevertheless was infused with a sense of reverence and a hunger for grace.

Sill grew up in the San Fernando Valley, north of Los Angeles. She exhibited both musical talent and a strong rebellious streak. Her participation in a series of armed robberies sent her to reform school during her teens; she led the school choir while serving time. After her release, she studied music at Los Angeles Valley College and played upright bass in local jazz clubs. A cycle of heroin addiction, prostitution,

and larceny held back her emergence as an artist. In the late 1960s, she became friends with bassist Jim Pons, who recorded her song "Dead Time Bummer Blues" with his band the Leaves and helped her secure a publishing deal with Blimp Productions. This led to the Turtles (Blimp's main recording act) releasing a version of her song "Lady-O" as a single in late 1969. Sill was gaining notoriety as a performer of her own material as well, prompting a young David Geffen to sign her to his newly established Asylum label. Pons, former Leaves bandmate John Beck, and engineer Henry Lewy coproduced most of her self-titled debut album, recorded over a two-year span and released in 1971.

Judee Sill is a remarkably well-realized first album. Its music interweaves strands of Bach-like classical melodies, campfire sing-along folk tunes, and Western movie soundtrack themes, often within the same song. The lyrics mix cowboy lingo with high-flown mystical invocations of divine beings—in fact, Sill seems obsessed with the idea of a "cowboy Christ" who will ride to her rescue. "Ridge Rider," "The Phantom Cowboy," and other tunes are landscapes of heaven as filmed by John Ford, vivid and haunting. In songs like "The Lamb Ran Away with the Crown" and "The Archetypal Man," she freely shuffles references to angels, demons, lambs, roses, and other Christian symbols, leaving room for various interpretations. "Jesus Was a Cross Maker" (the album's best known song, later covered by everyone from the Hollies to Warren Zevon) isn't about Jesus at all, but a false-hearted lover. For all its theological ambiguity, *Judee Sill* is clearly the work of an artist desperate to transcend the world, to receive "a kiss from God."

After touring the United States and Britain, Sill released a second Asylum album, 1973's *Heart Food*. If anything, the songs here express an even more intense yearning for contact with God. The "cowboy Christ" is back, galloping through "The Vigilante" and "Soldier of the Heart," saving Sill from the darkness. Her Savior is a loner, brave and pure—"blindly faithful but following none," as she puts it in "There's a Rugged Road." The album's final track, "The Donor," is a slow, brooding piece built around the liturgical phase *kyrie eleison* ("Lord have mercy"). This seems to be the prayer at the center of *Heart Food*.

The most striking thing about Sill's two Asylum albums are their lack of sensuality, their denial of the physical. If her life was mired in sex, dope, and self-destruction, her songs looked resolutely heavenward. They represented a dream of escape she never quite found. Sill lost her Asylum deal after *Heart Food* failed to sell and entered a downward spiral. Unable to restart her music career, she found work as cartoonist at a Los Angeles animation studio during the mid-'70s. Around this time, she turned to hard drugs again after suffering a severe back injury. She died of a heroin and cocaine overdose in late 1979.

Sill's two albums have recently been reissued on CD by Asylum in Japan.

Judee Sill (Asylum, 1971)
Heart Food (Asylum, 1973)

SIXPENCE NONE THE RICHER
Formed 1992 in New Braunfels, Texas

The wistful, quietly intelligent music of Sixpence None the Richer caught the ear of the mainstream pop world in 1999, when its single "Kiss Me" reached the top of the secular pop charts in the United States, Canada, Britain, Japan, and other

Sixpence None the Richer, with lead singer Leigh Nash (third from left) and guitarist Matt Slocum (far right)
Photo by Allen Clark

countries. The platinum-level success of the band's self-titled third album represented a major breakthrough for Contemporary Christian music, although neither "Kiss Me" nor its follow-up single, "There She Goes," were overtly Christian in lyric content. Still, Sixpence's huge international exposure encouraged other Christian bands to aim for large secular audiences.

Sixpence None the Richer was formed in 1992 by teenagers Matt Slocum (guitar) and Leigh Bingham (vocals). The group's name derived from a line in the C. S. Lewis book *Mere Christianity.* Initially based out of the Austin, Texas, area, the group released its debut album, *The Fatherless and the Widow,* on the R.E.X. label in 1993. *This Beautiful Mess* appeared two years later, featuring added band members Tess Wiley (guitar), Dale Baker (drums), and J. J. Plasencio (bass). Touring with such secular bands as 10,000 Maniacs and the Smithereens in the United States and Britain helped secure Sixpence a loyal following, and in 1996 the album won a GMA Dove for best modern/alternative album of the year.

An emphasis on sweet, folk-based melodies and thoughtful lyrics has distinguished Sixpence from the start. Slocum's songs often contain literary references and deal with themes of faith and self-doubt in personal, diary-like terms. Bingham tempers an innocent vocal air with a jazz singer's sense of timing. Sixpence's moody yet good-natured sound brings to mind the Sundays and similar 1980s British folk/pop groups. As Slocum and Bingham have matured, their music has grown less oblique and more accessible, with catchier hooks and better-realized lyric ideas.

The demise of the R.E.X. label and a subsequent contractual dispute kept Sixpence from recording for several years. The members scattered, leaving only Slocum and Bingham. Fortunately, the band was revived when veteran Christian artist/producer Steve Taylor agreed to work with the two and formed a record label, Squint Entertainment, to release their next album. A new backup roster, featuring guitarist Sean Kelly, bassist Justin Cary, and drummer Dale Baker, was recruited. The resulting album, *Sixpence None the Richer,* was released in 1998.

Sixpence None the Richer built upon the strengths of the band's first two albums with impressive results. Bingham (who became Leigh Nash after marrying Christian musician Mark Nash in 1996) sang with greater assurance, although her naïve, slightly old-fashioned vocal style remained her trademark. Slocum remained the principal songwriter, combining explicit biblical references with a more general sense of longing and spiritual hunger. Such album cuts as "The Waiting Room" typified his melancholy-tinged view of man's distance from God. The album as a whole benefited from Taylor's elegant production sense, which polished the band's ideas without making them too obvious or overtly commercial.

Previous Sixpence singles—most notably "Within a Room Somewhere" and "Thought Menagerie"—had received airplay on Christian stations. This time, Squint decided to work the single "Kiss Me" in mainstream markets. After months of limited success, the song took off in early 1999, thanks to its inclusion in the soundtrack to the film *She's All That*. In May of that year "Kiss Me" topped the Billboard U.S. singles charts for two weeks. Heavy video exposure and appearances on *The Tonight Show with Jay Leno* and other programs increased the band's momentum still further. "Kiss Me" went on to receive gold certification and a Grammy nomination for best pop performance by duo or group. The band's tours—most notably as part of Lillith Fair in 1998 and '99—continued to bring it to a widening mainstream audience.

The huge success of "Kiss Me" raised questions as to what truly constituted a Christian pop song. Controversy erupted when the Gospel Music Association declined to nominate "Kiss Me" for a GMA Dove Award due to its lack of overtly Christian content.

Sixpence followed "Kiss Me" with "There She Goes," a cover of a 1990 tune by the La's, a British secular band. In 2000, the band returned to the studio with producer Paul Fox (10,000 Maniacs) to record a new album, *Divine Discontent*. The demise of Squint Entertainment as an independent label in mid-2001 kept this project unreleased until October 2002, when it is scheduled to appear on the secular Reprise label.

The Fatherless and the Widow (R.E.X., 1993)
This Beautiful Mess (R.E.X., 1995)
Sixpence None the Richer (Squint, 1998)

MICHAEL W. SMITH
Born October 7, 1957,
in Kenova, West Virginia

One of Christian music's most successful crossover acts, singer/songwriter Michael W. Smith became something of a male counterpart to **Amy Grant** in the early 1990s. Voted one of *People* magazine's "50 Most Beautiful People" in 1992, his good looks are matched with an appealing voice and a knack for writing radio-friendly pop tunes. Smith achieved much popularity in the secular market with uplifting, theologically understated songs. In 2001, though, he returned to unmistakable Christian themes with his *Worship* CD.

Born and raised in a small West Virginia community, Smith lent his voice to both church choirs and rock bands in his youth. A songwriter since age six, he decided on music as a career after briefly attending college. In 1978 he relocated to Nashville, where he struggled with a drug habit and low self-esteem before recommitting his life to Christ. Things improved for him after he began working with the Christian band

Higher Ground and writing songs for Meadowgreen Music in 1981. The next year, he achieved a breakthrough hit with "How Majestic Is Your Name," recorded by **Sandi Patty**. He also toured as keyboardist and opening act for Amy Grant, paving the way for his emergence as a solo recording artist in 1983.

Smith's career took off quickly after the release of his Reunion debut album, *Michael W. Smith Project*. His first Christian radio hit, the chart-topping "Great Is the Lord," was a synthesizer-driven modern hymn. What set Smith apart from other writer/performers of inspirational material was the intimate quality of his voice,

defined by its light vibrato and hint of roughness. Rather than soar and exhort, Smith put his songs across with a quiet ache in his voice. This worked well on his 1984 single "Friends," a sentimental pop elegy that remains one of his best-loved songs. As a songwriter, he grew adept at describing the moral choices Christians face in everyday situations. "Rocketown" (1986) sketched the emptiness of the party life, while 1987's "Old Enough to Know" dealt with a teenager's struggle to remain sexually abstinent. Smith aimed his message at a young audience and sought to keep his music contemporary. From *The Big Picture* (1986) onward, he moved toward a more rock-oriented sound, adding hipper dance grooves and tougher-sounding guitars. The approach won him new fans, helping 1988's *i 2 (Eye)* become his first certified gold album.

By the end of the 1980s, Smith had racked up a long list of Christian radio hits and numerous awards, including a Grammy for best gospel performance, male (1984), and a GMA Dove for songwriter of the year (1986). His next step was to try for a mainstream audience. He got his chance when Geffen Records signed a distribution deal for the secular market with Reunion in 1991. Smith's songs and performing style were close enough to mainstream tastes that the leap was not difficult. *Go West Young Man* (1990) earned gold certification on the strength of "Place in This World," a song

Michael W. Smith
Photo by Allen Clark

of spiritual longing that soft-pedaled its references to the Deity. Cowritten with Amy Grant and Christian hit-maker Wayne Kirkpatrick, it became a number 6 secular hit. Smith fared even better with "I Will Be Here for You," a love song with only a hint of Christian content that topped both the Christian and secular singles charts that same year. The song was included on the certified-platinum CD *Change Your World*, which also contained such big Christian radio hits as "Somebody Love Me" and "Give It Away."

I'll Lead You Home (1995) took Smith to an even higher plateau. Produced by Patrick Leonard (known for his hits with Madonna, among others), the album's tracks are aggressive without being excessive, tastefully mixing rock, modern R&B, and a little country. Except for the title track (an Adult Contemporary secular hit), the songs here are explicitly Scripture-based. While it fell short of *Change Your World* in sales, *I'll Lead You Home* produced seven Christian radio hits, including "Cry for Love," "Breakdown," "I'll Be Around," and "Someday." It went on to receive a Grammy in 1996 for best pop/contemporary gospel album.

Though he largely retained the loyalty of his original audience, Smith's forays outside of Christian music were not beyond criticism. His 1997 single "Love Me Good," a modest secular hit, was disqualified from GMA Dove Award consideration because of its lack of Christian content. Sales of his albums continued to be strong—1998's *Live the Life* and 1999's *This Is Your Time* both went gold—and he easily could have edged further into the mainstream. Instead, Smith recorded a live praise album at a Florida church, released as *Worship* in 2001. Backed by a 23-member choir that included Amy Grant and members of **Plus One,** Smith played piano and led worshippers through such inspirational numbers as **Rich Mullins's** classic "Awesome God" and his own "Purified." *Worship* took Smith full circle, back to the prayerful expressions of "How Majestic Is Your Name" and "Great Is the Lord."

In addition to his recorded output, Smith has written a series of Christian-market books, including *Old Enough to Know* (1987), *Friends Are Friends Forever* (1997), *Cooking with Smitty's Mom* (1999), and *I Will Be Your Friend* (2001).

Michael W. Smith Project (Reunion, 1983)
Michael W. Smith 2 (Reunion, 1984)
The Big Picture (Reunion, 1986)
The Live Set (Reunion, 1987)
i 2 (Eye) (Reunion, 1988)
Michael W. Smith Christmas (Reunion, 1988)
Go West Young Man (Reunion, 1990)
Change Your World (Reunion, 1992)
The First Decade: 1983–1993 (Reunion, 1993)
The Wonder Years (Reunion, 1993)
I'll Lead You Home (Reunion, 1995)
Live the Life (Reunion, 1998)
This Is Your Time (Reunion, 1999)
Freedom (Reunion, 2000)
Worship (Reunion, 2001)

RANDY STONEHILL
Born March 12, 1952,
in Stockton, California

At the start of his career, singer/songwriter Randy Stonehill was the archetypal hippie for Jesus: painfully sincere, a bit ragged and comical, but nevertheless infused with a spiritual glow. Over the course of his 30 years in Christian music, he shed his counterculture naïveté and acquired a more mature perspective. But the sense of wonder and discovery that made his early recordings so distinctive continues to define his recent work. His melodic approach remains folk-rooted and his lyrics continue to leaven their earnestness with liberal dollops of humor.

Stonehill was born in Stockton, California, and spent most of his childhood in San Jose. By age 15, he had formed his own local rock combo. In early 1969, he met and was befriended by fellow San Jose musician **Larry Norman,** who asked him to sing on one of his recording projects. It was under Norman's guidance that Stonehill became a Christian—in fact, he came to know God for the first time while sitting in Norman's kitchen during the summer of 1970. The two of them began performing together, appearing at the few church-sponsored venues that would book long-haired Christian rock musicians. Stonehill began writing songs around this time—among his first was "Norman's Kitchen," a slightly loopy retelling of his

born-again experience. He also branched out into acting in 1970, starring in the Christian rock musical *Show Me!*

Born Twice, Stonehill's debut album, was released on Norman's One Way label in 1971. "Norman's Kitchen" and "Alright Now" typify this album's unaffected honesty and high spirits. Stonehill came across as a loose, playful singer and guitarist, his excesses checked by his compact, catchy pop tunes. In 1972, he had the dubious honor of appearing in the film *Son of Blob.* The following year, he took a detour into the secular music world, recording *Get Me Out of Hollywood* in London for Philips Records. With the exception of the apocalyptic "Puppet Strings," most of these songs are wistful musings about love in a James Taylorish vein. Philips wasn't happy with the album, and it remained unreleased in the States until 1999.

From there, Stonehill returned to Christian music, meeting new collaborators like **Keith Green,** with whom he cowrote the enduring "Your Love Broke Through" (later recorded by both Stonehill and Green, as well as **Phil Keaggy** and **Russ Taff**). Signing with Norman's new label, Solid Rock, Stonehill released *Welcome to Paradise* in 1976. This release was a major advance, the work of an artist finally hitting his stride. Such songs as "Keep Me Running" find a universality in Stonehill's own spiritual journey. *Welcome to Paradise* is widely regarded as Stonehill's best album; certainly it was the one that fully established him as an important Christian singer/songwriter. He went on to release a second album on Solid Rock four years later, *The Sky Is Falling*. This song collection swings between emotional extremes, brooding on mortality one minute ("Through a Glass Darkly,"' "Emily") and spoofing pop culture the next ("The Great American Cure"). Like its predecessor, *The Sky Is Falling* is unusually well produced for a '70s-era Christian market album, highlighting Stonehill's increasing vocal versatility and adept guitar work.

The 1980s found Stonehill moving to Myrrh Records and releasing albums on a nearly annual basis. *Between the Glory and the Flame* (1981) showed a New Wave rock influence and featured production input from **Daniel Amos**'s Terry Taylor. *Equator* (1983), also produced by Taylor, was a mixed bag of satiric topical tunes ("Big Ideas," "Cosmetic Fixation"), praise songs ("Light of the World," "World without Pain"), and Caribbean-style sing-alongs ("Shut De Do)." For all his quirkiness, Stonehill proved capable of writing hit material for Christian radio, including "Turning Thirty," "When I Look to the Mountains," "I Could Never Say Goodbye," and "Who Will Save the Children" (the latter recorded with Phil Keaggy).

The Wild Frontier, produced by **Dave Perkins** and released in 1986, saw Stonehill rocking harder than he had in years, barreling through such galvanizing tracks as "Here Come the Big Guitars" and "The Dying Breed." The rock hymn "Hope of

Glory" from this album brought him yet another Christian hit single. Perkins returned to produce his next release, *Can't Buy a Miracle* (1988), another strong effort that yielded the ballad "Coming Back Soon" and the upbeat rockabilly-styled "Brighter Day." From there, he grew more introspective on the **Mark Heard**–produced *Return to Paradise* (1989), then paired up again with Terry Taylor to record the Beatles-influenced *Wonderama* (1992). Wrapping up his tenure with Myrrh, he released 1994's *The Lazarus Heart* on his own Street Level label. Among his most successful albums, *The Lazarus Heart* spawned "I Turn to You," his first chart-topping single on Christian radio.

Stonehill has shown a remarkable ability to update his music without losing its essence. *Thirst* (1998), produced by Ragamuffin Band singer/guitarist Rick Elias, managed to blend fresh Celtic and even Middle Eastern influences into his approach. At the same time, he harked back to the Jesus Music fervor of his *Born Twice* days on "Fire" and "Father of Lights." Balancing the pathos of songs like "Little Rose" was the goofiness of "Baby Hates Clowns," a tune of no spiritual import whatsoever. *Thirst* testified to Stonehill's continued artistic vitality after nearly 30 productive years in Christian music.

In 2002, he cofounded the label Holy Sombrero with Ray Ware and Terry Taylor. Its first release was *Uncle Stonehill's Hat*, an album of whimsical children's songs.

Born Twice (One Way, 1971)

Get Me Out of Hollywood
(Polygram UK, 1973; Solid Rock, 1999)

Welcome to Paradise (Solid Rock, 1976)

The Sky Is Falling (Solid Rock, 1980)

Between the Glory and the Flame
(Myrrh, 1981)

Equator (Myrrh, 1983)

Celebrate This Heartbeat (Myrrh, 1984)

Love Beyond Reason (Myrrh, 1985)

The Wild Frontier (Myrrh, 1986)

Can't Buy a Miracle (Myrrh, 1988)

Return to Paradise (Myrrh, 1989)

Until We Have Wings (Myrrh, 1990)

Wonderama (Myrrh, 1992)

Stories (Myrrh, 1993)

The Lazarus Heart (Street Level, 1994)

Our ReCollections (Myrrh, 1996)

Thirst (Brentwood, 1998)

Uncle Stonehill's Hat (Holy Sombrero, 2002)

STRYPER
Formed 1983
in Orange County, California

Stryper was considered a bizarre novelty by many when it emerged from the Southern California heavy metal scene in 1984. Secular rock critics hotly debated the validity of a Christian metal band in the press; whether they were intrigued or amused, the four-member group reaped enormous publicity from it all. Stryper's brand of "heavenly metal" earned fans among secular metalheads and Christian rock enthusiasts alike, sustaining the group until its breakup in 1992.

The band evolved out of Roxx Regime, a Whittier, California-based metal combo founded by brothers Michael and Robert Sweet (singer/guitarist and drummer, respectively). Though raised in a Christian home, the siblings had fallen away from their faith until they experienced a spiritual renewal in late 1982. Rededicating their band to God, they added Oz Fox (born Richard Martinez) on guitar and Tim Gaines (born Tim Hagelganz) on bass. They dubbed themselves Stryper, derived from Isaiah 53:5 ("With His stripes we are healed). The name also was said to be an acronym for Salvation through Redemption Yielding Peace, Encouragement, and Righteousness.

Stryper's mix of head-banging rock and Jesus-driven lyrics caused considerable stir on the local club scene. The secular Enigma label signed the group and released its debut mini-album, *The Yellow and Black Attack*, in June 1984. National press coverage quickly followed, boosting record and ticket sales. The band's colorful yellow and black spandex uniforms emphasized its stance as rock'n'roll Christian soldiers. To further underscore the group's message, Michael Sweet often tossed Bibles into the crowd during concerts. The band repeated in interviews hat its music was intended to glorify Jesus. Not everyone in the Christian community saw it that way—Jimmy Swaggert called Stryper ungodly, and the Trinity Broadcasting Network refused to air one of its early videos. Such controversy only gained the band further attention.

After releasing a Christmas EP (featuring a blistering version of "Winter Wonderland") in December 1984, Stryper was back with its debut full-length album, *Soldiers Under Command*, in August 1985. This album revealed a solid rock unit with more going for it than hype—Fox was a fast-fingered guitarist in the Eddie Van Halen tradition, adding flash to the band's chant-along anthems. The harmony-laden "Reach Out" and the power ballad "Together as One" (the latter a Christian radio hit) showed songwriting skill, while the band's cover of "The Battle Hymn of the Republic" roused the faithful. After further touring, Stryper released *To Hell with the Devil* in 1986. This album contained the lushly melodic ballad "Honestly" (a hit single in both the Christian and secular markets) and ultimately earned gold certification. *In God We Trust* (1988) was a similar effort, spawning the singles "Always There for You" and "I Believe in You" (both big on Christian radio, less successful on secular). Both the album and its title track won GMA Dove Awards in the hard rock category in 1989.

By the time *Against the Law* appeared in 1990, Stryper was beginning to run out of steam. Michael Sweet decided to embark on a solo career in 1992, effec-tively ending the group. He went on to enjoy a measure of success on Christian radio in the mid-'90s, particularly with a remake of "Always There for You." Fox and Gaines formed their own band, Sin Dizzy, in 1994. In May 2000, the original Stryper lineup reunited to perform at a "first annual Stryper and Contemporary Christian Expo," held in Parsippany, New Jersey.

The Yellow and Black Attack (Enigma, 1984)
Soldiers Under Command (Enigma, 1985)
To Hell with the Devil (Enigma, 1986)
In God We Trust (Enigma, 1988)
Against the Law (Enigma, 1990)
Can't Stop the Rock: The Stryper Collection, 1984–1991 (Hollywood, 1991)
MICHAEL SWEET SOLO:
Michael Sweet (Benson, 1994)
Real (Benson, 1995)
Truth (2001)

RUSS TAFF
Born November 11, 1953,
in Farmersville, California

The fervent vocals of Russ Taff are among the most distinctive in Christian music. He made the transition from southern gospel–style singing with the Imperials to pop/rock as a solo artist in the 1980s. Taff went through further stylistic permutations before returning to Christian music in the late 1990s.

The fourth of five sons, Taff was reared in the Pentacostal faith by his evangelist father in a small Central California farming town. Singing in church at an early age, he was influenced by both white and black gospel (though forbidden to listen to secular pop music by his parents). At 15, he moved with his family to Hot Springs, Arkansas, where he formed the Sounds of Joy with guitarist James Hollihan, Jr. After several years with the band, he toured as a singer with evangelist Jerry Seville before joining the famed Imperials in 1977. Taff's reputation grew during his successful four-year tenure with the group. In 1981, he went solo and released his debut album for Myrrh two years later.

The music that Taff made during the 1980s was noticeably different from the harmony-centered southern gospel sounds of the Imperials. Such albums as *Medals* (1985) confirmed his abilities as a gritty rock singer, falling somewhere between John Fogerty and Eddie Money in vocal texture. There was a raw emotional edge to his voice that invoked the ecstatic church services of his youth. It helped him achieve an enviable string of Christian hits from his hugely popular 1983 single "We Will Stand" onward. *Russ Taff* (1987) was an especially strong effort, a bracing rock album featuring covers of such

tunes as **Dave Perkins**'s "Walk Between the Lines" and **Charlie Peacock**'s "Down in the Lowlands."

By the end of the 1980s, Taff had won eight GMA Dove Awards, including ones for male vocalist of the year in 1981, 1982, and 1984. The following decade saw him trying out new creative directions. *The Way Home* (1989) offered a stripped-down pop/ rock sound, while *Under Their Influence* (1991) celebrated the music of such gospel pioneers as Mahalia Jackson and Blind Willie Johnson. In 1994, he briefly replaced **Michael English** as a touring member of the harmonizing Gaither Vocal Band. The following year, he left Christian music to try his hand at secular country music, releasing *Winds of Change* on Reprise Records in 1995.

Taff met with limited success as a country singer, and returned to the Christian music world in 1997. Signing with Benson, he released *Right Here Right Now* in 1999. A heartfelt work mixing rock with traditional gospel, the album explored such personal issues as Taff's troubled relationship with his late father.

Walls of Glass (Myrrh, 1983)
Medals (Myrrh, 1985)
Russ Taff (Myrrh, 1987)
The Way Home (Myrrh, 1989)
Under Their Influence Vol. 1 (Myrrh, 1991)
A Christmas Song (Sparrow, 1992)
Winds of Change (Reprise, 1995)
Right Here Right Now (Benson, 1999)

JOHN MICHAEL TALBOT
Born May 8, 1954,
in Oklahoma City, Oklahoma

For a variety of reasons, singer/songwriter John Michael Talbot is in a category all his own. A Franciscan friar since 1978, he has devoted much of his prolific recording career to writing music rooted in ancient church tradition. A Catholic in a genre all but synonymous with evangelical Protestantism, his work has stood apart from Contemporary Christian music's trends and controversies. Talbot's art and life are very much of a piece—for the past two decades, he has lived out his spiritual ideals as a member of a small religious community in the Ozarks.

Talbot's creative path has been a long and unlikely one. Born in Oklahoma City and raised in Indianapolis, he and his older brother Terry seemed destined to become performing musicians. Their father, Dick Talbot, had been a violinist in the Oklahoma City Orchestra; mother Jimmie Margaret Talbot, a pianist, had inherited her love for music from her father, a singing Methodist minister. By age 10, Talbot was singing and playing guitar in local rock bands with Terry. These groups became more serious until, in 1968, the Talbot brothers formed the country/rock group Mason Profitt. The band sported frontiersman-style leather and buckskin outfits and performed songs with socially conscious protest messages. Mason Profitt went on

to release a series of albums on Warner Brothers Records before breaking up in 1973. Talbot dropped out of music, moved to an Indiana farm, and began exploring a range of spiritual traditions. He eventually became caught up in the Jesus movement and, together with Terry, recorded a Christian album for Warner Brothers, *Reborn*.

Signing with Sparrow as a solo artist, Talbot recorded a pair of folk-influenced pop albums, *John Michael Talbot* (1976) and *The New Earth* (1977). Together with Terry and songwriter Jamie Owens, he created the Christian musical *Firewind* (1976), with a cast featuring **Keith Green, Barry McGuire,** and members of **2nd Chapter of Acts.** Still spiritually restless, he put music aside for a second time and investigated the teachings of St. Francis of Assisi. This led him to embrace Catholicism and begin studies at a Franciscan retreat center in Indianapolis. In 1978 he joined the Franciscans as a Third Order lay brother and assumed vows of poverty, chastity, and obedience. Creating a monk's habit out of secondhand army blankets, he retreated to the woods to live a monastic existence.

At first, Talbot felt his monastic vows would mean the end of his musical involvements. He intended his next album, *The Lord's Supper* (1979), to be his last. Instead, this song cycle of contemplative music (released on Sparrow's sister label, Birdwing) ushered in a new phase of his career. The album's use of "The Apostles' Creed" and other centuries-old Christian texts were complemented by Talbot's classically influenced compositions. *The Lord's Supper's* positive reviews and strong sales inspired Talbot to release another album, *Come to the Quiet,* in 1980. That same year, he collaborated with his brother Terry on *The Painter,* a blending of folk and classical traditions recorded with the London Chamber Orchestra.

During the 1980s, Talbot drew further upon church music from the Middle Ages and the Renaissance for his own compositional direction. *For the Bride* (1981) was exemplary of his approach, alternating gently melodic passages with songs featuring Talbot's classical guitar and delicate tenor voice. In 1982, he released *Light Eternal,* a choral/orchestral album that earned a GMA Dove Award for worship music album of the year. Besides recording, Talbot performed his songs as part of worship services held at his hermitage. Music led him away from his retreat and toward greater involvement with fellow believers. In 1983, he moved to Eureka Springs, Arkansas, and founded the Little Portion Hermitage, a monastic community that grew to include singles and families as well as monks. Serving as general manager, Talbot lived and worked at the hermitage. He eventually resumed concert touring.

Albums of Talbot's sacred music continued to appear into the 1990s. Though his compositions were steeped in Catholicism, his work found considerable acceptance among Protestant listeners as well. In 1992,

he formed his own record label, Troubadour for the Lord. *Chant from the Hermitage* (1995) featured daily chants recorded at the Little Portion. In 1999, he returned to the sound of his earlier days with *Cave of the Heart,* which guest starred **Michael Card** and **Phil Keaggy** and found Talbot singing and playing in a folk/pop style. Tracks like "Glory to God" and "Common Fire" gave evidence that this master of monastic music could still rock a bit when he chose.

Talbot is also the author of more than a dozen books, among them *Music of Creation: Fundamentals of the Christian Faith* (Penguin Putnam, 1999). (Note: Discography is selective.)

John Michael Talbot (Sparrow, 1976)
The New Earth (Sparrow, 1977)
The Lord's Supper (Birdwing, 1979)
Come to the Quiet (Birdwing, 1980)
For the Bride (Birdwing, 1981)
Troubadour of the Great King (Birdwing, 1981)
Light Eternal (Birdwing, 1982)
Songs for Worship, Vol. 1 (Birdwing, 1983)
The Quiet (Birdwing, 1985)
Be Exalted (Birdwing, 1986)
Heart of the Shepherd (Sparrow, 1987)
Hiding Place (Sparrow, 1990)
The Birth of Jesus (Sparrow, 1990)
The Master Musician
    (Troubadour for the Lord, 1992)
Meditations in the Spirit
    (Troubadour for the Lord, 1993)
Meditations from Solitude
    (Troubadour for the Lord, 1994)

The John Michael Talbot Collection
　(Sparrow/Chordant, 1995)
Table of Plenty (Troubadour for the Lord, 1997)
Pathways of the Shepherd
　(Troubadour for the Lord, 1998)
Cave of the Heart
　(Troubadour for the Lord, 1999)
Simple Heart (Troubadour for the Lord, 2000)
WITH TERRY TALBOT:
The Painter (Sparrow, 1980)
No Longer Strangers (Sparrow, 1983)
The Talbot Brothers Collection
　(Sparrow/Chordant, 1995)

STEVE TAYLOR
Born December 9, 1957,
in Brawley, California

Brash and acerbic, singer/songwriter Steve Taylor has been an alternative force in Christian music since the early 1980s. Tagged "evangelical rock's court jester" at the start of his career, he gleefully satirized the shortcomings and blind spots of believers and the secular world alike. Taylor originally adopted a New Wave rock style, but his music has grown more diverse with time. Most recently, he's been active as a songwriter, producer, and record company executive.

The son of a Baptist minister, Ronald Stephen Taylor spent most of his childhood years in the Denver area. Though forbidden by his parents to listen to secular pop music until his midteens, he became a confirmed punk rock fan by the time he entered Biola University in Southern California. He began writing songs and, after failing to win interest from secular record companies in Los Angeles, returned to the Denver area to pursue music with local players. A stint working with Chuck Bolte's Jerimiah People, a Christian musical comedy group, led to an appearance at the annual Christian Artists Retreat in Estes Park, Colorado, in 1982. The highlight of Taylor's set was "I Want to Be a Clone," a scathing send-up of Christian conformity. Reaction to the performance was strong enough to secure him a deal with Sparrow Records.

Taylor made his recording debut with the *I Want to Be a Clone* EP in 1983. The disc's frenetic New Wave sounds and rapid-fire lyric lines earned him comparisons with Elvis Costello. The following year, he released his debut album, *Meltdown*. With a Johnny Rotten–like sneer in his voice, Taylor tore into secular materialism in songs like "Am I in Sync" and "Sin for a Season." Christian hypocrisy and clannishness were criticized in "Guilty by Association." The track that stirred the most debate, though, was "We Don't Need No Color Code," a pointed attack on the segregated dating policies of conservative Bob Jones University. While some in the Christian music community found it too radical, *Meltdown* sold 130,000 copies and went on to earn GMA Dove and Grammy nominations. Taylor sharpened his lyric thrust and added more musical substance on his next release, *On the Fritz* (1985). Produced by Ian McDonald (leader of the secular rock band Foreigner), the album yielded the Christian radio hits "This Disco (Used to Be a Cute Cathedral)" and "I Just Wanna Know." *On the Fritz* moved away from the brittle punk mannerisms of his early albums and toward a fuller, more serious sound. During this same time, Taylor was developing his skills as a video director, and went on to win a GMA Dove Award for the home video version of his 1986 live EP *Limelight*.

I Predict 1990 (released 1987) proved a landmark Christian rock album—lyrically sophisticated and musically diverse, it set a high mark for the genre. Taylor subtly probed the need for faith in "Harder to Believe than Not To" and took on 1980s-era greed with heightened ferocity in "What Is the Measure of Your Success." Sonically, the album mixed guitar-fueled rock with synthesizers and chamber music embellishments. Most of all, the album is remembered for "I Blew Up the Clinic Real Good," an ironic glimpse of an antiabortion extremist that was misconstrued by some as supporting clinic bombings. The fallout from this tune led to the cancellation of an Australian tour.

Feeling he had reached his potential as a Christian artist, Taylor decided to make a foray into the secular rock marketplace. Together with guitarists **Dave Perkins** and Lynn Nichols, bassist Wade Jaynes, and drummer Mike Mead, he launched a group

called Chagall Guevara and signed with MCA Records. The band's self-titled 1991 album was infused with Taylor's typically caustic wit and rampant idealism, evident in such tracks as "Escher's World" and "Violent Blue." Unfortunately, Chagall Guevara failed to find a large audience, and scattered after its first and only album. Signing with Warner Alliance, Taylor returned to Christian music with 1993's *Squint*, an album by turns brooding and aggressive in sound, with lyrics that are intricate and at times challenging; "Cash Cow," the album's final track, is nothing less than a mini-rock opera with a biblical setting. The single "Bannerman" brought Taylor his first Christian radio hit in more than six years. *Squint: Movies from the Soundtrack*, a home video featuring footage shot by Taylor in such exotic locales as Nepal and the Persian Gulf, appeared in 1994.

After the 1994 release of *Now the Truth Can Be Told* (a two-CD retrospective) and the live album *Liver* a year later, Taylor dropped out of sight as a recording artist. He remained active behind the scenes, most notably as the cowriter and producer of such **Newsboys** hits as "Shine," "Spirit Thing," and "Truth and Consequences." He also produced **Guardian**'s *Buzz* and *Bottlerocket* albums. In 1997, he launched Squint Entertainment, a record company funded in part by Gaylord Entertainment (then the parent company of Word/Myrrh Records). Seeking to find a middle path between the Christian and secular music worlds, Taylor assembled a diverse roster of pop, rock, and rap acts with crossover potential. The label's most impressive success was with **Sixpence None the Richer**'s self-titled album, produced by Taylor and containing the chart-topping secular hit "Kiss Me." Among Squint's other notable releases was *Roaring Lambs*, a multi-artist concept CD based on the writings of Christian author Bob Briner. Taylor contributed the quirky rocker "Shortstop" to the album.

Unfortunately, Squint ran into financial difficulties and ceased to function as an independent label in mid-2001. Taylor moved on to pursue other endeavors, including a long-germinating film project.

I Want to Be a Clone (Sparrow, 1983)
Meltdown (Sparrow, 1984)
On the Fritz (Sparrow, 1985)
Limelight (Sparrow, 1986)
I Predict 1990 (Myrrh, 1987)
Squint (Warner Alliance, 1993)
Now the Truth Can Be Told (Sparrow, 1994)
Liver (Warner Alliance, 1995)
WITH CHAGALL GUEVARA:
Chagall Guevara (MCA, 1991)

THIRD DAY
Formed 1994 in Marietta, Georgia

Third Day brings a deep southern earthiness to modern worship music. This Georgia-based quintet quickly gained a substantial following after the release of its debut album in 1996. Able to serve up pungent blues-rockers and sanctified ballads with equal ease, the band has often drawn upon Scripture for its lyric inspiration. The covey of GMA Dove Awards it won in 2001 testifies to its stature among Christian rock acts.

The group's roots extend back to 1991, when high school friends Mac Powell (lead vocals/acoustic guitar) and Mark Lee (guitar) began working together. Over the next four years, David Carr (drums), Tai Anderson (bass), and Brad Avery (guitar) were recruited into the lineup. Third Day's early local gigs drew much favorable word of mouth, as did its self-titled, independently released first album. Reunion signed

Third Day. Left to right: David Carr, Brad Avery, Mac Powell (leaning forward), Tai Anderson, and Mark Lee
Photo by Scott Greenwalt

the group in 1996, remixed the *Third Day* album and released it nationally. The singles "Love Song," "Forever," and "Praise Song" made the foursome a familiar presence on Christian radio almost immediately.

Several elements worked in Third Day's favor. The band's sound had a swampy, southern rock spirit to it, a hint of rebel pride amidst its reverence. Powell's deep-toned vocals were compelling, defined by a thick drawl reminiscent of rock's Darius Rucker and country's Travis Tritt. The songs on the first album were dialogues with God, intimate yet tinged with awe and grandeur. *Conspiracy No. 5* (1997) expanded the band's lyric focus somewhat, though its strong suit continued to be praise tunes like "My Hope Is You" (based on Psalm 25). *Conspiracy No. 5* solidified Third Day's place in the Christian market and went on to win a GMA Dove Award for rock album of the year in 1998 (with the track "Alien" winning for rock recorded song of the year as well).

In 1999, Third Day switched to Essential Records and released the rootsy CD *Time*. In some ways, this may be the definitive Third Day release—its marriage of Stones-ish blues/rock and backwoods preaching is hard to resist. Tracks like "Never Bow Down" have a defiant streak, while "I Have Always Loved You" is a ruminative expression of faith. The group's ensemble playing gelled especially well here, with guitarists Lee and Avery playing off each other nicely. *Time* earned the band a second Dove for

rock album of the year. Third Day's next move was to record a partially-live praise recording, *Offerings: A Worship Album* (2000). The material here is well chosen, ranging from covers of songs by **Michael W. Smith** ("Agnus Dei") and Bob Dylan ("Saved") to originals like "These Thousand Hills," an updating of the southern hymn tradition. This album proved Third Day's most successful to date, earning certified gold status. It led to a triumphant sweep at the 2001 Dove Awards, with the band winning for praise and worship album of the year, group of the year, and artist of the year.

After touring during the spring of 2001, Third Day released *Come Together*, an album steeped in late 1960s pop/rock sounds. The title track conjures up shades of the summer of love (in the name of Christ, of course); "I'm Still Listening" praises the Lord to a track with the bite of "Honky Tonk Woman." The mood here is not entirely retro—"My Heart" shuffles to a hip-hop groove. *Come Together* managed to broaden the band's sound without diluting its down-home flavor or country-bred evangelism. (A bit of trivia: Third Day reaffirmed its Georgia heritage by recording a Coca-Cola jingle in 1997.)

Third Day (Reunion, 1996)
Conspiracy No. 5 (Reunion, 1997)
Time (Essential, 1999)
Offerings: A Worship Album (Essential, 2000)
Come Together (Essential, 2001)

KATHY TROCCOLI

Born June 24, 1958,
in Brooklyn, New York

Embracing both inspirational songs and torchy romantic ballads, Kathy Troccoli occupies a distinctive niche among female Christian music singers. After an early 1990s foray into the secular market, she resumed recording primarily for a Christian audience.

Born in Brooklyn, Kathleen Colleen Troccoli spent much of her youth in the Long Island, New York, suburbs. She began her singing career as a nightclub performer while attending Boston's Berklee School of Music. In 1982, she relocated to Nashville, where she attracted the notice of Mike Blanton and Dan Harrell, managers of **Amy Grant.** Sensing her potential, they launched Reunion Records as a vehicle for her recording career. Troccoli established herself on the Christian airwaves almost immediately with her 1982 hit "Stubborn Love," co-written in part by Grant, **Gary Chapman,** and **Michael W. Smith.** Further singles—including "I Belong to You," "Talk It Out," and "All the World Should Know"—kept her a presence on Christian radio throughout the mid-'80s. Her albums *Heart & Soul* (1984) and *Images* (1986) received Grammy nominations. Toward the end of the decade, she stepped out of the spotlight for a time, searching for a way to cross over into the mainstream.

In 1987, she moved back to Long Island and sang on sessions for secular artist Taylor Dayne.

Troccoli took a shot at secular success with 1991's *Pure Attraction,* released by Reunion and distributed in the secular market by Geffen. "Everything Changes," written by mainstream hit-maker Diane Warren, became a Top 40 and Adult Contemporary hit as well as a Christian radio chart-topper. A well-produced showcase for her emotive, smoldering voice, the album was a credible bid for a larger audience. It also emphasized her songwriting, containing such original tunes as the 1992 Christian hit "Help Myself to You." Troccoli gained additional exposure in the mainstream through tours with Michael Bolton, Boyz II Men, and Kenny Loggins. She also recorded "I Can Hear Music" with the Beach Boys, which became an Adult Contemporary hit. *Pure Attraction* proved to be her commercial peak in the secular market, however, and the mid-'90s found her returning to more explicitly Christian material on such albums as *Sounds of Heaven* (1995).

In recent years, Troccoli has won particular favor as an interpreter of inspirational material. "I Will Choose Christ," released in 1996, and 1997's "A Baby's Prayer" (the latter a GMA Dove Award–winner for inspirational recorded song of the year) were among her standouts. The late '90s also saw her increasingly active as a speaker at Christian women's events, including Women of Faith, Time Out for Women, and Heritage Keepers. Her Dove-nominated song "Go Light Your World" served as the theme for the 1999 National Day of Prayer concert in Washington, D.C. In 2000, she released *Love Has a Name,* a largely self-written collection of faith-based songs that also included a cover of the Foreigner hit "I Want to Know What Love Is." Keeping her skills honed as a secular song interpreter, she contributed a version of "I Got It Bad (and That Ain't Good)" to the *Ultimate Ellington* CD (1999) and collaborated with **Sandi Patty** on *Together* (1999), an album of classic tunes by George Gershwin and other famed pop composers.

Troccoli has written or cowritten a number of inspirational books, including *My Life Is in Your Hands* (Zondervan Publishing, 1997) and *Falling in Love with Jesus* (Word Publishing, 2000).

Stubborn Love (Reunion, 1982)
Heart & Soul (Reunion, 1984)
Images (Reunion, 1986)
Portfolio (Reunion, 1987)
Pure Attraction (Reunion/Geffen, 1991)
Sounds of Heaven (Reunion, 1995)
Kathy Troccoli (Reunion, 1994)
Best of…Just for You (Reunion, 1994)
Corner of Eden (Reunion, 1998)
A Sentimental Christmas (Reunion, 1999)
Love Has a Name (Reunion, 2000)

MICHELLE TUMES
Born November 1, 1970, in Adelaide, Australia

By turns bouncy and solemn, Michelle Tumes's music has found a home on Adult Contemporary–formatted Christian radio stations. This classically trained Australian native first aroused interest in the States as a songwriter. Moving to the United States, she placed her material with other Christian artists before signing a recording deal with Sparrow. (**Sixpence None the Richer, Jaci Velasquez,** and **Point of Grace** would all eventually record songs by Tumes.) Her 1998 debut CD, *Listen,* presented her as a contemplative, somewhat mystical figure and yielded the singles "Please Come Back," "Healing Waters," and "Heaven Will Be Near Me."

In sonic approach, Tumes's work suggests a Christian version of New Age icon Enya, especially in its use of stacked vocals and sweetly ethereal melodies. These elements were accentuated on her next album, 2000's *Center of My Universe.* Coproduced by secular pop veteran David Leonard, the CD surrounded Tumes's serene vocals with percolating synthesizers and sleek string arrangements. "Heaven's Heart" and "Lovely" have a shimmering buoyancy to them that's hard to resist. In an un-Enyaesque move, she also included rock-oriented tracks such as "Do Ya," a catchy plea for love and acceptance. "Immortal" and "With the Angels" are softer meditations on God's presence in the physical world. If some of *Center of My Universe* seems derivative, it makes the album no less pleasing to listen to.

Tumes returned in 2001 with *Dream*, an album emphasizing her more upbeat side.

Listen (Sparrow, 1998)
Center of My Universe (Sparrow, 2000)
Dream (Sparrow, 2001)

JACI VELASQUEZ
Born October 17, 1979,
in Houston, Texas

In 1999, singer Jaci Velasquez made history by becoming the first Contemporary Christian artist to top the Latin singles charts. Her multicultural sound crosses both ethnic and theological boundaries in appeal, and her vivacious style and expressive vocals have launched her as a celebrity while still in her teens.

Velasquez received early inspiration from her parents, who toured with their own musical ministry. The youngest of five siblings, she was singing solos in church by age three. By the time she was 10, she was joining her father and mother on stage; in 1992, at age 13, she sang at the White House. A performance in Houston a year later led to a management deal, which in turn led to her signing with Myrrh Records. Her debut CD, *Heavenly Place*, was released in 1996 and yielded such Christian radio hits as "If This World," "Flowers in the Rain," and "Baptize Me." Overall, Velasquez's first album was a surprisingly mature effort for a 16-year-old, capturing both her fresh energy and polished versatility. Producer Mark Heimermann skillfully blended Latin elements with a mainstream pop sound, keeping things lively without distracting from the Christ-centered content. *Heavenly Place* went on to reach the gold sales mark and earned Velasquez a GMA Dove Award for new artist of the year in 1997; its track "On My Knees" won for inspirational song of the year.

Jaci Velasquez (1998) followed her first album in reaching gold certification. Songs such as "Glory" and "God So Loved the World" offered refinements of her debut's mix of evangelical sentiments and simmering rhythms. The following year, she signed with Sony Discos for distribution into the Latin music market, previously an unfavorable one for Christian artists. Though she had only begun speaking Spanish a few years earlier, she sang convincingly enough to make her 1999 album *Llegar a Ti* a surprising success. Its hope-filled title track became a number one Latin single in November 1999, making Velasquez an instant star in the Spanish-language media. As an evangelical Protestant singing to a predominantly Catholic audience, she faced many questions about her faith and her mission in the Hispanic press. Some of her original fans felt she might be leaving Christian music behind. In her interviews, Velasquez has dealt with these issues with the same sort of poise and maturity she has displayed on her albums.

Fears that Velasquez might be a mere teen phenomenon were put to rest by *Crystal Clear* (2000). This song collection combines the steamy with the sacred in a delicate but mostly successful balance. Tracks like "Escuchame" and "You Don't Miss a Thing" evangelize to a salsa beat, while the title track has a sleek, tribal-rhythm feel. Velasquez displays her diva credentials throughout, building to a stirring finale on "Just a Prayer Away," and with her breathy delivery adding unmistakably sensual touches. Lyrically, the content comes dangerously close to "Jesus-is-my-boyfriend" territory on "Imagine Me without You" and "Every Time I Fall"—without a close listening it would be easy to mistake these tunes as conventional love songs. Whatever its ambiguities, *Crystal Clear* was one of 2000's best Christian pop albums, the work of an artist on the ascent. (For more about Jaci Velasquez, see pages 102–105.)

Heavenly Place (Myrrh, 1996)
Jaci Velasquez (Myrrh, 1998)
Llegar a Ti (Myrrh/Sony Discos, 1999)
Crystal Clear (Word, 2000)
Christmas (Word, 2001)

VIGILANTES OF LOVE
Formed 1990 in Athens, Georgia

As their name implied, the Vigilantes of Love played a bit outside the rules during their 12-year run. Centered around singer/guitarist Bill Mallonee, this alternative rock/country group tried to straddle the Christian and secular music markets. Though they never achieved the commercial success they deserved, Mallonee and his bandmates recorded a series of well-realized albums distinguished for their lyric intelligence and pungent, rootsy musicality.

Influenced by both American folk/rock and British pop, Mallonee first gained attention in the late 1980s as part of the thriving rock scene in Athens, Georgia. From the start, his songwriting had an intensely visual quality, inviting comparisons with **Bruce Cockburn.** The characters populating his lyrics tended to be losers, outlaws, and victims, their misadventures played out against a backdrop of Christian faith. In the tradition of artists like **Mark Heard** and **Julie Miller,** Mallonee drew contrasts between Christian ideals and the everyday disappointments of the mortal world.

The Vigilantes of Love made their debut with *Jugular,* released on the independent Custom label in 1990. By the time of *Driving the Nails'* release the following year, Billy Holmes (bass, mandolin, guitar) and Travis McNabb (drums) were part of the band's frequently shifting roster. Signing with Mark Heard's Fingerprint label, Mallonee and his bandmates (now including bassist David Chalfant and guitarist Newt Carter) released *Killing Floor* in 1992. Coproduced by REM guitarist Peter Buck, this album won a measure of popularity among secular rock fans for its gritty edge and thoughtful lyric sensibility. An appearance at the Cornerstone festival that same year introduced them to a large Christian music audience for the first time.

Though their music improved with each release, the Vigilantes found it hard to connect with a large following. A deal with Capricorn Records gave them greater access to the secular market. Their three releases for the label—*Welcome to Struggleville* (1994), *Blister Soul* (1995), and *Slow Dark Train* (1997)—were substantial efforts, yet failed to elevate the group out of cult status. Mallonee hit his stride on these albums, reeling off sketches of desperate souls careening across vaguely southern landscapes. Such tunes as "Parting Shot" and "Bethlehem Steel" (from *Blister Soul*) displayed a knack for rapid-fire poetic imagery, underscored by Mallonee's rough-hewn yet tender vocals.

After completing their Capricorn stint, the Vigilantes released *To the Roof of the Sky* independently in 1998. This stripped-down collection mixed brooding country-ish tunes with chiming pop/rock numbers, all conveying Mallonee's distinctive mixture

Vigilantes of Love, with lead singer Bill Mallonee (far left)
Photo by Michael Wilson

of melancholy and optimism. After a series of almost continual lineup changes, the band settled into a relatively stable period with Jake Bradley on bass and Kevin Heuer on drums. They were on hand for 2000's *Audible Sigh,* arguably the band's strongest album. Mallonee's familiar topics of damaged love and free-floating depression were restated here with more clarity and wry humor. Buddy Miller's production input gave *Audible Sigh* a ragged-in-the-right-places sound, similar to the moody country ambiance found on his wife Julie's albums. A Christian vision of redemption runs through such darkly evocative tunes as "Solar System" and "Resplendant," the latter featuring Emmylou Harris's vocals.

Summershine (2001) took the band in a somewhat different direction, using 1960s-era rock (specifically that of the Beatles and the Byrds) as its main departure point. The results were pleasing, if less compelling than on *Audible Sigh.* As in the past, the album satisfied the Vigilantes' loyal following but didn't add many new converts. Still on the outskirts of Christian music circles and not quite in sync with the alt-rock crowd, the group's considerable virtues remained underappreciated. Wearied from a decade's worth of touring and record-making, Mallonee decided to break up the Vigilantes and pursue a career under his own name. His debut solo release, *Fetal Position*, was set to appear in the summer of 2002.

Jugular (Custom, 1990)

Driving the Nails (Core, 1991)

Killing Floor (Fingerprint, 1992)

Welcome to Struggleville
    (Capricorn/Fingerprint, 1994)

Blister Soul (Capricorn/Fingerprint, 1995)

VOL (compilation) (Warner Resound, 1996)

Slow Dark Train
    (Capricorn/Fingerprint, 1997)

To the Roof of the Sky (Meat Market, 1998)

Live at the 40 Watt (Paste, 1998)

Audible Sigh (Compass, 2000)

Summershine (Compass, 2001)

WHITEHEART
Formed 1981 in Nashville, Tennessee

Two things are key to remember about the band Whiteheart. One is that its brand of melodic Christian hard rock was played with a clean and sharp edge by exceptionally good musicians. The other is that the group experienced a dizzying number of changes during its 16 years of existence. Somehow, it managed to keep its level of musical quality high and score a long streak of hits despite membership shake-ups, label shifts, and a nasty public scandal.

Keyboardist Mark Gersmehl and guitarist Billy Smiley—who at the time were both members of the Bill Gaither Trio's touring band—formed the nucleus of the band in 1981. Completing the roster were guitarist/vocalist Dan Huff, drummer David Huff, bassist Gary Lunn, and lead singer Steve Green. It was Green who chose the name "Whiteheart" in reaction to a video he saw by Joan Jett and the Blackhearts. Signing with Myrrh, the group released its self-titled debut album in 1982. Among *White Heart*'s highlights was "Everyday," a duet by Dan Huff with **Sandi Patty.** The singles "He's Returning" and "Carry On" gave the band a presence on Christian radio in 1983.

That same year, Green decided to embark on a solo career and was replaced by Scott Matthiesen (a.k.a. Scott Douglas).

The band's career began picking up speed after the release of its second album, *Vital Signs*, in 1984. The stirring "We Are His Hands"—featuring a backup chorus with such notables as **Amy Grant** and **Russ Taff**—became its first big Christian radio hit. The band toured extensively, impressing audiences with its instrumental prowess and sense of rock showmanship. *Hotline*, released in 1985, promised to keep the momentum going. Then Dann and David Huff left the group for session work and were replaced by guitarist Gordon Kennedy and drummer Chris McHugh. Scott Douglas left under uglier circumstances—in 1986, he was convicted of sexually related crimes and sentenced to 15 years in prison. (He was released in the mid-1990s.) The band chose its roadie/bus driver Ric Florian to replace him.

Whiteheart entered its prime with Florian as front man. Signing with Sparrow, the band released *Don't Wait for the Movie*, an assured modern rock performance. Besides its big Christian hit "How Many Times," the album featured such topical material as "King George" (a protest against restrictions on Christian free speech) and "Dr. Jekyll and Mr. Christian" (a swipe at religious hypocrisy). *Emergency Broadcast* (1987) and *Freedom* (1989) continued to add refinements within the group's basic framework.

Florian became an expressive interpreter of the band's material (largely written by Gersmehl and Smiley). Poetic, melodically rich tunes like "The River Will Flow" and "Desert Rose" were among the group's best hits from this period.

By 1988, Lunn had been replaced on bass by Tommy Sims; a year later, Sims, Kennedy, and McHugh departed. Filling their slots with guitarist Brian Wooten, bassist Anthony Sallee, and drummer Mark Nemer, Whiteheart bounced back with 1990's *Powerhouse*. Nemer was replaced by Jon Knox (also a drummer with **Adam Again**) for *Tales of Wonder* (1992), an album that mixed acoustic and electric instrumentation to pleasing effect. The group's lineup held in place to make *Highlands* (1993), an album tinged with Celtic and progressive rock influences. Polished songwriting, focused musicianship, and Florian's supple vocals held the band together through all these comings and goings.

In 1995, Whiteheart moved to the secular Curb Records label, bringing in John Thorn to replace Sallee on bass. Two final albums, *Inside* and *Redemption*, appeared in 1995 and 1997. Gersmehl, Smiley, and Florian embarked on a brief tour in 1997, then closed the book on the band at last. A number of the band's alumni have distinguished themselves in other projects, particularly Dann Huff (now a top-flight session guitarist and producer) and Tommy Sims (a Bruce

Springsteen tour band member and co-writer of the Grammy-winning Eric Clapton hit "Change Your World.") Original singer Steve Green has enjoyed a lengthy career as an inspirational singer/musical minister.

White Heart (Myrrh, 1982)
Vital Signs (Myrrh, 1984)
Hotline (Myrrh, 1985)
Don't Wait for the Movie (Sparrow, 1986)
Emergency Broadcast (Sparrow, 1987)
Souvenirs (Sparrow, 1990)
Powerhouse (Star Song, 1990)
Tales of Wonder (Star Song, 1992)
Highlands (Star Song, 1993)
Nothing but the Best: Rock Classics
   (Star Song, 1994)
Nothing but the Best: Radio Classics
   (Star Song, 1994)
Inside (Curb, 1995)
Redemption (Curb, 1997)

ZOEGIRL
Formed 1999

Launched as a wholesome alternative to Britney Spears and similar secular acts, ZOEgirl caught on with Christian teens in a big way after the release of its self-titled debut album. Singers Chrissy Conway, Alisa Girard (daughter of **Love Song**

singer/keyboardist Chuck Girard), and Kristin Swinford were brought together to create the group, which derives the first part of its name from the Greek word for "life." Released by Sparrow in 2000, *ZOEgirl* matched the trio's closely harmonized vocals with uplifting dance/pop tracks. The group quickly found a niche on Christian radio, scoring hits with such singles as "I Believe" (a danceable declaration of faith) and "Anything Is Possible" (a praise song set to a sleek R&B groove). After the album's release, almost constant touring with **Carman, Clay Crosse,** and **Nichole Nordeman** helped secure the group's following. ZOEgirl's stage show features choreography as well as music (still something of a novelty in the Contemporary Christian genre).

ZOEgirl became the fastest-selling debut in Sparrow's 25-year history. The group's follow-up CD, *Life,* appeared in 2001. A bit more guitar-oriented than the first album, this release featured songs written by the group that concentrated on teen-related issues. Songs like "Plain" and "Dismissed" sought to promote self-confidence and strength of character in young women. Late 2001 saw ZOEgirl resuming its busy concert schedule as *Life* showed signs of duplicating the first album's success.

ZOEgirl (Sparrow, 2000)
Life (Sparrow, 2001)

CHRONOLOGY
OF CONTEMPORARY
CHRISTIAN MUSIC

1950 Word Records, Inc. is founded by Jarrell McCracken

1960 **Amy Grant** is born in Augusta, Georgia

1962 **Steven Curtis Chapman** is born in Paducah, Kentucky

1965 The Billy Graham Association produces *The Restless Ones*, one of the first Christian-themed films to feature rock instrumentation on its soundtrack

1967 Ralph Carmichael creates the early Christian pop/rock musical *Good News*; Ray Hildrebrand releases *He's Everything to Me* on Word

1968 Christian hard rock group **Agape** forms in Southern California; bizarre Christian cult group **All Saved Freak Band** forms in Ohio; the Salt Company, an important early Christian coffeehouse/music venue, opens in Los Angeles; *Joseph and the Amazing Technicolor Dreamcoat* premiers in Britain; Calvary Chapel begins ministering to long-haired youth in Costa Mesa, California; pioneering Christian music disc jockey Scott Ross begins broadcasting in upstate New York

1969 **Larry Norman** releases his seminal *Upon This Rock* album; Top 40 hits such as the Edwin Hawkins Singers'

"Oh Happy Day" and Lawrence Reynolds's "Jesus Is a Soul Man" praise God on the secular airwaves

1970 **Love Song** forms in Southern California; Word releases LP of Ralph Carmichael/Kurt Kaiser musical *Tell It Like It Is*; Jesus Music trend on Top 40 radio continues with such hits as Norman Greenbaum's "Spirit in the Sky" and Judy Collins's version of "Amazing Grace"; groundbreaking Faith Festival is held in Evansville, Indiana; Knott's Berry Farm in Orange County, California, inaugurates Christian music concerts

1971 **Randy Stonehill** releases his debut album *Born Twice*; Christian-themed musicals *Godspell* and *Jesus Christ Superstar* are staged in New York City; early Christian music magazine *Rock in Jesus* begins publication; Calvary Chapel starts its Maranatha! Music label; Bob Larson publishes attack on Christian pop music, *Rock and the Church*

1972 Word launches rock subsidiary Myrrh Records; major Christian music festival Explo '72 is held in Dallas, Texas; **Larry Norman** releases his acclaimed LP *Only*

Visiting This Planet; **2nd Chapter of Acts** releases its debut single "Jesus Is"; **Resurrection Band** forms in Milwaukee, Wisconsin; **Petra** forms in Ft. Wayne, Indiana; Pat Boone starts Lamb and Lion Records

1973 **Phil Keaggy** releases his solo debut album *What a Day*; three-day Jesus '73 festival is held in central Pennsylvania

1974 **Daniel Amos** forms in Orange County, California; Word Records is purchased by ABC Entertainment Corporation

1975 **Larry Norman** launches Solid Rock Records; **Love Song** disbands

1976 Sparrow Records is founded by former Word employee Billy Ray Hearn; **Daniel Amos** releases its debut album; **Randy Stonehill** releases his landmark *Welcome to Paradise* LP; **John Michael Talbot** releases his first solo album

1977 **Amy Grant** releases her debut album; **Keith Green** releases his debut LP *For Him Who Has Ears to Hear*; **DeGarmo & Key** release their debut album *This Time Thru*; Debby Boone's spiritually tinged hit "You Light Up My Life" tops the secular charts; **Rebecca St. James** is born in Sydney, Australia

1978 *CCM* magazine begins publication; **Don Francisco's** "He's Alive" becomes a huge hit on Christian radio; **Dallas Holm & Praise** release massively popular single "Rise Again"; **Mark Heard** releases *On Turning to Dust*

1979 Bob Dylan releases his first Christian album, *Slow Train Coming*; **Sandi Patty** releases her debut album *Sandi's Song*; **Amy Grant** releases her classic single "Father's Eyes"; **Petra** enters the front ranks of Christian rock with *Washes Whiter Than*; **Bruce Cockburn** releases his career landmark LP *Dancing in the Dragon's Jaws*; **Larry Norman** and **Barry McGuire** perform at the White House; **Jaci Velasquez** is born in Houston, Texas

1980 Bob Dylan's Christian-themed "Gotta Serve Somebody" wins Grammy Award; evangelist Jimmy Swaggert publicly condemns all rock music, secular or Christian, as sinful

1981 **DeGarmo & Key's** *This Ain't Hollywood* becomes the first Christian rock album to be nominated for a Grammy; **Steve Camp** releases his career-defining single "Run to the Battle"; **Daniel Amos** releases its cult favorite *Horrendous Disc*; **Gary Chapman** wins a GMA Dove for songwriter of the year; Sparrow Records signs a secular distribution deal with MCA; CBS launches its short-lived Priority Records label in the Christian market

1982 **Keith Green** is killed in a plane crash in Lindale, Texas; **Amy Grant** releases her platinum-selling *Age to Age* album and marries **Gary Chapman**; **Sandi Patty** wins a Dove for artist of the year; **Carman** releases his debut album; **the 77s** release their debut album *Ping Pong Over the Abyss*; **Kathy Troccoli** scores her initial hit with "Stubborn Love"; **Twila Paris** makes the singles charts for the first time with "Humility"; **Whiteheart** releases its debut album

1983 **Steve Taylor** releases his debut *I Want to Be a Clone*; **Michael W. Smith** releases his first hit single, "Great Is the Lord"; **Amy Grant** wins her first Doves, including artist of the year and album of the year; **Michael Card** wins a Dove for songwriter of the year, with his song "El Shaddai" winning for song of the year; **Sandi Patty** and duet partner Larnelle Harris win a Grammy for "More than Wonderful"; **Russ Taff** scores his first (and biggest) hit as a solo artist with "We Will Stand"; **Leslie Phillips** releases her debut *Beyond Saturday Night*

1984 **Stryper** releases its debut *The Yellow and Black Attack*; **the 77s** release their album *All Fall Down* to the secular market via A&M; **Charlie Peacock** releases his debut *Lie Down in the Grass*; Youth Choir (later renamed **the Choir**) forms in Los Angeles; **Twila Paris** scores an enormous hit with "The Warrior Is a Child"; **Whiteheart** releases its breakthrough song "We Are His Hands"; **Steve Taylor** takes on Bob Jones University's segregated dating policies in the controversial "We Don't Need No Color Code"; first Cornerstone music festival is held in rural Illinois

1985 **Amy Grant** achieves Contemporary Christian music's first secular crossover hit with "Find a Way" and wins Grammy for her album *Unguarded*, as well as a Dove for *Straight Ahead*; **Sandi Patty** and Larnelle Harris win a Grammy for "I've Just Seen Jesus"; **Michael W. Smith** wins a Dove for songwriter of the year; **DeGarmo & Key**'s video for "Six Six Six" is initially rejected by MTV

1986 **Michael W. Smith** scores chart-topping Christian hits "I Know" and "Rocketown"; **the Newsboys** form in Australia; **Adam Again** releases its debut album *In a New World of Time*; **Carman** releases anthemic hit single "The Champion"; **What? Records** begins to release albums by Christian artists in the secular market with limited success

1987 *The Joshua Tree* by Christian-inspired band U2 wins a Grammy; **Margaret Becker** releases her debut *Never for Nothing*; Eddie DeGarmo cofounds ForeFront Records; **Amy Grant** releases "The Next Time I Fall," a secular chart-topping duet with Peter Cetera

1988 **Rich Mullins** releases *Winds of Heaven, Stuff of Earth* and scores a hit with the worship classic "Awesome God"; **Leslie Phillips** changes her name to **Sam Phillips** and releases her first album for the secular market, *The Indescribable Wow*; **2nd Chapter of Acts** disbands

1989 **dc Talk** releases its debut album; **Steven Curtis Chapman** wins his first Dove for "His Eyes"; reggae group **Christafari** forms in Los Angeles

1990 **Mark Heard** releases the acclaimed *Dry Bones Dance* on his own Fingerprint label; **Charlie Peacock** emerges as a Christian radio hit-maker with "Big Man's Hat" and "Almost Threw It All Away"; **Julie Miller** releases her debut album *Meet Julie Miller*; **Point of Grace** forms in Arkadelphia, Arkansas

1991 **Amy Grant** releases her multi-platinum album *Heart in Motion*, containing such major secular hits as "Baby, Baby" and "That's What Love Is For"; **Out of the Grey** releases its debut album and racks up its first hit single, "Wishes"; **Kathy Troccoli** scores a secular pop hit with "Everything Changes"; **Petra** wins four Doves, including group of the year

1992 **Mark Heard** dies of a heart attack near Los Angeles; **Michael English** wins a Dove for new artist of the year; **Michael W. Smith** has big secular hit with "I Will Be Here for You"; **the Choir**'s Steve Hindalong produces his groundbreaking *At the Foot of the Cross* worship album; **Twila Paris** wins a Dove for *Sanctuary*; Word Records is purchased by

Thomas Nelson Publishers; Sparrow Records is purchased by EMI; **Sixpence None the Richer** forms in New Braunfels, Texas

1993 **Steve Taylor** returns to the Christian market with *Squint*; **Steven Curtis Chapman** wins a Dove for *The Great Adventure*; **Point of Grace** makes singles charts for the first time with "I'll Be Believing"; **Ashley Cleveland** makes her Christian market debut with *Bus Named Desire*; **Sixpence None the Richer** releases its debut album *The Fatherless and the Widow*

1994 **Jaci Velasquez** releases her debut album *Heavenly Place*; **Amy Grant** releases another huge seller, *House of Love*; **the Newsboys** deliver their signature hit "Shine"; **Michael English** wins four Doves, then returns them after confessing to an extra-marital affair; **Sandi Patty** confesses to having an affair following the announcement of her divorce; **Rebecca St. James** releases her debut album; **Point of Grace** wins Dove for new artist of the year; **Jars of Clay** forms in Greenville, Illinois; **Third Day** forms in Marietta, Georgia; **Carman** performs before a crowd of 71,000 in Dallas, Texas, setting a Christian concert record

1995 **dc Talk** releases its Christian anthem "Jesus Freak"; **Jars of Clay** scores a hit on both Christian and secular charts with "Flood"; **Amy Grant** scores the biggest Christian hit in four years with "Helping Hand"; **DeGarmo & Key** disband

1996 **Charlie Peacock** launches his re:think label, aiming for both mainstream and Christian markets; **MxPx** releases its cult favorite *Life in General*; **Michael English** releases his secular album *Freedom*; Word is purchased by Gaylord Entertainment; **Avalon** releases its debut album, as does **Third Day**; **Jars of Clay** wins Dove for new artist of the year

1997 **Rich Mullins** dies in a car accident in LaSalle County, Illinois; **Bob Carlisle** achieves a huge secular hit with "Butterfly Kisses"; **Steve Taylor** launches Squint Entertainment; **Caedmon's Call** releases its debut album; **Delirious** tops singles charts in Britain with "Deeper"; **dc Talk** achieves its first crossover hit with "Just Between You and Me"; **Amy Grant** releases *Behind the Eyes*

1998 **Michael English** returns to Christian music with *Gospel* album; **Steven Curtis Chapman** contributes "I Will Not Go Quietly" to the soundtrack of the Robert Duvall film *The Apostle*; **MxPx** releases *Slowly Going the Way of the Buffalo* into the secular market; **Third Day** wins its first Dove for "Alien"

1999 **Sixpence None the Richer**'s "Kiss Me" becomes the year's biggest pop single in the U.S; **Jaci Velasquez** tops the secular Latin singles charts

with "Llegar a Ti"; the Gospel Music Association announces new lyric criteria for Dove Award nominations, disqualifying "Kiss Me"; **P.O.D.** releases its major crossover album *The Fundamental Elements of Southtown*; **Amy Grant** and **Gary Chapman** divorce

2000 Gene Eugene (of **Adam Again**) dies of natural causes in Huntington Beach, California; **Nicole C. Mullin** releases her massive worship hit "Redeemer"; OneDay, a worship event attended by 40,000, is held near Memphis; **Michael English** is charged with illegally obtaining drugs; Christian artists contribute to the soundtrack CD of CBS-TV miniseries *Jesus*; such groups as **Plus One** and **ZOEgirl** tap into large Christian teenage market

2001 **Third Day** wins three Doves, including group and artist of the year; Squint Entertainment is absorbed by Word Records, which in turn is purchased by Warner Music Group; longtime Christian label Benson Records shuts down; **dc Talk** members Toby McKeehan, Michael Tait, and Kevin "Max" Smith each release solo albums; Salem Communications finds growing success with "Fish" syndication format on Christian radio stations across the U.S.; **P.O.D.** continues its success in the mainstream with the release of *Satellite*

AFTERWORD

February 6, 2002: ABC NEWS.com carries a story about Contemporary Christian music's status as "the fastest-growing segment of the music industry." Using the group Plus One as a departure point, the brief article emphasizes the increasingly mainstream look and sound of the genre's artists. *CCM* magazine editor Matthew Turner is quoted as describing Christian music as "great music from people of faith that just so happen to follow Jesus Christ." Also interviewed is Jaci Velasquez, who comments: "It's a business for us too.... But the fact that we get to change people's outlooks on [a] certain part of life makes it worth it." The subtext is that these entertainers are reasonable people who won't preach too loudly at nonbelievers, who know how to fit comfortably into the American cultural mix.

The above story pretty much could've been written five or 10 years earlier—it's how the secular media covers Contemporary Christian music when they desire to put a positive spin on things. (The other common treatment is to ridicule the music and portray its exponents as finger-pointing squares and/or hypocrites.) Here again is the familiar paradoxical face that Christian artists show to the secular world: inoffensive and "normal," yet profoundly different below the hip veneer. And the

secular media tend to accommodate this, to treat Christian pop music like a new health fad that people are getting into. It's easier than actually talking about the beliefs that the music conveys, which risks controversy and complaints from advertisers and the public. The idea that a form of entertainment might be highlighting—or even promoting—division in society doesn't make for a nice, safe "lifestyle" story.

Contrast this desire to present Contemporary Christian music as the work of those who "just so happen to follow Jesus Christ" with the prophetic, confrontational music of a Larry Norman or a Keith Green. "I Wish We'd All Been Ready" resisted easy digestion by the entertainment mainstream—its distinction didn't lie in how similar it was to a Christ-free pop song. Songs like this are still being written, but you don't tend to read about them in the secular media. Fervently Christian material—whether recorded by a dance/pop artist like Rebecca St. James or a Goth-metal group like Saviour Machine—rarely reaches the ears of those outside the faith. The evidence that this may be changing is inconclusive at best.

As I mentioned in the introduction, this book is not about the pros or cons of fundamentalist Christianity or any other faith. It's concerned with a type of pop music that emerged 30-some years ago and has since expanded and mutated. And what seems clear in 2002 is that the Contemporary Christian music industry has followed a growth pattern laid down three decades ago by secular rock'n'roll, its supposed moral nemesis. Both musical genres were born out of rebellion against the mainstream, both had their periods of separatism and defiance, and both eventually rounded off their corners and accepted their places in mass society. As R&B artist Swamp Dogg once put it, they didn't sell out as much as they bought in.

Yet many of the Christian artists are not quite falling into line. Their albums are riddled with ambivalence about a believer's place in this world. The self-declared Jesus freaks are having an identity crisis. "My Bible tells me that Christianity and the whole message of Christ will never be popular," dc Talk's Michael Tait says. Still, he and many of his peers are constantly trying to engage secular culture on its own terms and preach to those outside the choir. These musicians don't come across as outsiders; they don't reject most of the trappings of the mainstream. But they live in fear of modern America compromising not only their art, but their relationship with God. Rebecca St. James goes to the lengths of having others dip into secular music and videos on her behalf; Steven Curtis Chapman keeps up with the latest pop tunes but tries to keep the carnal content at bay. All are gingerly navigating a morally ambiguous world while trying to remain apart from it, a difficult balancing act to maintain.

The phrase "accountability" comes up a lot when talking to Contemporary Christian artists. Chapman, for one, places great emphasis on spiritual oversight from pastors and friends outside the music business. When Charlie Peacock and Sparrow Records had a disagreement over the moral implications of "Kiss Me Like a Woman, Love Me Like a Man," an outside evangelical authority was brought in as a referee. Artists working within the Christian music industry are held to account on both a business and a spiritual level—they have to sell records *and* keep from falling into spiritual error. Serving God and the bottom line simultaneously presents artists with a unique set of challenges. Having to square the circle between the businessperson's needs and the Lord's standards makes for a tight space in which to create music.

The fact that the three leading Christian labels—Word, Sparrow, and Reunion—are owned by secular conglomerates adds yet another odd twist to the situation. In effect, the parent companies (Warner Music Group, EMI, and Zomba) are funding the musical ministries of artists who consider secular entertainment decadent if not demonic. The lines of accountability seem to grow more tangled each year.

Can meaningful, artistically valid music come out of a system like this? Certainly, it's not hard to crank out disposable "Jesus Lite" pop hits that are innocuously "positive" enough to please a wide audience. Music with more substance—which is spiritually potent and risks offending someone—may have a harder time surfacing. On one end there are the potential dangers of the standard of "acceptability" that Christian artists are expected to meet. In effect, the Christian music industry might become a denomination with little room for heretics and dissenters. Angry prophets in the tradition of Norman and Green may no longer be tolerated. On the other end of the spectrum are the subtler voices of artists who are deeply Christian but expect a close listening from their fans. Twenty years ago, they found homes at Christian labels that didn't mind putting out a few "artsy" albums now and then. The pressures of commerce may preclude this now.

Christian and non-Christian music fans have a common foe: banality. Original, uncompromised art created to honor God advances both the cause of faith and of art itself. And it has something to say to everyone, including the nonbeliever. It requires a willingness to face an artist's vision of a world beyond this one. I wish we all were ready.

SOURCES AND CONTACTS

A number of important Christian artists have released hard-to-find recordings via smaller record labels. To make obtaining their music easier, I've included below a listing of independent record companies (organized by artist) and how to contact them.

AGAPE
Hidden Vision Records
P.O. Box 23508
Tucson, AZ 85734-3508

ALL SAVED FREAK BAND
Hidden Vision Records (*see* Agape)

THE CALL
Conspiracy Music
P.O. Box 461975
Los Angeles, CA 90046
http://www.conspiracymusic.com

GARY CHAPMAN
(self-released albums)
http://www.garychapman.com

THE CHOIR
(self-released albums)
http://www.thechoir.net

CHRISTAFARI
Lion of Zion Records
http://www.christafari.com

ASHLEY CLEVELAND
204 Records
http://www.ashleycleveland.com

DANIEL AMOS
(self-released albums)
Galaxy 21 Music
9 Music Square South #387
Nashville, TN 37203
http://www.galaxy21music.com;
http://www.danielamos.com

DANIELSON FAMILE
Secretly Canadian
1021 South Walnut
Bloomington, IN 47401
http://www.secretlycanadian.com

Tooth & Nail Records
P.O. Box 12698
Seattle, WA 98111
http://www.toothandnail.com

FIVE IRON FRENZY
Five Minute Walk Records
2056 Commercial Ave.
Concord, CA 94520

DON FRANCISCO
(self-released albums)
http://www.donfrancisco.com

KEITH GREEN
Last Days Ministries
825 College Blvd., Suite 102, #333
Oceanside, CA 92057
http://www.lastdaysministries.org

MARK HEARD
Fingerprint Records
P.O. Box 197
Merrimac, MA 01860

HOME SWEET HOME RECORDS
6301 N. O'Connor Rd., Building #1
Irving, TX 75039
http://homesweethomerecords.com

INNOCENCE MISSION
What Are Records
2401 Broadway
Boulder, CO 80304
http://WhatAreRecords.com

JOY ELECTRIC
Tooth & Nail Records
(*see* Danielson Famile)

GLENN KAISER
Grrr Records
939 W. Wilson Ave.
Chicago, IL 60640
http://www.grrrrecords.com

MXPX
Tooth & Nail Records
(*see* Danielson Famile)

LARRY NORMAN
Solid Rock Records
3760 Market NE, Suite 306
Salem, OR 97301
http://www.larrynorman.com

RESURRECTION BAND
Grrr Records
(*see* Glenn Kaiser)

THE 77S
(*Fools of the World*)
Galaxy 21 Music
(*see* Daniel Amos)
http://www.77s.com

RANDY STONEHILL
Solid Rock Records
(*see* Larry Norman)

JOHN MICHAEL TALBOT
Troubadour for the Lord
350 CR 248
Berryville, AR 72631
http://www.johnmichaeltalbot.com

INDEX